War and Society in Europe 1618–1648

War and Society in Europe 1618–1648

J. V. POLIŠENSKÝ
PROFESSOR OF HISTORY AT
CHARLES UNIVERSITY, PRAGUE

WITH THE COLLABORATION OF
FREDERICK SNIDER
ASSISTANT PROFESSOR OF HISTORY AT
OHIO STATE UNIVERSITY

CAMBRIDGE UNIVERSITY PRESS
CAMBRIDGE
LONDON NEW YORK NEW ROCHELLE
MELBOURNE SYDNEY

Published by the Press Syndicate of the University of Cambridge
The Pitt Building, Trumpington Street, Cambridge CB2 1RP
32 East 57th Street, New York, NY 10022, USA
296 Beaconsfield Parade, Middle Park, Melbourne 3206, Australia

First published 1978
Reprinted 1979

First printed in Great Britain by
Western Printing Services Ltd, Bristol
Reprinted in Great Britain by Weatherby Woolnough, Wellingborough, Northants

Library of Congress Cataloguing in Publication Data
Polišenský, Josef V.
War and society in Europe, 1618–1648.
Includes index.
1. Thirty Years' War, 1618–1648. I. Snider,
Frederick, joint author. II. Title
D258.P644 940.2'4 77-71423
ISBN 0 521 21659 1

TO THE MEMORY OF
S. H. STEINBERG
B. F. PORSHNEV
O. ODLOŽILÍK

Contents

Preface

This is not another attempt at a straightforward history of the conflict commonly known as the Thirty Years' War. Even from a narrow unashamedly Central European viewpoint, such an attempt would be rash; but perhaps I shall undertake it once the edition of the *Documenta Bohemica Bellum Tricennale Illustrantia* is completed.

I have worked on this book for nearly thirty years. The result of my labours should primarily serve future research. It should inform the reader (and the prospective historian) of the present state of our knowledge about the main theme: the interrelationships among different aspects of society, politics and ideas in a period of military and political crisis of continental dimensions. I do not pretend to have solved all the problems, because I am aware that we all exist in a three-dimensional world. We are shaped by the past and the future alike; with our ideas of the future and from our vantage point in the present we are continually reshaping our conception of the past, which also shapes us. I am glad that I can once again agree with my friend Christopher Hill about each generation's need to have history rewritten – an idea superbly expressed in his *Change and Continuity in Seventeenth Century England.*

Thus each of these chapters begins with a word about problems and sources. It is my belief that the historian's profession consists in the search for new problems and, if possible, the attempt to solve them. To do this, he has to find the appropriate methods and suitable source material. Most of the documentation used in this volume comes from the archives and libraries of Czechoslovakia. It was my great privilege to be able to help save and open for research the former private archives in my country. To offer them to the historians of all lands makes all the years spent in bringing them together a labour of love. So it is to my friends, the archivists and librarians, whom I must have exasperated with my insatiable thirst for more books and documents, that I must express my thanks before all.

Next come my former students. They were usually the innocent audiences on whose intellect I was trying to sharpen my muddled ideas. One of them deserves a special mention: Dr Frederick Snider has spent many days travelling with me from one archive to another. He also translated most of the chapters and participated especially in formulating the contents of Part Two. But he is a competent historian himself, and he is in no way responsible for any errors that may be found in this volume.

I must also express my gratitude to the Academia Publishing House and the Böhlau Verlag for permission to reprint material.

The dedication records my continuing debt to three friends whose kindness and wisdom have helped me in different ways. They all died prematurely, but for me and for others they opened up new fields for research.

J. V. Polišenský

Note. Seventeenth-century usage in the rendering of proper names was flexible and no attempt has been made in this volume to render it strictly consistent.

Czechoslovakia Locations of archives and libraries

* State Regional Archives
† Central State Archives
‡ Branches of State Archives
§ District and Municipal Archives, State Libraries

	Czech, German, Hungarian
*	**Banská Bystrica**, Neusohl, Besztercebánya
§	**Banska Štiavnica**, Schemnitz, Selmecbánya
§	**Bardejov**, Bartfeld, Bártfa
‡	**Benešov**, Beneschau
* †	**Bratislava**, Pressburg, Pozsony
* §	**Brno**
‡	**Bytča**, Bicse
§	**České Budějovice**, Budweis
‡	**Český Krumlov**, Krumau
§	**Český Sternberk**,
§	**Cheb**
§	**Chomutov**, Komotau
‡	**Děčín**, Tetschen
§	**Frýdlant**, Friedland
§	**Holešov**
§	**Horšovský Týn**, Bischofteinitz
§	**Jablonec nad Nisou**, Gablonz
‡	**Janovice-Rýmařov**, Römerstadt
§	**Jihlava**, Iglau
‡	**Jindřichův Hradec**, Neuhaus
§	**Kežmarok**, Käsmark
*	**Košice**, Kaschau, Kassa
‡	**Klatovy**, Klattau
§	**Komárno**, Komorn, Komárom
§	**Kremnica**, Kremnitz, Körmöczbánya
‡	**Křivolát**, Pürglitz
§	**Krnov**, Jägerndorf
§	**Kroměříž**, Kremsier
‡	**Levoča**, Leutschau, Löcse
§	**Liberec**, Reichenberg
‡	**Libochovice**
*	**Litoměřice**, Leitmeritz
§	**Louny**, Laun
§	**Mikulov**, Nikolsburg
‡	**Mnichovo Hradiště**, Münchengrätz
§	**Nitra**, Neutra, Nyitra
§	**Nové Hrady**, Gratzen
§	**Nové Zámky**, Neuhäusel, Ersékújvár
‡	**Olomouc**, Olmütz
*	**Opava**, Troppau
*	**Plzeň**, Pilsen
* †	**Praha**, Prag
‡	**Prešov**, Preschau, Eperjes
§	**Rimavská Sobota**, Gross-Steffelsdorf, Rima-Szombat
§	**Roudnice**, Raudnitz
§	**Rožnava**, Rosenau, Rozsnyó
§	**Rychnov nad Kněžnou**, Reichenau a.d. Kn.
§	**Skalica**
§	**Sokolov**, Falkenau
§	**Stará Lubovna**, Alt-Lublau
§	**Šumperk**, Mähr. Schönberg
§	**Teplice**, Teplitz-Schönau
*	**Třeboň**, Wittingau
§	**Trenčin**, Trentschin, Trencsén
§	**Ústí nad Labem**, Aussig
*	**Zámrsk**
‡	**Žitenice**, Schüttenitz
‡	**Žlutice**, Luditz
§	**Znojmo**, Znaim
§	**Zvolen**, Altsohl, Zolyom

0
100 miles
0
150 km
Děčín
Litoměřice
Žitenice
Mnichovo Hradiště
Cheb
Žlutice
Prague
Zámrsk
Pilsen
Benešov
Janovice–Rýmařov
Opava
Olomouc
Klatovy
Jindřichův Hradec
Brno
Kroměříž
Třeboň
Bytča
Levoča
Prešov
Český Krumlov
Banská Bystrica
Košice
Kremnica
Banská Štiavnica
Bratislava

Introduction

SEVENTEENTH-CENTURY STUDIES AND THEIR CONTEMPORARY SIGNIFICANCE

At about the same time that the Fourth Meeting of Czechoslovak Historians reached the conclusion that the seventeenth and eighteenth centuries form a period which deserves more attention, similar opinions began to be expressed elsewhere. This was not purely a matter of chance. The French Marxist writer, Pierre Daix, in his article 'The unknown 17th century', pointed out that historians have until now concentrated more on the sixteenth and eighteenth centuries, which seem on the surface to have been far more 'revolutionary'. 'Our knowledge of the seventeenth century is minimal and is riddled with misunderstanding; it is high time for a revision.'[1] Essentially the same sentiments have been expressed by Pierre Vilar in his studies of the Spanish 'Golden Age' and historical reality, by Pierre Chaunu in his *Civilization of Classical Europe*, Pierre Goubert in his captivating monograph *Louis XIV and Twenty Million Frenchmen*, and Fernand Braudel in his brilliant, but slightly specious, *Material Civilization and Capitalism*.[2] All this agrees substantially with the conclusions of the historians who, in a number of articles in *Past and Present*, saw the period 1560–1660 as a European crisis, with those of the Soviet historians, B. F. Porshnev, N. A. Chistozvonov and M. A. Barg, and finally with the opinions of a group of Americans who place the beginnings of the early modern age in the period 1550–1650.[3]

But the idea that the seventeenth and the twentieth century have a great deal in common, that the former was a period not only of change, but of substantial and revolutionary change, is nothing new. Voices asking whether we are not living again in the seventeenth century, whether the twenty-year period between the World Wars was not merely a truce separating two sections of a new Thirty Years' War, came to be heard as early as the beginning of the Second World War.

This question was also asked at least in passing by a historian well acquainted with the Thirty Years' War, the late Otakar Odložilík.[4]

However I believe today that this train of thought is not taken into account often enough. Historians who lived through the Second World War and the following thirty years are perhaps too much aware that we are not living in the seventeenth century, but in the twentieth, in which human society has reached new heights of technical achievement and has come within reach of universal destruction – things undreamt of even by the chiliastic writers of the seventeenth century. But if contemporary historiography continues to betray a spiritual kinship with a period long vanished, it is a manifestation of the collective experience of people taught by Marx and Freud, Lenin and Einstein, shorn of the shallow optimism which characterized the liberal and nationalist historians of the last century. For our immediate forebears so many problems seemed so simple partly because they did not consider them to be problems at all, partly because they were unwilling or unable to grasp the mentality of preceding generations.

Today historians have discarded most of their illusions about the public response which scholarship will evoke and stand slightly puzzled before new tasks. It is not very difficult to show that traditional historiography worked with myths, legends and stereotypes. It is far more difficult to show what the 'new historiography' should look like. Of course, Fernand Braudel was easily able to demonstrate the absurdity of the notion of the 'encirclement of France' in the sixteenth and seventeenth centuries, and Gaston Zeller has demonstrated that the thesis of a struggle for the 'natural' frontiers of France is unacceptable. But this does not mean that there was no struggle between Habsburgs and Bourbons for hegemony in Europe. The difference is that our explanations are not merely personal, as they were when much was written about the statesmanship of Henry IV, the cruelty or benevolence of Ferdinand II, the genius of Richelieu and Wallenstein. For us the problem is to understand how a ruler as an individual carried out his policies, how he managed his power apparatus, which in a society divided into classes had its characteristic features, its interests and traditions. This means that the historian cannot get along without 'political' history, that he cannot neglect demography, the history of administration, social movements, quantitative history. Without them it is almost impossible to understand economic problems. Nor can he do without the study of mentality, collective psychology or cultural history. All this means that the tasks of the historians studying the society of the seventeenth century are far more difficult today than they have ever been before. To study the biological conditions of life is no simple matter, and it is only with the greatest caution that quantitative methods can be applied to materials from a pre-statistical age. Neither bureaucracies nor social movements can be studied in isolation, as we have come to realize in the last decades, and as for the study of mentality, we stand only at the very beginning.[5] But that people living in the last quarter of the twentieth century, readers of Franz Kafka, James Joyce and even Vladimir Nabokov, can blink in astonishment at the unexpected parallels between two centuries so widely separated by the gulf of time and by the illusory idea of mechanical progress, has been shown in a new way by Robert Mandrou in his stimulating book about the inquisition and persecution of witches in seventeenth-century France, and by Christopher Hill in his *World Turned Upside Down.*[6]

The change in our thinking about the seventeenth century and its central politico-military conflict, the Thirty Years' War, can be seen from a glance at two American university textbooks written by the same group of authors: Crane Brinton, John B. Christopher and Robert Lee Wolf. In their earlier book, called *Modern Civilization. A History of the Last Five Centuries*, the authors explain the origin of modern civilization (that is, Western civilization of the twentieth century) mostly from the foundations laid in the eighteenth century. The Thirty Years' War is here seen as a series of dynastic–religious wars without any further significance. By contrast the more concise *Civilization in the West* published later in 1964, presents the seventeenth century as a period of social, political and spiritual ferment which reached new heights when it began to accomplish something new. As a result of the purgative Thirty Years' War and the English Revolution, France and England faced each other in a contest for hegemony in Europe and overseas.[7]

Briefly, the unity of feudal and Catholic Europe was shattered in the first half of the sixteenth century. On this point, A. G. Dickens, J. H. Elliott and Heinrich Lutz agree, and Lutz declares that in the middle of the sixteenth century the European continent presented the spectacle of *Christianitas afflicta*, the broken and suffering Church.[8] According to the circle of historians around the journal *Past and Present* a 'European Crisis' begins with the Dutch Revolution. Dutch historians, who do not believe in a general European crisis, emphasise the aspect of revolution, which they analyse in the wake of A. Meusel and K. Griewank.[9] For them the Thirty Years' War was an episode in the Eighty Years' War between the Netherlands and Spain, and it can in fact be so considered if we place it in the line of development which begins with the Dutch Revolution of the sixteenth century and ends with the English Revolution of the seventeenth.

All this means that historical interest in the Thirty Years' War has increased. Not that it is equally strong everywhere. It is for instance not particularly noticeable in a region where we would expect to find it: in the German-speaking areas. This is surprising, particularly for the Marxist historians, who can rely not only on the chronological writings of Marx or the popularizing work of Mehring, but also on the pioneering studies of A. Meusel and K. Griewank. During the 1930s and the Second World War, the Thirty Years' War was used as something of a bogeyman by Nazi propagandists and others, perhaps because the seventeenth century was the field of a number of historians in exile: C. F. Friedrich, V. Valentin, D. Gerhard. For this reason the first postwar work on the Peace of Westphalia and the conflict between the principles of representative monarchy and absolutism was done by West German historians. But in the past decade German historiography has taken up the problems of the Thirty Years' War only in the work of Fritz Dickmann, F. H. Schubert, Dieter Albrecht, and H. Langer in the German Democratic Republic. But the most stimulating contributions have come from German-speaking historians living outside Germany — above all Hans Sturmberger in Austria and S. H. Steinberg in Britain.

Steinberg's work, which often betrays a polemical tone, differs from the parochialism of French and German historians. Steinberg repeatedly points out that in the period in which the foundations of modern Europe were laid general European problems naturally assumed greater significance. The same tendency is to be noted in the work of Spanish historians who have freed themselves from the bogeyman of hypernationalism, as well as in the writings of those historians who have chosen to study the seventeenth century in a global rather than a European context.

In the present situation the study of the Thirty Years' War is not only justified as history, but also opens up unexpected prospects. It is of course necessary to agree on what we mean by the Thirty Years' War. In 1954 I defined it as a political conflict which was the logical result of a crisis in the policies of the old feudal ruling classes in various regions of Europe. Because in Bohemia this political and social crisis had deep economic roots, I believed that its analysis would enable us to place this troubled period of Bohemian history in the larger context of the historical development of European society. It now seems that this view was not wide of the mark and that it was of some use.

It was taken up ten years later by Theodore K. Rabb in his introduction to a collection of articles about the Thirty Years' War: 'Today there can be no doubt that the war must be seen as a phenomenon embracing the whole continent, which influenced the history of international relations and the internal development of most European countries.'[10]

SOURCES AVAILABLE FOR THE STUDY OF THE STRUCTURE OF SEVENTEENTH-CENTURY SOCIETY

The logical first step toward the serious study of the Thirty Years' War or any of its aspects is to place it in proper relation to the most significant revolutionary conflicts of the time, that is the Dutch and English Revolutions. After studying English policy on the Bohemian question of 1618–20 I reached the conclusion that

> diplomatic history makes no sense without an explanation of the structure of a given society. If we fail to consider that Jacobean England was a society in transformation, headed towards revolution, her policies will seem to us hopelessly chaotic. Furthermore, however important and interesting the relations between England and Bohemia before the Battle of the White Mountain may have been, their significance was less than that of those between Bohemia and the Netherlands. For it was not England and France, but the Netherlands on the one hand and the Vatican and the Spanish Habsburgs on the other, who were the active elements in European politics in the years 1618–20. The social and economic foundations of European policy at the beginning of the Thirty Years' War are better explained by the example of the Netherlands, the most advanced of all European states at that time, than by the English example.[11]

It has become clear, however, that the confrontation between diplomatic partners is an imperfect reflection of reality. The relationship, say, between Bohemia and the Netherlands is comprehensible 'only against the background of a changing European society'.[12] But what was the character of this social change? Gerhard Ritter has suggested that in the second half of the sixteenth century, during a structural crisis, there arose in western Europe 'modern anti-feudal states' (as Fernand Braudel called them): the Netherlands, England and France.[13] In central Europe this crisis was not resolved, according to Ritter, and the corollary was that 'the repercussions of the religious wars of the sixteenth century' were delayed, and were transformed into a conflict among the great national states of modern Europe'.[14] Ritter's explanation of the Thirty Years' War thus returned to the traditional forms, which were taken up by A. Meusel in his studies in German history. A departure from this traditional picture of unchanging society and changing conditions of social and political conflict was made by Dietrich Gerhard in his attempt to explain the history of European society on the threshold of the modern age as a struggle between feudal societies, whose democratic aspects Gerhard overestimates and the levelling effects of absolute state power. Gerhard's approach was thoroughly political; he attempted to prove that regionalism and feudalism (or rather, representative institutions) distinguished Europe from Russia and America, and that this development took place primarily during the conflicts of the sixteenth and seventeenth centuries.[15] Gerhard's challenge was not taken up, as far as I know, except by some Dutch historians. They mentioned his thesis in their discussion of the conservative character of the Dutch Revolution of the sixteenth century which began as a feudal opposition to Spain and was led to a victorious conclusion by burghers, who promptly fell over each other in their scramble to gain admittance into the nobility. Fernand Braudel's thesis about the decline of late Renaissance Italy is similar (*la faillite de la bourgeoisie*). The social basis of power conflicts in the sixteenth and seventeenth centuries, however, has been shown more clearly – by F. H. Schubert in his studies of the Netherlands at the beginning of the Thirty Years' War, and by others elsewhere.[16]

In 1966 an international colloquium on *Problems of Social Stratification* was held at Paris under the direction of Roland Mousnier.[17] As far as it is possible to judge from the publication which resulted from the colloquium, the theme was conceived too broadly, certainly too broadly for our purposes. Four of the contributions were devoted chiefly to problems of the seventeenth century: I. Schöffer spoke on the social structure of the United Netherlands in the seventeenth century, G. E. Aylmer on 'Caste, estates and classes in seventeenth-century England', F. L. Carsten on Brandenburg-Prussia in the sixteenth and seventeenth centuries, and J. A. Maravall on the divisions in Spanish society as revealed in the comedies of the Golden Age. These studies by no means cover the whole of Europe and cannot be compared with the more ambitious attempt by E. J. Hobsbawm, or with several studies by Christopher Hill, which deal with trends common to all of Europe. Since the work of Hobsbawm and Hill will be discussed later, it will be sufficient to say here that in the last decade attention has centred on the study of the social structures of two countries whose rivalry was proverbial for three generations of Europeans and even eclipsed the traditional antithesis between Europe and the Turkish Orient: the Netherlands and Spain.

In considering Dutch work, we can agree substantially with Schöffer's idea that during the Eighty Years' War (from the beginning of the rebellion against Spain to the middle of the seventeenth century) a type of society was formed in the Netherlands, which later blended with its English rivals and partners, to oppose the type of society represented by France under Louis XIV. In contrast to Dietrich Gerhard, the Dutch historians affirm that feudal institutions continued to exist into the seventeenth century, but in name only. In reality they had vanished. A new 'model' of society and state had emerged, with the burgher regents as the new 'élite'. This bourgeois élite showed a marked upward mobility in the first half of the seventeenth century and a general process of 'aristocratization' in the second. Here one's position in society was determined by property and affluence. Both were paid for by larger groups, the 'small men' who in urban areas represented 80 to 90 per cent of the population, and the growing numbers of *Lumpenproletariat.* In the Netherlands, however, there were differences not only between the élite and the poor *non possidentes*, but also between the western maritime provinces, Holland and Zealand, where the middle class predominated, and the eastern provinces, Geldern and Overijssel, where the 'old society' survived. Its representatives, together with the Calvinist clergy and some of the the guild craftsmen, formed a political and religious opposition to the patrician regents from the western provinces, those Erasmian-oriented Arminians in whom Trevor-Roper sees the real pioneers of capitalism throughout Europe.[18]

According to Maravall and Salomon, Spanish society was no less complex than Dutch society.[19] Salomon finds no balance between the two most important social classes in Castile: the powerful aristocracy and the feeble bourgeoisie. Nor is it possible to speak of a Spanish or Castilian 'absolute monarchy,' which, according to the Marxist view, demands a balance among social forces within a society that had been upset by a pre-revolutionary crisis. The monarchical-aristocratic state lived off the peasantry and rents from landed property. Both Salomon and Maravall have given special attention to the decline of a narrow segment of wealthy peasants, *villanos ricos*, who struggled with the *hidalgos* and landless *labradores* alike. So small a group was unable to influence the deeper, essentially medieval, social structure, in spite of what the authors of a number of contemporary economic tracts, or playwrights like Lope de Vega may have thought.[20]

José Gentil da Silva concludes that in the struggle between old and new social forces, which elsewhere in western Europe led to revolutionary changes, the 'Spanish case' is interesting because Spain distinguished herself from the rest of Europe by being the first European country to extend her power overseas.[21] It seems, however, that the situation in Spain was not greatly different from that in a number of regions in central and southern Italy, and that similar regions, declining into economic dependence, may be found outside the Mediterranean area, in Poland and the Baltic.[22]

Between these two limited sixteenth- and seventeenth-century 'models' – the Atlantic or Maritime and the Mediterranean, the Netherlands and Spain (which themselves were full of internal tension and do not represent static social organisms) – lay, of course, a 'middle Europe' which followed neither of these patterns or models completely. According to Miroslav Hroch and Josef Petráň, the southern part of central Europe (the Bohemian Crownlands, Lower and Upper Austria) formed a typically 'transitional' region, where neither of the economic tendencies had managed fully to win out. Therefore it is precisely in these areas that it would be fruitful to explore the influence of the war on the structure of economy and society. And this is exactly the aim of the present volume.

From the work that has been done so far it is clear that the structure of society in Bohemia before the Thirty Years' War was by no means static, that the bourgeois elements, in spite of their political defeat in 1547, had not been destroyed, and that possibilities for social development towards modern structures remained very real. It also seems clear from the so far partial results of sociographical analysis that the Bohemian nobility was subjected to thorough-going changes after the Battle of the White Mountain, chiefly by the confiscation of estates; it is possible to speak of a 'restructuring' of the whole of Bohemian society. This research, as far as it concerns the nobility, rests on the confiscation protocols from 1621 to 1634, evidence later collected against noblemen who were politically active in the Estates' government between 1618 and 1620, and on the records of the Diet concerning the acceptance of foreigners into the Bohemian nobility; after the Renewed Constitution of 1627, there are the appropriate documents collected in the *Tabulae regni.* Only some regional and local studies are available for the bourgeoisie and the peasantry.

The changes in the composition of the ruling class, plotted on a map, show that the most obvious transformation took place within the baronial Estate, whose holdings, especially in the border regions where latifundia had been prevalent since the Middle Ages, were acquired by the 'new nobility', cosmopolitan in background, who were generally military men or administrative officials. This 'new nobility', contrary to the expectations of Bohuslav Balbín, blended with the rest of the feudal community after one or two generations; in fact it showed such vitality that its descendants maintained their position as landlords through the land reforms of 1918, down to 1945 and 1948. Less clear but deeper and equally lasting were the effects upon the lesser nobility, which was only able to maintain itself on the economic periphery of Bohemia and Moravia, and for the bourgeoisie, including the urban intelligentsia. Here the changes were slower but far more fateful, because in fact they resulted in the destruction of the middle class; the Czech bourgeoisie had to regroup and re-form itself in completely new circumstances during the so-called 'national awakening' of the late eighteenth and early nineteenth century.

If it were possible to speak at all of acts of justice in history, if it were possible to gather all the debts of the seventeenth century into one account and transfer it to a completely different age, one would have to conclude that only the twentieth century, in the land reforms after the Second World War, brought satisfaction to those who work on the land. Perhaps the written records which survive from the age of patrimonial administration could be counted on the credit side. Bohemia, which in the seventeenth century suffered a fateful blow when any chance for further development in continuity with the past was destroyed, is now in a key position as far as historical research into the period of the Thirty Years' War is concerned. For the 'new nobility' after the Battle of the White Mountain was composed chiefly of generals and colonels of the Imperial army, military purveyors and entrepreneurs, who left behind a rich body of evidence. These records are now in Czechoslovakia for good reasons. First, the written records were considered, not always justifiably, as a guarantee of payment of debts owed by the Emperor to their possessors. Thus the widow of General Buquoy, who was killed at Nové Zámky in Slovakia in 1621, received, along with his personal property, the archive of his military chancery. The debts owed Buquoy were paid with the estates of south Bohemian rebels, and his military chancery remained the pride of the family, the basis of its continued social splendour, and the proof of its title to landed property. In other cases family papers were moved from Vienna or from estates outside Bohemia, ending up in Bohemia or Slovakia when the Viennese quarters of the families became too cramped, or when they decided to renovate Bohemian châteaux which had stood empty in the preceding years. This happened, for instance, to the papers of the Schwarzenbergs and the Metternichs.

Secondly, for a number of these families — for instance the Fürstenbergs, Windischgrätz, Herbersteins, Thuns, and others – their Bohemian, Moravian or Slovakian estates were the material foundation of their social pre-eminence and political power. This means that, besides documents resulting from official, military, administrative or diplomatic activities, as well as papers of a purely personal character, there can be found in these patrimonial archives an important class of records dealing with the administration of the estates. These papers are of great importance because they record the activity of feudal entrepreneurship. They include accounts, correspondence, rent rolls, inventories, instructions and the like – materials which have not been preserved elsewhere or at least are difficult to discover. The earliest belong to the period before the Thirty Years' War, and in some cases they have been preserved in unbroken series from the last decades of the Thirty Years' War down to the twentieth century. This means that the contents of the family or 'patrimonial' archives offer not only new and often most valuable source material for political and military history – that is, the history of events – but also make possible, now and in the future, the study of a thoroughly 'modern' set of problems: the history of 'structures'.

For the period of the Thirty Years' War we may say that both groups of documentary evidence are of equal importance. Of course, studies of the modern type are possible chiefly where there is the opportunity of working with comprehensive groups of documents which have been left intact: manorial registers, or diplomatic and military chanceries. About a dozen of these chancery archives have been preserved. They include the military archives of Buquoy, Wallenstein, Collalto and Gallas, and the military–diplomatic archives of the Lobkowicz, Schwarzenberg, Dietrichstein and Piccolomini families, sometimes supplemented by the family archives of the Waldsteins, Thuns, Colloredo-Mansfelds, and Schlicks. The family archives of Hungarian magnates preserved in Slovakia are generally far less complete, largely as a result of the 'millennium campaign' at the end of the last century, which led to the transfer of much of the material to Budapest. But the archives of the Thurzo, Pálffy, Illésházy and Koháry families serve as an important complement to the materials in the Bohemian archives. The contents of these more or less organic units are supplemented by the papers of several dozen members of the 'new' and 'old' Bohemian nobility. The former include the papers of a mixture of Spanish, Italian, Flemish, Walloon, Austrian, German and English soldiers of fortune. Verdugo, Marradas, Caretto-Millesimo,

Braida, Lamboy, Belrupt, St Hilaire, Aldringen, Clary, Eggenberg, Herberstein, Metternich, Morzin, Leslie, all stand side by side with members of old Bohemian families: Adam Waldstein, Slavata, Martinic, Kaplíř, Vratislav of Mitrovice, Kolovrat, Kinský, Kaunitz and others. All have left evidence which is often indispensable and difficult to match either in extent or accessibility elsewhere. In general it may be said that these documents at least partially supplement those of the central government of the Austrian monarchy, now deposited at Vienna or Budapest. Often they supply papers which are not available in the central archives: drafts, memoranda, accounts; on the other hand they contain relatively few fair copies and finished documents.

The origin of these documents naturally produces certain difficulties and shortcomings. First, it is clear that the individuals involved all belonged to one party, that of the Habsburgs and the Catholics. Their opponents, including the members of the Estates' opposition, did not preserve their papers, or carried them into exile, or else purposely destroyed them. The papers of the anti-Habsburg party, therefore, have only been preserved when they were used as evidence against members of the defeated opposition, or when they were incorporated into the archives of one of the victors. Some such material was seized and kept by Wallenstein.

Generally speaking, the nationalization of the estates after 1945 and more than twenty years' work by archivists since then has helped to create a comprehensive body of material which will have a permanent effect on research into the history of the seventeenth to the nineteenth centuries both in Czechoslovakia and abroad, just as medieval studies were stimulated by documents collected during the English Reformation in the sixteenth century, or modern studies by the centralization of the papers of Ancien Régime aristocrats in the French National Archive after 1789. It is perhaps not too much to say that a perspective for the study of the Thirty Years' War has been opened which may be compared with the possibilities created by the October Revolution after 1917 for the study of international relations in the age of imperialism.[28]

The character of the documents brings us to a further conclusion. It has already been mentioned that this wealth of documentary evidence was used chiefly to guarantee the material claims of the 'new nobility' upon the Emperor. In this respect its composition is one-sided. At the same time, however, it makes possible a new investigation into the material aspect of the conflict, revealing the military and administrative apparatus in its functions, and enables us to understand the dialectical relationship between the infrastructure and superstructure.

PROBLEMS OF PERIODIZATION

From the foregoing it is clear that a new periodization of the Thirty Years' War should be based on an analysis of the social structures of both sides, the Habsburg–Catholic camp and the anti-Habsburg 'Great Coalition' whose formation had been attempted as early as 1618–20 by the leaders of the Bohemian Rebellion. While the class structure of the first remained relatively static, that of the second changed constantly. The anti-Habsburg camp was from the beginning a free grouping of 'maritime' powers under the leadership of the United Netherlands, the heirs of the Dutch Revolution of the sixteenth century. From 1621 the Estates General attempted by means of financial subsidies to enlarge this grouping into a coalition reaching into central and eastern Europe. This effort reached its zenith with the Hague Coalition of 1625, embracing the United Netherlands, England, Lower Saxony, Denmark and Norway (and in the original conception also Sweden), the central European followers of Frederick of the Palatinate, and Transylvania. After the collapse of Denmark in 1629, the United Netherlands initiated the formation of an alternative alliance with Sweden, supported unofficially by France from 1631, and openly after 1635. In this period the non-feudal character of the anti-Habsburg camp was weakened by the beginnings of the social and political conflict in England. After 1635 the Dutch receded from their position of leadership in the anti-Habsburg group, while the importance of France increased. A process of re-feudalization began in Sweden similar to the 'aristocratization' of the Netherlands. After the withdrawal of the Netherlands and revolutionary England, the anti-Habsburg coalition, in which the German princes and the Imperial Estates (Saxony, Brandenburg-Prussia, Hesse-Kassel) increasingly asserted themselves, became an alliance which in its class composition could scarcely be distinguished from its enemy.[24]

This means that the usual division of the conflict along territorial lines (the Bohemian War, the Danish, Swedish, Franco-Swedish phases, etc.) is of merely practical significance. In any case, work by F. L. Carsten and S. H. Steinberg, has shown that its value is only relative, and Steinberg has actually suggested a widening of the period into a 'war for European hegemony' lasting from 1609 until 1660.[25] This principle would, of course, allow one to push the beginning of the period back to 1567, as is usual in Dutch historiography. But since the Thirty Years' War remains a clear historical category, its traditional termini of 1618 and 1648 may be preserved, though the former will for some purposes have to be stretched back to 1617 (as John Rushworth did even in the seventeenth century), and the latter will have to be extended to enable us to glance at the diplomatic aftermath – in some cases as late as 1651.

Of the chronological dividing lines the period 1625–9, the period of the Hague Coalition, is clearly distinguishable from the preceding period, when it was impossible to overcome localization of the conflict. A second watershed would seem to be the year 1635, the year of the Peace of Prague and at the same time the end of the localization of the conflict in central Europe. Finally there is the critical year 1643, in which the very existence of an anti-Habsburg coalition was called into question.

PART ONE

PROBLEMS IN THE HISTORY OF THE THIRTY YEARS' WAR

I

Attempts at a reinterpretation of the conflict

PROBLEMS AND SOURCES FOR THE HISTORY OF THE THIRTY YEARS' WAR

Of the older work appearing in the 1930s, most of it in the years immediately preceding the Second World War, the books by the German Günther Franz, the Frenchmen Georges Pagès and V. L. Tapié, and the Soviet historian O. L. Veinstein and the popular English book by C. V. Wedgwood are still useful.[1]

The Soviet historian V. M. Alekseyev has written a book on the Thirty Years' War intended for a wide audience, based chiefly on the findings of Soviet historical scholarship.[2] The author of another attempt at a 'new explanation' of the conflict, S. H. Steinberg, tried to explore its origins on a very wide basis. Thus he took account of work by east European, including Czechoslovak, historians. Apparently in reaction against the thesis, pressed by the Nazis, of the catastrophic results of the War and the possibility of its repetition, Steinberg underestimated the concrete consequences of the conflict and even doubts the validity of the concept of a 'Thirty Years' War'. This is how the phrase appears – in quotation marks – in the English version; they are absent in the German edition, apparently in deference to his German readers.[3]

Steinberg's conclusions are disputed by Theodore K. Rabb in his sober study of the results of the Thirty Years' War on the German economy, which was published in 1962.[4] Rabb is also the editor of an interesting anthology published for American university students, in which the differing views of a number of historians are placed side by side.[5]

More interesting are works which conceive the Thirty Years' War as a historical category in the development of society in the sixteenth and seventeenth centuries. In the opinion of most of the historians who participated in the discussion of a 'general crisis of the seventeenth century' which ran from 1954 to 1962 in the pages of *Past and Present*, the war speeded up developments already in progress. These views, later collected and published as *Crisis in Europe 1560–1660*,[6] were later supplemented by Henry Kamen's work (1965) on the relationship of the war to the general European crisis.[7] This study, also published in *Past and Present*, suggests that the economic situation in Germany after the war was a result of the crisis, that the war worsened the economic malaise, but did not cause economic regression. Kamen's argument is weakened by his exclusive concentration on German conditions. The different situation in central Europe was explored by the present author in the same number of *Past and Present*.[8]

Along with these studies, to a greater or lesser degree influenced by Marxism, there exist, of course, other views of the crisis, which are strongly represented in modern French historiography. The conclusions of Roland Mousnier come close to the traditional view.[9] The crisis has been examined more sensitively by Robert Mandrou,[10] Pierre Vilar,[11] and Pierre Chaunu.[12]

If we view the Thirty Years' War as a manifestation of the crisis or crises of the sixteenth and seventeenth centuries, then we must study the function of the conflict in regard to the Eighty Years' War between Spain and the Netherlands and to the English Revolution and the revolutionary movements of the 1640s.

An extensive literature on the character of the Spanish monarchy in the sixteenth and seventeenth centuries has appeared in the last few years. The gist of the discussion on this theme was presented in a survey published in 1963.[13] Later followed a series of important studies by the Hungarian historian Tibor Wittman, who concluded that 'mediterranean absolutism' of a Spanish type had to be distinguished from absolutism in western and eastern Europe.[14] Wittman's thesis was criticized by A. N. Chistozvonov,[15] who maintains that it is possible to manage with two types of feudal absolute monarchy: a feudal-serf type and a type which integrates itself into capitalism. This distinction, however, cannot be made to apply to Spain.

A different view was put forward by the French Marxist historian Noel Salomon in his studies of the Castilian countryside.[16] According to Salomon, the Spanish monarchy lived on the production of the peasantry and the shepherds and on the exploitation of land rents. At the end of the sixteenth century there was no equilibrium of forces between the aristocracy and the bourgeoisie in Castile, and therefore no Spanish 'absolute monarchy'. Close to this view are the authors of the latest survey of Spanish history, products of the 'Barcelona School' and the influence of its leader J. Vicens Vives.[17] Juan Reglá sees the 'Golden Age' only in the realm of the spirit and regards the Spanish intervention in central Europe as a catastrophe for both Bohemia and Spain. On the battlefields of central Europe the representatives of the 'new order' – that is, the Europe of modern states – confronted those of the 'traditional order' – hierarchically divided feudal society. The Spanish historian thus reaches precisely the opposite conclusion to that reached by Bohdan Chudoba in his study of *Spaniards in the Battle of the White Mountain*.[18]

Chudoba's work is cited in neither of two later publications which deal, directly or indirectly, with Bohemian–Spanish relations in the period of the Thirty Years' War. The more important of these, a study of Wallenstein and his position between the Holy Roman Empire and Spain, was written by Emilio Beladiez and published in 1967.[19] Unfortunately the author was not interested in the roots of the Bohemian conflict nor in the motives for Wallenstein's policies. Bohemian affairs also lie at the heart of the latest biography of Count Gondomar.[20] Both works cover the traditional territory of diplomatic and military history and do not search for a deeper significance in the war.

Nor were such questions, surprisingly enough, posed by those Dutch historians who in the past decades have been concerned with the Eighty Years' War and the revolutionary aspects of the Dutch revolt. This is true both of the influential survey of the Eighty Years' War written during the Second World War by J. Presser and his collaborators,[21] and of individual chapters in the great history of the Netherlands, presided over in its infancy by J. M. Romein.[22]

The character of the Dutch Rebellion (conservative according to Geyl and Rogier, and non-conservative according to H. A. Enno van Gelder) was the subject of a discussion between 1954 and 1956 in the journal *Bijdragen voor de Geschiedenis der Nederlanden*.[23] The revolutionary character of the rebellion has been championed by the Marxist historian E. Kuttner,[24] and by Tibor Wittman and A. N. Chistozvonov, cited above. Their views have been collected and summarized by me in a study published in 1958,[25] and in a later work by the American historian Gordon Griffiths.[26] A Dutch assessment of Griffiths' conclusions has been provided by Ivo Schöffer,[27] who has also published a concise survey of the history of the Dutch Revolution[28] and a stimulating inquiry into the relationship between the Dutch Golden Age and the European crisis.[29]

Ivo Schöffer is also the author of a history of the English Revolution of the seventeenth century,[30] but the standard works on this subject remain Christopher Hill's studies, the most recent of which appeared in 1974.[31] Work by the 'radical conservative' H. R. Trevor-Roper shows a welcome polemical strain.[32]

The late Soviet historian B. F. Porshnev has frequently devoted attention to the revolutionary waves of the seventeenth century. In 1964 he published an augmented version of an earlier study of the relationship of the masses to the feudal régime and to bourgeois revolutions.[33] His best monograph, devoted to the situation in Europe before the conclusion of the Peace of Westphalia and the outbreak of the Fronde in France, was prepared for publication in French by Robert Mandrou,[34] who himself has published two interesting studies of Ancien-Régime France.[35] It may be said that French historians in particular have devoted a great deal of thought and attention to a new picture of the seventeenth century. The brilliant work by Fernand Braudel, Pierre Chaunu and others, however, often cannot hold its own when confronted with available factual material. Far more useful, it seems, is the work by Roland Mousnier and, particularly, Robert Mandrou, who combine a theoretical approach with the analysis of very extensive archival material.

The incorporation of the Thirty Years' War into the process of change undergone by European society in the first half of the seventeenth century has been studied by S. H. Steinberg, a historian in the old German tradition of independent conception distinguished by a rare understanding of new developments. There could be no question, of course, of his testing his conception against the sources, because at a time when a new interpretation was wanted, they were at once extensive, diverse in content, form and language, widely scattered, and not easily accessible.

The weakness of most of these attempts at a new interpretation of the Thirty Years' War is that they are grounded in speculation and therefore fulfil the requirements of formal logic rather than of historical reality. Too often the authors have been dependent on what they found in the available historical literature, which is often defective and hopelessly outdated. Therefore even the highly original theses of E. J. Hobsbawm or H. R. Trevor-Roper are in the end unconvincing.

Certainly the difficulties are at their most severe when it comes to a general reinterpretation of the conflict. Since the conflict was European-wide and lasted the span of a generation, it affected many countries and regions and left its documentary evidence in all of them.

Earlier Czech historians were aware of this, when from the 1860s they gathered material from Bohemian archives, and later photocopies from foreign archives for the series of documents published under the title *Bohemian Diets* (*Sněmy české*), which was to conclude with the minutes of the Diet between 1618 and 1620. The State Central Archive in Prague still preserves a large number of copies of varying value, some of which have not yet been worked through. Of course, these papers are of secondary value and cannot be substitutes for work with the originals. Besides the archives it has also been necessary to consult the resources of many libraries. Transcripts available in the State Central Archive at Prague include materials from Spanish archives (Simancas, Madrid); Italian archives (the Vatican Library, Venice); from the archives at Brussels and Copenhagen. Further transcript materials are available in the Historical Institute of the Czechoslovak Academy of Sciences (chiefly valuable material from the Hague, obtained by the late O. Odložilík) and at the State Archive at Zámrsk (where they are catalogued with the family archive of Colloredo-Mansfeld).

The difficulties are particularly acute for the historian who strays from the better worn paths of military and political history. Modern scholars, attempting to clarify the complex but very real connections between social, economic, cultural and political developments, cannot count on obtaining sufficient documentation from a few archives only. And, since they deal with a set of problems whose existence was not even suspected by earlier archivists, they cannot expect to find documentation ready-made for a given topic. Roughly speaking, sources for these problems will be found in all archives and libraries where there are documents dealing with the seventeenth century. In this book these materials will be described in the following chronological chapters (always at the point where the documentation applies the most or for the first time); it is therefore appropriate at this stage to review the archives and libraries in Czechoslovakia where they are preserved.

The first place belongs, of course, to the State Central Archive in Prague, especially its first section. The old registry was abandoned in the eighteenth century, to be replaced by the system called the 'Old Section' (*Stará manipulace*), in which documents were distributed under alphabetically arranged subject headings. There is also a volume of similar material in the later 'New Section' (*Nová manipulace*). Other important collections include the Bohemian Court Chancery (*Česká dvorská kancelář*) (e.g. documents concerning Wallenstein), Records of the Chamber (*Komorní knihy*) (containing a calendar of correspondence of the chancery of the Directorate for 1618–19), the

Register, the 'Militare' (which can be approached through Líva's edition of the registers), Autographs, the Bohemian Section of the Hofkammer, Wallensteiniana, Jesuitica, etc.[36]

Little of the former Bohemian Land Archive has been preserved in the original. Here the collections include the Bohemian Crown Archive, the Archive of the Bohemian Estates (containing the *Tabulae regni*, Incolationes, and Admittance certificates granted to foreign families), the Appellate Court (*Apelační soud*), Patents; and finally there is a collection of transcripts and microfilms. The archive of the Prague archbishopric, which has not yet been extensively investigated, and that of the Prague Metropolitan Chapter are under the professional supervision of the State Central Archive. Archives of other Church institutions are heterogeneous. Some of the most interesting of them, for example the Capuchin Archive, are depleted because of loans to Rome made over several decades which have not been returned. Some documents have remained in Vienna, and therefore the artificial collections, such as 'Bohemia–Moravia–Silesia' are often fragmentary. The archive of the Charles University possesses quite rich sources for the sixteenth and seventeenth centuries. Largely untapped is the wealth of the Prague Municipal Archive, particularly the collections 'Civic Protocol Books' and 'Parish Registers'. But work here is difficult because most of the catalogue was destroyed by fire in 1945.

The older collections of Prague libraries are indispensable. These include the University Library (part of the State Library) with its collections of manuscripts and rare books, and the Library of the National Museum (which also contains the Dobrovský–Nostitz and the Kinský libraries). The Strahov Monastery Library (now part of the National Museum of Literature) is also valuable for this period.

The State Regional Archive at Prague is useful for the seventeenth century chiefly in its second section, which is located at Benešov, with facilities also at Křivoklát and Mnichovo Hradiště. The core of the collection at Benešov are the archives of the families of Šternberk, Chotek and z Vrtby; here also are the registers of the royal domains of Poděbrady and Brandýs-nad-Labem. The Šternberk Family Archive is complemented for the period of the Thirty Years' War by the collection of pamphlets at the castle at Český Šternberk. At Křivoklát, where the remarkable Castle Library remains intact, are the archives of the Martinic family, the papers of the bailiff Kolenec and some other less extensive family papers. The archive at Mnichovo Hradiště possesses a large collection of Waldstein family papers, concerning chiefly Albrecht Wallenstein, but also two of his relatives – Adam

Waldstein and his son Max. This collection, one of the most important sources for the Thirty Years' War, is augmented by the library of the castle (which once belonged to the Waldstein family of Duchcov) with its rich stock of pamphlet literature.

As at Mnichovo Hradiště, so in other regions family archives have been gathered into one place during the past twenty years. In southern Bohemia the regional depository is the State Archive at Třeboň with branches at Jindřichův Hradec and Český Krumlov. The Rožmberk Family Archive and that of the Buquoys are at Třeboň. There, too, is a rich district and municipal archive with the important town registers. The core of the collection of the State Archive at Jindřichův Hradec are the family archives of the lords of Hradec, the Slavata and Černín (Czernin) families. There are also papers from the family of Vratislav of Mitrovice. In the District and Municipal Archive at Jindřichův Hradec are the (incomplete) papers of the public prosecutor Přibík Jeníšek of Újezd. The branch at Český Krumlov contains papers of members of various branches of the Schwarzenberg family; close by is the Castle Library, dating from the time of the Eggenbergs and Schwarzenbergs.

In České Budějovice is a District and Municipal Archive with a remarkable collection of transcripts, town registers, and correspondence and drafts of the city's agents. Also valuable are the pamphlets from the period of the Bohemian War which have been collected in the Library of the South Bohemian Museum at České Budějovice.

The resources of the State Archive at Pilsen dealing with the Thirty Years' War are in its second section, located at Klatovy and in the section's branch at Žlutice. At Klatovy are the family archives of Krakovský-Kolovrat (of Březnice), Trautmannsdorf (of Horšovský Týn), Kaplíř ze Sulevic, Nostitz-Rieneck (of Planá); at Žlutice are the archives of the Verdugo, Contreras and Nostitz-Rieneck (of Sokolov) families. Nor should the District and Municipal Archives at Pilsen and Cheb be overlooked. The museum at Cheb has a large collection of material on Wallenstein.

The north Bohemian sources have so far been those most accessible to research because of the publication of guides to the Archives. But since the volume of material that has been preserved in this region is so large, much work in the way of cataloguing still remains to be done. The State Archive at Litoměřice has its second section at Žitenice, with branches at Děčín, Libochovice and Jablonec. There are important District and Municipal Archives at Litoměřice, Liberec, Ústí-nad-Labem, Děčín, and Teplice. The core of the holdings at Žitenice are the papers of various branches of the Lobkowitz family. At Libochovice are family papers of Dietrichstein-Herberstein and a few of Kaplíř ze Sulevic. The collection at Děčín is very rich for the sixteenth and seventeenth centuries. Here are the family archives of Thun-Hohenstein and Clary-Aldringen (of Teplice). These have been joined in recent years by other documents, which are now being sorted out, including the Clam-Gallas papers and others. The episcopal library at Litoměřice complements the Waldstein library at Mnichovo Hradiště.

Most of the rich resources of the State Archive at Zámrsk have been catalogued and arranged in the last few years; they include muniments of several families: Piccolomini (of Náchod), Kolovrat (Rychnov), Colloredo-Mansfeld (of Opočno) (which has an extensive collection of transcripts from Vienna, particularly from the Kriegsarchiv), Leslie (of Nové Město-nad-Metují), Kinský (of Chlumec-nad-Cidlinou and Kostelec-nad-Orlicí), Schlick (of Jičíněves), and others.

One of the most valuable archives for our purposes is the State Archive at Brno, containing the family archives of Dietrichstein, Kaunitz, Magnis, Rottal, Chorinský, Collalto, Serényi, Tiefenbach, Žerotín, and others. Also important for the seventeenth century are the papers of Moravian administrative offices (Gubernium, the office of the Moravian Lieutenant-Governor) and a number of artificially arranged collections.

Also important are the Municipal Archive at Brno and the municipal and district archives at Jihlava and Znojmo. Other district archives in Moravia are at Olomouc (the Dudík Collection), and Kroměříž (now transferred to the District Archive at Holešov). The Silesian District Archives (Opava and Krnov) are less important for this period.

The State Archive at Opava has branches at Olomouc and Janovice-Rýmařov. The most important sources are at Olomouc, which administers the archepiscopal archive (from Kroměříž, which complements the materials of the Dietrichstein Collection in the State Archive at Brno, cited above) and the archives of the Olomouc Chapter, Consistory and University. The Olomouc Archive also administers the important Chapter Library with its large manuscript collection. The Archepiscopal Library remained in the castle at Kroměříž. At Janovice-Rýmařov are smaller family collections of Podstatský-Liechtenstein (of Veselíčko; a second part, from Telč, is at Brno) and Belrupt (of Chudobín).

The organization of archives in Slovakia is somewhat different from that in Bohemia and Moravia. For the Czech lands it is only the records of the central administrative institutions which must be sought in Vienna; for Slovakia, on the other hand, the Central Archive at Budapest is indispensable. But there remains in Slovakia an important network of documents originating in the offices of the counties (*komitáty*). There were sixteen of these administrative units in Upper Hungary, and in many cases their records have been preserved intact from the sixteenth century down to their dissolution in 1922. A second characteristic group of Slovak documents are those of the *loca credibilia*, which until 1874 performed the functions of public notaries. A third group are archives originating with economic enterprises belonging to the monarch or administered by royal chambers or committees (mining, coinage, etc.). Then there is a wealth of material in municipal archives and libraries, the most important of which are the archives at Bratislava, Košice, Kremnica, Levoča, Bardejov, Banská Bystrica, Trnava and Banská Štiavnica.

The Slovak State Central Archive at Bratislava in its second section possesses a series of family archives which are valuable for the sixteenth and seventeenth centuries. A significant, though incomplete, collection is the central archive of the Pálffy family. The Zay-Uhrovce Collection with its remarkable materials for the study of the history of Protestantism in Slovakia, is complemented by records from the former archive of the Slovak National Museum at Martin. The Central Mining Archive at Banská Štiavnica has been reorganized and made independent of the Central Archive at Bratislava.

The Bratislava State Archive contains the registers of the counties of Bratislava and Trenčin and also the Illésházy Family Archive. Its branch at Nitra contains the documents of the counties Nitra, Tekov and Komárno. The archive of the Nitra cathedral chapter is rich, but family archives for the seventeenth century are lacking here.

More valuable is the Municipal Archive of Bratislava, with its town registers, and its documents concerning the Estates Rebellion and the Turkish War. The collection *Varia* includes transcripts from Roman and Florentine libraries. The Municipal Archive at Skalica is useful for the history of emigration after the Battle of the White Mountain. The State Archive at Banská Bystrica has a branch at Bytča. At Banská Bystrica are the documents of the counties of Gemer and Zvolen, a collection of Turkish documents *Rimavská Sobota*, and a collection entitled *Documenta Historica* beginning in 1647. The Family Archive of Koháry-Coburg is significant for the history of the wars against the Turks. At Bytča are the papers of the counties of Orava, Turiec, and Liptov, fragmentary genealogical material concerning the Rákóczi family, and papers of George Thurzo and his descendants in the Thurzo-Bytča Family Archive.

The network of central Slovakian archives is completed by the municipal archives at Kremnica, Banská Bystrica, Banská Štiavnica and Žilina, mentioned above.

The State Archive at Košice contains the records of Abauj and Turnia and has branches at Levoča and Prešov. At Levoča are the records of the county of Spiš (Szepes) and the archive of the Horváth-Stansith-Strážky family. At Prešov are valuable records from the Šariš county and some family papers, particularly those of Drugeth-Andrássy (of Humenné). In this region the network is completed by the municipal and district archives at Košice, Prešov, Bardejov, Kežmarok (with a branch at Stará Lubovňa), Levoča and Rožňava.

Many Slovak libraries have been preserved intact from the sixteenth century because the censorship of the Counter-Reformation was not as strict here as in the Bohemian lands. The University Library at Bratislava has many early printed works and a collection of Turkish documents. The Central Library of the Slovak Academy of Sciences at Bratislava contains the library of the Protestant secondary school with its valuable manuscript collection, which is similar in character to the libraries of the Protestant communities at Kožmark, Levoča, and Bardejov. The libraries of Prešov and Košice also have materials concerning the seventeenth century.

Sources for the history of economic and social change in the sixteenth and seventeenth centuries are widely dispersed, and in the final analysis it is necessary to compare the documents of the patrimonial administration, as far as is possible, with the fragmentary remains of the records of the district administration (in Slovakia the counties) with those of the land administration (which are lacking for Slovakia), and finally with the equally incomplete materials preserved in the central Habsburg archives at Vienna or Budapest. This is of course only possible in certain optimal cases, because a coherent economic policy found expression with the beginnings of Austrian cameralism (*i.e.* mercantilism). For the present the most appropriate beginning would be an analysis of specific phenomena, for example of non-agricultural economic activities of feudal entrepreneurs, for which sufficient material is conveniently available.

In conclusion some of the sources for political history should be mentioned. Their volume is too great to allow an exhaustive survey here, but a good example is provided by the materials available for the study of the 'Spanish' court party. A sketch of the programme of the radical wing of the 'Roman', *i.e.* Catholic, party, which later coalesced into the 'Spanish' party, is found in a document preserved in two Church archives – that of the Olomouc cathedral chapter and the Prague archepiscopal archive. An important figure in Moravia was Cardinal Dietrichstein, whose family and personal papers have been preserved chiefly in the Dietrichstein Family Archive in the State Archive at Brno. But his correspondence is widely dispersed; it is also to be found in the Kroměříž Archive, and in a number of Bohemian archives. The Dietrichsteins were joined at the end of the sixteenth century by members of other Catholic families (Berka z Dubé and Lobkowitz) and by some converted Protestants (K. Podstatský of Prusinovice, Albrecht Wallenstein and others).

In Prague the 'Spanish' party gathered around the court and the salon presided over by Dona Maria Manriquez de Lara, who had married into the Pernštejn family. Her daughter Polyxena became the wife first of the Supreme Burggrave William of Rožmberk, later of the Supreme Chancellor Zdeněk Lobkowitz. The correspondence of the Pernštejns and Lobkowitzes together with the papers of related families (Manriquez de Lara, Cardona, and others) are now to be found chiefly in the State Archive at Žitenice.

Spanish manuscripts and books are in the collections of the Lobkowitz Library (now in the University Library at Prague), the Nostitz Library (administered by the Library of the National Museum at Prague), the Eggenberg section of the Castle Library at Český Krumlov, the former archepiscopal library at Kroměříž, and the Chapter Library at Olomouc, the remains of the Dietrichstein Library at Mikulov (now in the University Library at Brno), and elsewhere. Further indications of the extent of this kind of documentation and the opportunities it affords future scholarship will be given in the following section.

SPANISH AND DUTCH MODELS OF SOCIETY IN BOHEMIAN LIBRARIES

The relationship between political, cultural, social and economic developments in central Europe at the beginning of the seventeenth century is a problem which historians so far have tended to ignore. Two attempts have been made to throw light on at least a part of this group of problems. Both of them deal with the nature of political thought in Bohemia before the Battle of the White Mountain.

One, by Bohdan Chudoba, begins from the thesis, put forward by Josef Pekař, of the predominance of a Latin, Catholic 'culture' over a

Germanic, Protestant 'culture' – though it is necessary to add that Pekař later repudiated this view and maintained that 'the Battle of the White Mountain did not result in the victory of a higher culture'; what interested him here, he continued, was primarily 'a dynamic national consciousness' – a vantage point from which he was able to deliver mutually incompatible judgements. Chudoba attempted to ascertain the political views of the chief representative of the 'Spanish' party at the Prague court, Zdeněk Lobkowitz, by analysing the political literature in the Lobkowitz family library – the so-called Roudnice Library.[37] The results of his research were published in an article entitled '*Politica* from the Roudnice Library (the representation of Renaissance political theory in the library of a Bohemian statesman at the beginning of the 17th century)'.[38] Another approach, involving the analysis of the written documentation and the theoretical basis of the practical politics adopted by the Estates opposition, was chosen by Otakar Odložilík in a paper read at the International Congress of Historical Sciences held at Zürich in 1938. All we have, unfortunately, is a summary which shows that Odložilík dealt with three problems in political thought in early seventeenth-century Bohemia: the discussion about the elective character of the Bohemian Crown, the question of the hereditary rights of the Habsburgs, and the issue of justifiable rebellion against a tyrant.[39]

It would be tempting to compare the political writings of both parties, the 'Spaniards' and the Estates' opposition, and conclude that the Catholic, pro-Habsburg group was inferior. The political perspectives of Daniel Adam of Veleslavín, Kocín of Kocínet, Pavel Skála ze Zhoře in his commentaries on Bodin, and Comenius in his use of Campanella (as the author of the *Spanish Monarchy*), are certainly wider than those of most of the leading nobles. Jáchym Ondřej Schlick in 1617 had a clear conception of the significance of the conflict over the Habsburg claim to the Bohemian throne. Václav Budovec of Budov's *Antialkoran* even understood that Europe, confronted with the example of an 'oriental' civilization represented by the 'Tyrannical Monarchy' of the Turks, itself contained two 'models' of state and society: the Spanish absolute monarchy (more absolute by reputation than in fact) and the model of a representative monarchy controlled by Estates, whose closest realization was the United Netherlands.[40]

It is not difficult to demonstrate that the last Smiřickýs, Kinskýs, lords of Roupov, and Karel of Žerotín the Elder, were all strongly under the influence of a western type of culture whose impulses came from the Netherlands, from Huguenot France, and partly even from

Elizabethan England and from Switzerland. What is difficult is to link their cultural orientation to their political sympathies, their views of society, and their economic practices. The linkage is partly evident perhaps only in the case of the Smiřickýs, whose close connections with the United Netherlands, lasting to the death of Albrecht Jan Smiřický in November 1618, coincided with the implementation of progressive economic principles.[41] The connections are not so clear in the case of Karel of Žerotín, who in general reveals himself as more of an Erasmian than a Calvinist. We know nothing of the Smiřický library, but a portion of the Žerotín library survived destruction in the last war and is preserved at Wrocław. We know something of Václav Vilém of Roupov's close connection with the University at Altdorf, which together with Heidelberg and Herborn acquainted Bohemian students with the political views of Althusius and Grotius and with the principle of confederation, on which the United Netherlands was founded and of which, except for Switzerland, they represented the sole European example.[42] In Comenius we see today the typical apologist for the Netherlands, as well as the admirer and indeed the propagandist of the Protestant–Humanist ideal, which widened from its original Bohemian national and religious limits to embrace the whole of the *Corpus evangelicorum*, and which finally, in the *General Considerations on the Amendment of Human Affairs*, expanded further to encompass all mankind.[43]

On the basis of what we now know about political thought in the society of the Bohemian Estates we may conclude that the court factions of the 'Spaniards' and the nucleus of the radical 'Dutch' opposition were only unsubstantial fringe groups, with sharply conflicting views, particularly on the distribution of power, but by themselves of little practical significance. If we analyse the political manoeuvres of Vilém Slavata and compare them with the political principles that he later expressed in his *Historical Writings* (*Historické spisování*), we may say that in the years before the Bohemian Rebellion he was more interested in power than in the purity of political principle. Neither then nor later did he distinguish himself in the field of political thought, but rather in the realm of practical power politics; when he later searched for ideological foundations for his political career, he named among his mentors the Jesuit teachers at the Prague Clementinum, with the Englishman Edmund Campion at their head.[44]

Because Spanish universities were not normally visited by Bohemian students and the opportunity to become acquainted with Spain was limited to a few noblemen and to members of the Society of Jesus, the

Bohemian intelligentsia was made up mostly of former students at West European universities – Altdorf, Heidelberg, Herborn, Leyden, Saumur, Geneva, Oxford. Most members of the Estates of course inclined toward the Erasmian ideal of reasonable moderation, religious toleration, political equilibrium, and the search for new paths in art, philosophy and history. These disciples of Erasmus of Rotterdam, whose writings are well represented in the libraries for instance of the burghers of the town of Louny, could certainly sympathise with the mannerist culture of Rudolph II's court at Prague, and with attempts to restore peace in the West and gather the forces of Europe against the Turks.[45] Rudolph's political programme finally collapsed, but the year 1609, it seemed, brought at least the illusion of equilibrium between the 'Spaniards' and their opponents at the court, between Catholics and non-Catholics. When it became apparent that the balance was only illusory and that the court of the Emperor Mathias was henceforth in the hands of the 'Spaniards', some of whom moved from Prague to Vienna, the 'moderate' group was split. Some, like the physician and historian Jan Jessenius, joined the opposition. His former colleagues and friends, J. M. Wacker, Nostitz and Eggenberg, by contrast, joined the Imperial faction.[46] The Bohemian War destroyed these divisions in Bohemian public opinion, and of course also terminated one line of development. It also caused the destruction of much historical material. The library of Jessenius was confiscated and distributed among the libraries of various Church institutions; the private libraries of the burghers of Louny were purged of suspicious books by Jesuits under the supervision of Huerta's Spaniards and ended in monastic libraries at Chomutov and elsewhere; the library of the physician Borbonius was taken by the Lobkowitz family. At the same time the libraries of Rudolph II and the Rožmberks disappeared; the library of Cardinal Dietrichstein at Mikulov was carried off to Sweden, including its copy of *Don Quixote* who in 1619–20 appeared as an allegorical figure in the Cardinal's correspondence.

This demonstrates that the Cardinal had read Cervantes' novel, but since he too belonged to those 'Spaniards' who were interested in the problems of practical politics and not at all in theories, it is impossible to find in his extensive political correspondence much evidence for any far-reaching speculation. Certainly he felt close ties with Spain, forged by his birth and background, and he considered the King of Spain to be the natural head of that politico-religious power group to which he gave allegiance. What he thought about Castilian society or the Spanish monarchy it is impossible to tell. But it is perhaps symptomatic that for his Spanish and Italian correspondence he employed one 'Italian' secretary, and that in his library, as in others of the period, books in both these languages were classed under the heading 'Italian'. Perhaps instead of a 'Spanish' model of civilization we should be thinking in terms of a Spanish–Italian or 'Mediterranean' model.[47]

Some of the hazards of the methods employed by Bohdan Chudoba are immediately obvious. Before we can draw any conclusions from the character of a library owned by some figure active in politics, we must first establish when the library was collected, whether those books which could have served as a stimulus to actual political activities were really present, and, if they were, whether he in fact read them. These things can be ascertained only very rarely in the case of Lobkowitz. The early catalogues have not survived, and the pre-nineteenth-century catalogues which have been preserved are of little help for our purposes. From these we learn only that the Lobkowitz library at Roudnice did not correspond to the Pernštejn library, which was given to the Clementinum at Prague, and that it did not correspond to the Rožmberk library. Did Zdeněk Lobkowitz add books to the collection, or was this chiefly the work of his wife Polyxena? From the correspondence that has survived it is clear that Zdeněk never learned Spanish very well, and that Polyxena never took the trouble to write legibly. Chudoba believes that those bindings stamped with a tower and the motto *Inconcussa manet* belonged to Polyxena, and that the device was a sort of ex-libris. A note in Lobkowitz's own hand has been found in one book, Burghard's *De autonomia:* 'Omni studio universisque machinamentis, ferro ac igne abscindere a corpore morbum, a vita luxum, ab animo ignorantiam, concordiae discordiam, civitati seditionem oportet.'[48] But the note is not dated, and we find a very similar phrase in one of Jessenius' books. Both wished surgically to remove social evils, but they probably identified them quite differently.

In contrast, for example, to Johann Ulrich von Eggenberg, Lobkowitz never quoted when or where he acquired a book, never made notes in the margins (the usefulness of these has been shown in a study of pre-Rebellion historical literature in Prague libraries[49]), and never revealed in his journal entries his impressions of his reading. He therefore leaves us baffled. In the Roudnice library we find side by side Machiavelli and Bodin, Guevara, Bellarmin and Juan de Mariana – defenders of the absolute power of rulers and its opponents, monarchists and critics of absolute and universal monarchy. But besides books the Lobkowitzes also possessed political writings in manuscript form, and part of this collection was absorbed into the so-called Lobkowitz

Library in Prague (where it now forms section 65 of the University Library). Here we find the same universality of taste: the *Relazioni* of Bentivoglio and the writings of Amandus Polanus; Guicciardini's description of the Netherlands next to Paolo Sarpi; a textbook *Auxilios para bien governar una monarquía catholica* next to Grotius' *De jure belli ac pacis*, Machiavelli's *The Prince* next to his republican *Discorsi*; the Protestant Chytraeus together with orthodox and heterodox Catholics. With this sort of material it is impossible to describe 'the character of the political thinking of the Bohemian nobility at the beginning of the Baroque period, the impulses on which it fed and the extent of its horizons', as Chudoba himself finally came to realize.[50]

If we survey Lobkowitz's correspondence or his journal entries (both of which, however, are fragmentary for the years 1618–20), the Council protocols for 1600–06 and his commentaries on the commissions for the Renewed Constitution, we can conclude that after the Battle of the White Mountain he was pressing for a restoration of the situation before 1609, but that he was not prepared to go further. In the 1620s neither Lobkowitz nor Martinic stood for the principle of absolute monarchy, which was possibly supported only by Slavata. We cannot entirely agree with Tapié's conclusion that Lobkowitz 'like Richelieu wished to enhance the will and authority of the ruler against the proper interests of the nobility; like Colbert he laid the foundations of the administrative monarchy'.[51]

We are a good deal better served by two other libraries, those formed by two prominent members of the 'Spanish' party, Johann Ulrich von Eggenberg and Otto von Nostitz.

For the Eggenberg library, today a part of the Castle Library at Český Krumlov, we have two older catalogues and one modern one. On the basis of catalogues dating from 1721 and around 1780, and of *supralibros* and characteristic white bindings, it has been possible to establish the nucleus of the old Eggenberg library.[52] That part of it which dealt with politics, history and belles lettres was divided among various languages as follows:

Books published	*1500–50*	*1551–1600*	*1601–50*	*1651–1700*	*1701–50*	*1750–*	*No date*	*Total*
Spanish	1	12	28	3	–	–	2	46
Italian	7	73	126	127	25	16	23	397
French	–	2	24	283	90	100	11	510
German	1	–	4	39	12	41	7	104
Latin	–	2	–	5	–	1	–	8
	9	89	182	457	127	158	43	1,065

The Eggenberg library in the time of Johann Ulrich (d. 1634) was thus 'modern' and predominantly Italian and Spanish; his heirs quickly gave it a more French character (in the second half of the seventeenth century), probably because the last Eggenbergs belonged to the circle around Charles of Lorraine. In 1721 there were eighty-five *hispanica*, of which fifty-three remain today (the catalogue lists only forty-four: it appears, therefore that the number fluctuated greatly in the eighteenth century and that some of the books were introduced by the first Schwarzenbergs). The dates of the *hispanica* that have been preserved suggest that Johann Ulrich began to buy Spanish books on his journey to Spain (1600–01) and that from that time he bought steadily more – with an obvious preference for belles lettres (Cervantes, Lope de Vega, but also Quevedo), and historical and geographical literature. It is noteworthy that the library was plentifully supplied with descriptions of Spanish America.[53] There are also, to be sure, political writings in the library, but they cannot be shown to have been instrumental in forming or supporting the owner's political outlook.

The Nostitz Library (today called the Josef Dobrovský Library) had its origins in the library of Otto von Nostitz for which there exist several partial bound catalogues from the seventeenth and eighteenth centuries and a twentieth-century card catalogue. J. V. Šimák published a list of the manuscripts in 1910. According to the catalogues, there were eighty-eight Spanish books, ten translations from Spanish into French, six into German, twenty-one into Latin, two into Dutch, seven into Italian. The French translations were mainly belles lettres, and the German mainly military, religious, and also a translation of Campanella's *Spanish Monarchy*. Latin translations touch religious, military, and political matters: Saavedra, Sánchez, Antonio Pérez (who was also translated into Dutch in 1596). The Italian translations included Guevara and religious literature.

The Spanish books themselves were published between 1551 and 1679, so that the literary influence is of approximately the same period as in the Eggenberg library:

Books published:	1551–1599	22
	1600–1649	48
	1650–1679	18

The oldest book is Juan Luis Vives' *Introducción a la sabiduría*, a Spanish translation from the Latin, published in 1551 at Antwerp. For the second half of the sixteenth century the dominant categories are religion, military affairs, poetry and politics (Antonio de Guevara,

F. L. Gomara, Hernán de Acuña, Antonio de Ferrera). For the first half of the seventeenth century there are more belles lettres (Quevedo, Pícara Justina, Góngora and others), more travel books (descriptions of the Escorial), and the indispensable Antonio Pérez who seems to have been a best-seller for a long time. The general character does not change for the third quarter of the seventeenth century, except for the introduction of a number of Spanish versions of atlases printed at Amsterdam by Blaeuw.[54]

A survey of the libraries of Lobkowitz, Eggenberg and Nostitz thus reveals substantially the same picture. In all three families there was evidently a deep interest in Spanish writing and culture. It would be logical to expect such an interest in Spanish authors who were in some way connected with the central European milieu, or with some of the central European noble families. It is no surprise, therefore, to come across the poems of Cristóbal de Castillejo, the *Araucana* of Ercilla, or the writings of Hurtado de Mendoza. But it is interesting to find both humanist works (Vives, Guevara) and, in growing proportion, mannerist and early baroque writings by Quevedo, Góngora, Campanella (the *Spanish Monarchy*), together with translations from the Italians Botero, Paolo Sarpi (attacking the Roman Curia), Antonio Pérez (attacking Philip II), Mexía's history of the conquest of Mexico and the bitter indictment of it by Bartolomé de Las Casas. The presence of Cervántes and Lope de Vega can be explained by the current fashion; writings concerning the *romanceros*, and even theoretical treatments of them, descriptions of the New World, all point to the existence of a specialized interest. A number of Spanish romances from the mid-sixteenth century found their way into the University from the Hybernian Monastery in Prague. The foundation of this monastery was aided by the Contreras and Verdugo families. All this can be established; but it does not follow that those individuals who were interested in Spanish culture automatically adhered to the Spanish political programme. We know, certainly, that the Protestant Karel of Žerotín recommended a Spanish voyage to his youthful relatives, that some of the Prague patriciate forced to emigrate because of their religion could read Spanish, or that even Comenius in his *Secular History* considered the Spanish monarchy to be the successor of the Biblical Four Kingdoms. Even the exiled historian Pavel Ješín of Bezděz, author of the *Memorial to the Bohemian Heroes* ... published in the Netherlands in 1621, had, on his own testimony, some friends among the Jesuits and knew Spanish.[55]

But what came into conflict on the battlefields were not 'cultures'.

as Josef Pekař maintained, nor even conceptions of civilization – that is, certain notions of erudition and thought, of state and society, or of life and death. These conceptions come into conflict only when they become parts of an ideology. By civilization we usually mean today a certain level in the development of a society, characterized by the complexity of phenomena which determine the character of various facets of society and their interrelationships. In Spain, around the beginning of the seventeenth century, a part of a conception of civilization – which fell far short of embracing all its aspects and certainly did not include its better facets – became the Decalogue of the government. Whatever conflicted with this Decalogue, or with the principles it contained, fell at once outside the law: this included much of the heritage of Spanish humanism and the Erasmian tradition in Spain. The struggle over Vives, more sympathetic to Comenius than to Nostitz, over Las Casas, Ponce de León or Francisco de Vittoria, was carried on in central Europe as well as Spain, within individual social groups, and probably within individuals themselves. But the simple analysis of the contents of libraries cannot tell us much about political conviction.

This does not mean that we must give up trying to explain the complex relationships between economic, cultural and political development. The Battle of the White Mountain really was a conflict between two forces which represented two different programmes. In this sense it is proper to speak of a conflict between two power groups who adhered to two models of an idealized civilization. But the delineation of this relationship is not aided by the simple identification of culture with politics, or by hasty conclusions about the relation between politics and economics. We must accept the reality that all these relationships arose and existed in a certain social milieu. Therefore, if we wish to elucidate the development of European thought and avoid distorting it, we must use more sophisticated methods.

2

The Bohemian War 1618–20

PROBLEMS: SOME ATTITUDES

Austrian and German historians have done much work on the beginnings of the central European crisis. The survey of Austrian history by Hugo Hantsch presents a conservative, pro-Habsburg view;[1] the liberal textbook by Erich Zöllner, *Geschichte Österreichs*,[2] attempts a more balanced assessment of the conflict. The interesting work by the Austrian historian Hans Sturmberger,[3] taking a similar approach, expresses doubts whether either the Spanish or the Austrian Habsburgs were striving for absolutism. Like Sturmberger, Grete Mecenseffy sympathizes with Austrian Protestantism and the Estates' community, and there is a well-written survey of the situation by Karl Richter.[4]

V. L. Tapié has devoted much attention to the seventeenth century in his studies of methods and problems in the history of central Europe.[5] Habsburg problems have also been dealt with by A. Wandruszka[6] and the Italian R. Belvederi.[7] The articles by R. F. Schmiedt[8] are also useful.

The monograph by J. B. Novák, *Rudolf II and his Fall*,[9] has not yet been surpassed. The biography of the 'Saturnian Emperor' by Gertrude von Schwarzenfeld[10] applies a more literary treatment and was apparently inspired by G. R. Hocke's work on Rudolphine Prague, the centre of European mannerist culture. But the best books now available are *Rudolf II and his World* by R. J. W. Evans and *Bohemia and the Netherlands in the 16th Century* by E. H. N. Mout.[11] The work of Belvederi and Sturmberger is complemented by useful studies by the late Tibor Wittman on the crisis in the régime of the Austrian Habsburgs.[12]

Work by Czech and Slovak historians for this period is collected in a selective bibliography published in 1960 for the Congress of Historical Sciences held at Stockholm.[13]

Earlier work dealt chiefly with problems in administration,[14] while more recent studies have concentrated on economic and social conditions in Bohemia before the Battle of the White Mountain. Taxation, earlier studied by A. Gindely and O. Placht, has been taken up more recently chiefly by M. Volf,[15] V. Pešák[16] and J. Kolman.[17] The burden of taxation, of course, depended upon the fluctuating value of money, and therefore the 'price revolution' of the sixteenth and seventeenth centuries has been a topic of permanent interest to historians. Josef Janáček studied the price controls imposed by Rudolph II,[18] and later the Polish historian S. Hoszowski published a stimulating article on the influence of the price revolution in the lands of central Europe.[19] Tibor Wittman has discussed conditions in Hungary in the framework of the European economy,[20] and Josef Petráň has returned to the problems suggested by Hoszowski's article.[21] Useful material may also be found in a collection of papers on the history of prices and wages in the sixteenth and seventeenth centuries.[22] These studies have been used by Miroslav Hroch and Josef Petráň in their discussion of crisis and regression in Europe.[23]

The greatest interest has centred around the economy of feudal estates before the Battle of the White Mountain and the question of the position of the serfs. The pioneering work by V. Pešák on the economy of the Smiřický estates has been continued in studies by J. Křivka, J. Jirásek and A. Míka. Particularly noteworthy are articles by Josef Válka[24] and Josef Petráň;[25] František Matějek has explored conditions in Silesia.[26] So far we lack studies of the economy of the estates of small and middling noblemen and of the towns – whose holdings represented two-thirds of the landed property in Bohemia in the period before the Battle of the White Mountain. Some fundamental questions have therefore remained unsolved, although the printed source collections (such as the *Bohemian Diets – Sněmy české*, and the *Bohemian Archive – Archiv český*) together with the rich documentation preserved in the archives, provide ample research opportunities.

The discussion of the so-called Second Serfdom (conducted by A. Míka, J. Petráň, J. Válka, A. Matějek and others) has clarified some aspects of the economic and social situation, but so far it has not led to any more general conclusions. Josef Petráň's study of the class conflict and its function in Bohemian society before and after the Battle of the White Mountain[27] is useful for its methodology.

Work in the history of the towns of Bohemia and Moravia has been rather uneven. Josef Janáček, author of some of the chapters of the *History of Prague*,[28] is the only historian to explore conditions in other towns as well – e.g. Jihlava and others. František Kavka has published an interesting monograph on Bohemian towns in the first half of the sixteenth century,[29] and Jaroslav Marek has written on royal towns in Moravia in the fifteenth and sixteenth centuries.[30] The large group of unfree towns, which held an important place in the economic life of the Bohemian lands, still awaits systematic historical investigation. In my study of the Thirty Years' War, I analysed conditions in at least one of these, the Moravian town of Zlín. Also there is the incomparable history of Pelhřimov, written with obvious devotion by Josef Dobiáš. The (unfortunately) still unpublished study of Uherský Brod by Josef Válka demonstrates what can be gleaned from civic registers for the solution of concrete problems.[31]

Political thought in Bohemia before the Battle of the White Mountain presents a difficult problem. The sources are the manuscripts and printed works forming the contents of sixteenth- and seventeenth-century libraries, and also contemporary literature. A large portion of the libraries existing then, of course, were carried off at the end of the Thirty Years' War to Sweden. The fate of one of these, the Rožmberk library, has been studied by Emil Schieche.[32]

It is difficult, however, to determine when individual books were acquired by libraries, and whether they were read. The exception to this is the collection of Eggenberg, who regularly noted next to the ex-libris when and where he acquired each book, and sometimes entered a pithy judgement of his opinion of the book. The remnants of his library are now part of the Castle Library at Český Krumlov. Only in cases such as this is it possible to reach any firm conclusions, as B. Baďura and I showed in a review of B. Chudoba's *Spaniards at the Battle of the White Mountain.*[33]

Of prime significance for this period are J. B. Novák's *Rudolf II and his Fall*, mentioned above, and K. Stloukal's *Papal Policies and the Imperial Court at Prague at the Beginning of the Seventeenth Century.*[34] J. Matoušek dealt with the eastern policy of Rudolph in a monograph published in 1935;[35] František Hejl has written more recently on Polish policy toward the Habsburgs, and a Polish view has been presented by W. Konopczyński.[36]

Like Bohdan Chudoba, Grete Mecenseffy has been interested in relations between the Austrian and the Spanish Habsburgs,[37] and in the same field Charles Howard Carter has concentrated on the diplomatic aspect.[38] A far more modern approach is that of the British hispanist J. H. Elliott in his stimulating survey of Spanish history in the sixteenth and seventeenth centuries.[39] Elliott's monograph *The*

Revolt of the Catalans[40] is the most significant contribution to the study of the Spanish rôle in European politics in the seventeenth century to appear in recent years.

J. Janáček minimized the international significance of Rudolphine Prague in the political and cultural life of Europe before the outbreak of the Thirty Years' War. A similar view was taken earlier by Kamil Krofta in his apology for old Bohemia published just before the Second World War.[41] Editions of source material have brought forward new evidence which seems to raise one's opinion of Bohemian society of this period. These include Rezek's edition of the *Memoirs* of Mikuláš Dačický z Heslova (1880), Tieftrunk's edition of Pavel Skála's *Bohemian History from 1602 to 1623* (1867), as well as the volumes in the series *Bohemian Archive* and *Bohemian Diets*, and Pavel Stranský's *The Bohemian State* (1940). Newer editions include V. Pešak's *Protocols of the Bohemian State Council, 1601–1610* (1952), and this author's edition of the historical writings of Ondřej z Habernfeldu and Pavel Skála ze Zhoře.[42] I have published a general survey of new editions in collaboration with J. Kolman.[43]

I have also published two studies of the struggle for power and the political crisis in the period before the Battle of the White Mountain;[44] and with J. Hrubeš I have studied public opinion in Bohemia in connection with the Turkish Wars and the Hungarian Revolt.[45]

In 1894 F. Kameníček published a collection of sources for the rebellion of Bocskai;[46] a popular selection from these was published by me under the title *Liber tristitiae et doloris.*[47] The most popular Hungarian work on this theme is a book by K. Benda, though the later study by Tibor Wittman, mentioned above, should not be overlooked.[48]

The political crisis which led to the defenestration of 1618 is illuminated by studies devoted to members of the 'old' Bohemian nobility and the 'Spanish' radicals. Václav Březan's biography of the last Rožmberks has been re-issued by J. Dostál;[49] the latest treatment of the anti-Habsburg activities of Petr Vok of Rožmberk is by O. Hulec.[50] Karel Stloukal, whose first work was devoted to the youth of Cardinal Dietrichstein, has investigated the end of a related family, the lords of Hradec, whose heir was Vilém Slavata.[51] František Hrubý and Otakar Odložilík have investigated the activities of two typical representatives of the society of the Estates in Moravia, Ladislav Velen of Žerotín[52] and Karel of Žerotín the Elder.[53] Studies by J. Glücklich and V. Kybal,[54] published nearly a century ago, pointed out the connection between the Bohemian political crisis and the more general conflict between the European Great Powers.

In the last decades, too, the Bohemian War has received a good deal of attention from both Czech and other historians. Gindely's *History of the Bohemian Rebellion*, though now nearly a century old, has not been surpassed.[55] Two different views of the Bohemian situation were presented by the conservative Josef Pekař[56] and the liberal Kamil Krofta.[57] The state of our knowledge of the period of the Thirty Years' War has been summarized in articles collected under the rather unfortunate title *The Period of the White Mountain and Albrecht Wallenstein*,[58] with contributions by O. Odložilík, J. Prokeš and K. Stloukal. At the same time J. Prokeš published a calendar of part of the correspondence of the Bohemian directorate for 1618 and 1619.[59]

New approaches to the study of the Bohemian War were sought by V. L. Tapié and Josef Macůrek. Tapié was interested in relations between Bohemia and France,[60] and the Czech translation of his book *The Battle of the White Mountain and French Policy* was prepared by Zdeněk Kalista.[61] Josef Macůrek was concerned with Bohemian-Polish relations.[62] The Silesian question at the beginning of the Thirty Years' War has, of course, also been dealt with by Polish historians, most recently W. Czapliński.[63] Josef Macůrek also published a number of articles on this question in the Wrocław journal *Sobótka* between 1947 and 1951; and together with M. Rejnuš has also explored the connections between the Bohemian lands and Upper Hungary. The latest additions to the Turkish aspect of the conflict were written by the Austrians R. Neck and R. Heinisch and by the Rumanian Cristina Rotman.[64]

I have myself dealt with this same general problem in monographs concerning the attitude of progressive Western lands toward the Bohemian uprising.[65] A similar study of Bohemian–Spanish relations has not yet been published. I have published a study of the Swedish position on the Bohemian War together with M. Hroch.[66] B. Badura has studied the question of the Valtelline,[67] and Zdeněk Šolle has sketched Charles Emmanuel of Savoy's position on Bohemia. S. Pánek has written on military aspects of the war, and V. Líva has published a register of the section 'Militare' in the State Central Archive at Prague.[68] J. Dobiáš has investigated the military events of 1618;[69] the march on Prague is covered in Kalista's edition of Buquoy's itinerary[70] and in an article by František Hrubý.[71] M. Volf published a series of articles on the war in southern Bohemia, based on the Buquoy Archive (now part of the State Archive at Třeboň),[72] and a study of the 'Attempts of the patriciate of Budweis to join the Bohemian uprising in 1618'.[73] The most detailed study to date of the defenestration of

Prague is an article by Fridrich Macháček published in 1908, and there is a new book by Josef Petráň.[74]

The most original work on the Bohemian War by a foreign historian comes from the Austrian Hans Sturmberger: *Aufstand in Böhmen.*[75] Materials for studying the policies of the German allies of the Bohemian uprising are found in the Palatinate correspondence preserved in the State Archive at Munich, in the correspondence of Christian of Anhalt (State Archive, Oranienbaum-Magdeburg), and the correspondence of Johann Ernst of Saxe-Weimar (State Archive, Weimar). For Habsburg policy, the most important materials are in the Haus- Hof-und Staatsarchiv at Vienna, and in the archives at Munich, Madrid and Brussels (the correspondence of Diego de Zeelandre from Vienna). D. Albrecht has used the Munich sources for a study of the policy of Maximilian of Bavaria.[76]

The meetings of the Estates and Diets for 1618–20 are described in Skála's *History* (Library of the National Museum at Prague), and in the printed *Articles of the Diet* (the most complete collection of which is in the State Central Archive, Prague). R. Stanka has written on the confederations of 1619,[77] and a new study is being prepared by V. Vaněček. The rôle of the lesser nobility in the uprising is illustrated in the protocols of evidence compiled by the prosecutor Přibík Jeníšek of Újezd, in the Municipal Archive at Jindřichův Hradec. Helmut Weigel[78] and I. G. Weiss[79] have studied the policy of the Palatinate, and A. Wandruszka has found Italian sources for the Battle of the White Mountain.

There can be no doubt that the problem of the Battle of the White Mountain is one of the fundamental questions of Bohemian national history, and that it is also closely connected with problems in European history. A clear attitude on the Battle of the White Mountain has always been an essential part of any discussion of 'the meaning of Czech history'.

The plain task of the historian now is to review these current ideas and to replace the century-old account by Anton Gindely. At the same time it is obvious that the contemporary historian faces a far more difficult task than did his famous predecessor, who could concentrate on political history even though he was aware of its limitations. Gindely knew that future generations of scholars would broaden their interest to include the fields of social and economic development. This, however, was not grasped by his followers, that generation of historians who searched through European archives and in the collections of the former Bohemian Crown Archive in Gindely's tracks to collect material for the great edition of *Bohemian Diets*. It seems that it was the First World War and the creation of the independent Republic which reduced the urgency of this task. In consequence the historians did not bring their work to its conclusion while conditions were relatively favourable.

In the second half of the twentieth century historians are faced with a series of basic tasks: to deal with the social structure of the Estates, to analyse their politically active elements, to assess the relationship between Bohemian society and European political thought, to evaluate the Estates' Confederation of 1619, and so on. On the other hand, it is a decided advantage that the historian today has at his disposal a whole series of sources that Gindely did not use or that were not available to him, even though they were and are located in Bohemia. In this respect the situation a century later is far more propitious.

SOURCES

Sources for the history of the Bohemian War have only been preserved in haphazard fashion. Quite naturally, our most valuable material comes from members of the victorious Habsburg party, since those documents were customarily preserved which could later be used to secure compensation from the Emperor.

The core of this documentation are the military chancery of Buquoy and the correspondence of some of the leaders of the Habsburg camp: Zdeněk Lobkowitz, Vilém Slavata, Cardinal Dietrichstein, and others The Dietrichstein correspondence, which was widely dispersed, has been laboriously collected and is now concentrated chiefly in the State Archive at Brno.

Historians are becoming increasingly aware of the significance of another branch of the evidence, that left by the 'neutrals', Adam of Waldstein, Šternberk, and in Moravia Karel of Žerotín the Elder. The activity of the Directorate and the Palatine government and their administrative organs is far more difficult to reconstruct, doubtless because after the Battle of the White Mountain many people made vigorous efforts to obliterate all trace of their doings. The largest mass of evidence consists in the papers of the Confiscation Commission and other commissions and in the records of the public prosecutors. Most valuable are the protocols of the prosecutor Přibík Jeníšek of Újezd, and the original records of dissolved administrative offices, obtained by the enlightened chronicler Jan Jeník z Bratřic who used them in the volumes of his collection entitled *Bohemica*, compiled at the end of the eighteenth century. Some idea of the contents of the chancery of the Directorate can be gained through calendars which have been preserved, and also from indications in Pavel Skála's *Ecclesiastical History.* These are only indications. Transcripts of correspondence were gathered in Skála's *Prolegomena*, which is lost. Wallenstein's military chancery preserves fragments of the military correspondence of the government of the Estates; these materials are not found in the military fonds of the archives which were published by V. Líva.

These basic sources are augmented by smaller archival collections in Bohemian and Slovak archives. There is rather more material for Moravia, since that province did not suffer the same degree of administrative reorganization as took place in Bohemia.[80] These collections include the correspondence of the Thurzo family, concerning the relation of Upper Hungary to the Bohemian rising as well as the papers of Verdugo and Nostitz, Martinic and Aldringen. Also valuable are the remnants of the correspondence of the Thurns, Tiefenbachs, Collaltos, Colloredos, and Zdeněk Lev Libštejnský-Kolovrat. All these of course betray the social and political attitudes of the writers. Most of the state archives and libraries contain minor additions to this mass of material.[81] I shall describe here those collections which concern the period of 1618–20. Other collections, which chiefly concern later periods, will be mentioned only briefly.

The Military Chancery of Buquoy

This collection is deposited in the State Archive at Třeboň, in the section entitled 'Nové Hrady Historical Archive'. It is divided into three parts, organized in a rather unfortunate fashion by earlier archivists. As all three sections contain interrelated documents, they will be brought together in due course under the title 'Buquoy Family Archive' and will be arranged chronologically. But the present division is thus: I. *Geschichte des Grafen K. B. Buquoy*; II. *Dreissigjähriger Krieg*; III. *Kriegssachen–Neue Folge.*

The first section (call-number G B) contains mainly biographical materials, papers dealing with the administration of family property in Bohemia, the Netherlands, and so forth. Another, larger, part of this section contains 634 items of Buquoy's correspondence between 1618 and 1621, that is, from the period of his command on Bohemian and Hungarian battlefields. The correspondence is arranged inconveniently according to the organization of the *Almanac de Gotha*: first come letters to the Emperors Mathias and Ferdinand II, the archdukes, to

Maximilian Duke of Bavaria, to officers and courtiers; then come letters to lesser administrative institutions, Church institutions, towns, domains, etc., which deal primarily with the logistic problems of Buquoy's army in Bohemia.

The second and most important section (*Dreissigjähriger Krieg*, call-number D K) contains materials from the period 1618–48, particularly those dealing with Buquoy's estates (Nové Hrady, Rožmberk, Libějovice – together about forty documents). There are about 155 documents concerning the progress of the war. The section has been divided into ten subsections, the documents being arranged chronologically in each. The first subsection contains material dealing with southern Bohemia, while the second covers rather more ground: news of military action in Bohemia, Moravia, Hungary, the Palatinate, chiefly between 1618 and 1621. About fifty documents are missing from the original collection: they were exchanged in 1878 for other family documents. There are also materials dealing with the policies of the Austrian Estates; reports from the court, lists of officers, and so forth. After 1621 the documents deal chiefly with the military career of the general's son Karl Albert.

The third section (*Neue Folge*, call-number N F) is a collection of about 320 more recently acquired documents, bought between 1888 and 1901. From the period 1618–21 there is Buquoy's important correspondence with Baltasar de Marradas and Verdugo, commanders of armies paid by the Spaniards. It includes correspondence with the Court War Council and political reports from various parts of Europe. It is difficult to detect any systematic organization in this section; there have, however, been attempts to gather the letters together according to their authors. As far as language is concerned, the Buquoy papers are a good example of a cosmopolitan archive: most of the documents are in German, followed by Spanish, French, Italian, and to a lesser extent Latin and Czech, with a few letters in cypher. All together there are about 1,260 documents.

A copy of the register of this archive exists in the District and Municipal Archive at České Budějovice. Section II was transcribed for the former Bohemian Land Archive (*Archiv země české*) and is now in the State Central Archive at Prague.[82]

The State Archive at Brno

This archive, the second largest for the period, includes fragments of the *Estates Register* (*Stavovská registratura*), containing noblemen's notes of sums owed them by the government of the Margraviate; letter books of the Directorate from May to September 1619 (about 640 documents), chiefly concerning the May and August meetings of the Diet; finally there are letters of fealty, a collection of patents, pamphlets and leaflets. Since this kind of material has only rarely been preserved from the period of the uprising in Bohemia and Moravia, these documents are of particular significance. The letter books have the call-number A-3, Estates Manuscripts no. 82. Notes concerning the Diets (Estates Manuscripts, nos. 20–22) include deleted portions of the meetings; the fragments of the Estates' correspondence are contained in the papers of Ladislav Velen of Žerotín (*Bočkova sbírka*, G-1); the same material is in the 'New Collection' (*Nová sbírka*, G-2). The 'Patents' (G-18) and 'Leaflets' (G-17) provide information about developments in Moravia and their public impact. There are also some important documents in the 'Manuscript Collection' (*Sbírka rukopisů*, G-10) – for instance, an index of the correspondence of the city of Olomouc during the years of the uprising.[83]

An important complement to these fonds is the 'Collection of Transcriptions of Select Documents' from the period of the uprising in Moravia, in 1619–20, originally intended as an appendix to the printed edition of *Moravian Correspondence and Documents, 1625–36*.[84] This collection also includes some documents from foreign archives (Vienna, Munich, Wrocław, Innsbruck and Dresden).

Besides this, the Brno archive contains rich family archives, of which the most important for this period are those of the Žerotíns, Collaltos and Dietrichsteins.

The Žerotín Family Archive

Letter book no. 16 of this collection (call-number G-78) contains a calendar of the German correspondence of Karel of Žerotín the Elder: summaries of letters to the Emperor, to Cardinal Dietrichstein, Rudolf von Tiefenbach and H. Stitten, to June 1619. There are also extracts from Žerotín's journal for November 1618. There is no material here for that branch of the family to which Ladislav Velen of Žerotín belonged.

The Collalto Family Achive

The collection G-169 of the State Archive at Brno is divided into three sections, of which the first, dealing with the seventeenth century, has three parts: the archive of the Tiefenbach family, the archive of the Counts of Thurn, and the archive of the Princes Collalto-Treviso. The Tiefenbach Archive contains letters of the Imperial Commander Rudolf and his brothers Friedrich and Sigmund, who joined the uprising. There are only a few papers from the years 1618–20; there are more for this period in the correspondence of Veit von Thurn with members of the Bohemian nobility (the 'Thurn Archive'). The correspondence of Rambold Collalto runs to 1630 and is important chiefly in the latter part of the 1620s, which will be discussed in more detail below. For the period 1618–20 there is correspondence between R. Collalto and Cardinal Dietrichstein and with Wallenstein, both from 1616. There are also letters from General Buquoy and his second in command from 1614. Finally there are Imperial rescripts from the year 1618.[85]

The Dietrichstein Family Archive

This collection (call-number G-140) is composed of seven parts: the 'Historical Archive', the 'Dietrichstein Family Archive', the 'Pruskovský Family Archive', the 'Leslie Family Archive', 'Related and Unrelated Families', 'Legal Representatives', and 'Court Cases'. These documents are complemented by the so-called *Grosse Korrespondenz* transferred to Brno from Prague in 1959, and the 'Unbound Correspondence' (*Volná korespondence*) deposited in the archepiscopal archive formerly at Kroměříž, now in the State Archive at Olomouc. Copies of the catalogue of the 'Unbound Correspondence' are in the State Archive at Brno in the collection G-83 (*Matice moravská*) and transcripts of Dietrichstein's correspondence in German from the period of the uprising are in the Kroměříž collection (*Universita Olomouc*). For practical purposes the *Grosse Korrespondenz* begins in 1621 and will be discussed below, while the 'Unbound Correspondence' will be examined separately.

The 'Historical Archive', containing the Cardinal's correspondence with the court and with innumerable foreign and Bohemian correspondents, is primarily valuable for the period after 1621. But the section 'Morava' contains a subheading 'Mährische Rebellion' (f. 199), dealing with the year 1619, in which are letters of the Captain of Mikulov, Henry Bruce, and J. Horský, running from July to the end of the year 1619. Also there are some letters of Ladislav Velen of Žerotín, Dampierre, Alonso de Castro, Pavel Michna of Vacínov, and much of this material is important for the study of the struggle for Moravia.

Correspondence with the Emperor for the year 1618 is in section f. 199.

The Dietrichstein Family Archive contains the Cardinal's correspondence for 1620 and 1621 (f. 845, 946), most of which is in Italian and addressed to various Church dignitaries.

The 'Unbound Correspondence' of Cardinal Dietrichstein

Dietrichstein's correspondence between 1617 and 1620 has been most plentifully preserved in the collections of the Olomouc archepiscopal archive, under the title *Volná korespondence* (call-number V.K.), which until 1964 was deposited at Kroměříž with the Archepiscopal Library (which contained some complementary manuscripts) and the Gallery. These documents were then moved to Olomouc, where they were augmented by related documents that had formerly been in the collection of the Olomouc Chapter Archive. In the reorganized collection, the most important section for our purposes is the one entitled 'The Olomouc Archdiocese', with its subsection 'Episcopal Correspondence' (letters received dating from 1503; letters sent dating from 1540).

A calendar of the correspondence from 1617–20 contains information about the beginnings and the course of the rebellion in Moravia, military and also diplomatic activities, and information about taxation. There is correspondence here from the period when the Cardinal took over the administration of taxation from Karel of Žerotín, and also correspondence which he maintained with Mathias, with Ferdinand, Cardinal Khlesl and with the Directorate. In addition there is his correspondence with commissioners and with military leaders of both sides, including Albrecht Wallenstein, Jiří of Náchod, and Peter Sedlnický of Choltice. On the Italian and Spanish side there are letters from the Cardinal's Italian and Belgian connections (Roque de Ayerbe, Giulio Ginnani, Amaro Méndez Feijóo, M. Somogy) and from relatives in Spain (the Marchioness of Mondéjar and others).

Besides military actions (Dampierre's campaign, the struggle in the south), there is also information about attempts to get aid from Madrid and documentation about the first signs of the conflict in the Valtelline.[86]

In the collection of the Olomouc Chapter there are some important individual documents, for example a letter from the Captain-General Ladislav Velen of Žerotín to the Chapter in March 1620.

Dietrichstein's position as the leading representative of the 'Spanish' party in Moravia expanded to include all of Bohemia with the removal of the Court and the Supreme Chancellor Zdeněk Lobkowitz to Vienna. The Lobkowitz correspondence is an important part of the State Archive at Litoměřice in its branch at Žitenice.

The Family Archive of Lobkowicz of Roudnice

In this collection the period 1617–20 is represented in the section entitled 'Correspondence of Zdeněk Vojtěch Lobkowicz (1568–1628)', containing twenty-three documents (call-numbers B 209–231). This correspondence is the basic source for our knowledge of the relations between individual members of the Court party, including Vilém Slavata, Adam of Šternberk, Pavel Michna of Vacínov, Jaroslav Bořita of Martinic, and Adam Waldstein the Younger. Among Lobkowitz's foreign correspondents there were Spanish diplomats and soldiers: the Ambassador Oñate, Baltasar de Marradas, Baltasar de Zúñiga, G. Tilly, M. Werdeman and others. These documents are augmented by the correspondence of Zdeněk's wife Polyxena, *née* Pernštejn 1566–1642).

In the Lobkowicz Family Archive are also the papers of the Chancellor's son Wenceslas Eusebius and his wife, including the correspondence of Wenceslas Felix Pětipeský of Chyše and Egerberk, a member of the Estates' Directorate. There is also important material for the Estates' Rebellion in section IX (call-number Q 14/3–6). The correspondence of Zdeněk and Polyxena Lobkowitz, mostly in Spanish and in Polyxena's case almost illegible, has been preserved for the later period as well. Its tone is increasingly pessimistic, in spite of the economic improvement, created chiefly by the efforts of Polyxena at the time of the confiscations. There is material on the meetings for the Renewed Constitution; but more important for the history of the Thirty Years' War is the correspondence of Wenceslas Eusebius Lobkowitz (1609–77), who, though he grew up under the influence of Wallenstein, nevertheless in 1636 became a member of the Court War Council, in 1644 its Vice-President, and in 1650 its President. This correspondence will be discussed below.[87]

The significance of the Lobkowitz correspondence is all the greater because of the disappearance of most papers of the other leaders of the Court party, such as Martinic and Slavata. The Martinic Archive was destroyed as early as the seventeenth century, and the so-called Smečno Calendars, located at the State Archive at Křivoklat, begin only in 1622 and are valuable chiefly for the years 1643–50. No trace has been found of Martinic's manuscript 'Memorabilia Jaroslai Bořitae à

Martinic 1597–1619'. Two manuscripts in the National Museum, which have been connected with Martinic and contain descriptions of the uprising (*Aufstand in Böhmen*, MSS KNM VI G 2; VIII A 18), date from the 1640s, and though based on older material (perhaps on reports sent to Lobkowitz at the time of the uprising), are also dependent on Slavata's *Memoirs*.

The Family Archive of Slavata of Chlum and Košumberk

This collection is deposited at Jindřichův Hradec and contains the manuscript of Slavata's *Historical Writings* (*Historické spisování*) (call-numbers 84–97; books 1–14, the tenth volume is in the State Archive at Mnichovo Hradiště). Other materials in the collection include drafts from 1622 and materials for the *Historical Writings* (call-number III A 1, boxes 11–14). There is also family correspondence with Jaroslav Bořita of Martinic, Adam Waldstein the Younger and Karl von Liechtenstein (III A 2b, boxes 15–17). Boxes 18 and 19 (call-number III A 30) contain documents concerning the defenestration and the Rebellion. The historical section also contains transcriptions from other archives, chiefly the Lobkowicz Family Archive.[88]

Materials in the State Central Archive, Prague

The State Central Archive contains most of the materials for the activities of the central administration of the Directorate and of the Palatine government between 1618 and 1620. Most of this has only been preserved in fragmentary form and is not conveniently organized.

The 'Crown Archive', an exception to this, contains primarily documents dealing with fundamental problems of domestic and foreign policy. There is diplomatic material connected with the so-called Oñate Agreements of June 1617, and most of the extant material on the confederations among the Estates of the Bohemian Crownlands, and their federation with the Estates of Upper and Lower Austria and Hungary in 1619, is also here. The last document of this sort is the Articles of Confederation with the Estates of Transylvania, signed at Banská Bystrica in August 1620.[89]

The whole of the section 'Militare' is important, and for our period the guide is the third volume of the series by František Roubík and V. Líva, though it is important to note that Líva's registers are not always accurate and do not include all the documents contained in the collection (for instance, documents dealing with attempts to pacify the troops' financial complaints and to gain new sources of financial aid in November 1620). In the Palatine period this collection includes diplomatic as well as military documents, for example notes of the negotiations of Christian of Anhalt in Austria, the correspondence of Frederick of the Palatinate with Gabriel Bethlen, letters from Nürnberg, etc.[90]

The collection 'Old Section' (*Stará manipulace* – call-number S.M.) is inconveniently arranged. Correspondence with the Emperor Mathias in 1618–19 is under the call-number K (*i.e. Kaiser*) II 11/134; further, K. 1/137 contains diplomatic correspondence of Frederick of the Palatinate with Bethlen, letters of Johann Georg of Saxony, etc. K. 182, K. 187, K. 109/14 contain the foreign correspondence of the government of the Directorate from the spring of 1618, with Hamburg, Breslau and the German princes. K. 109/15 is correspondence with Johann Georg of Saxony; K. 109/2 are papers of the Viceroy Karl von Liechtenstein from 1621. Other important call-numbers are E 3/8 (*Eger*), containing correspondence with that city; G 4/7 (*Gesàndschaften*), and L 34 (*Lusatia*).

Meetings of the Diet between 1618 and 1620 have not been preserved in the *Tabulae regni*. Therefore we must rely on the printed *Articles of the Diet* (*Sněmovní artykuly*), which are deposited in the State Central Archive and in libraries in Prague, in both their Czech and German series. The Articles, of course, sketch only the results of the meetings of the Diet and tell us nothing of the course of the meetings themselves. Information on this score must be looked for in the correspondence of the participants (some of this is in the Transcription Collections of the State Central Archive – *Opisové sbírky*), or in the commentaries of contemporaries (Pavel Skála ze Zhoře, Vilém Slavata, Pavel Stránský).

Less extensive collections of similar material are in the Archive of the Archbishopric of Prague (under the heading *Miscellanea et Emanata*, containing the correspondence of Archbishop Lohelius), and the Archive of the Court Chamber. Jaroslav Prokeš has published a 'Protocol of the Correspondence of the Chancery of the Bohemian Directorate, 1618–1619' in the series *Sborník archivu ministerstva vnitra*. There probably exist further fragments as well – for example MS 1045 in the State Central Archive, 'Reports from the Office of the Lieutenant-Governors', beginning in 1611, running to 1620, and containing an alphabetical index of correspondence received. The handwriting corresponds to that of J. Longo, the secretary who wrote what remains of the correspondence for 1619.[91]

Important original documents may be found in the collection *Bohemica* of Jan Jeník z Bratřic (MS in the Library of the National Museum, Prague). This contains mainly newsletters, Articles of the Diet and archival materials that were once in various municipal archives.[92] Similar in content is another rich collection of pamphlets in the Castle Library at Mnichovo Hradiště (section 42, *Tricennale Bellum*, volumes LXI–LXXII, nos. I. 17.173–17.517; other parts of the collection are under different headings – *Anglica et Hollandica*, etc.).

There is also a group of documents formerly in the Vienna Archive, which have been transferred to the State Central Archive at Prague. These are in the collection *Bohemia–Moravia–Silesia* and were once in the section *Bohemica*, fasc. 46ff. of the Haus- Hof- und Staatsarchiv in Vienna. Among these documents should be mentioned the manuscript by G. Tschernembl ('Allerhandt memorabilia ...'), whose fate has been traced in J. Sturmberger's biography of Tschernembl (336ff.). Tschernembl's 'Memorabilia' are more informative than the comments by Zdeněk Lobkowitz for the period 1618–21, preserved in the manuscript collection of the Lobkowicz Library (now in the University Library, Prague, call-number VII ad. 118, 121). Fragmentary commentaries in Latin, Czech and German are preserved in the pages of the *Kalendář hospodářský a kancelářský*, published by Mikuláš Pštros.

The following smaller collections should be mentioned:

The Papers of Johann Aldringen (d. 1634), in the State Archive at Děčín ('Family Archive Clary-Aldringen'), concern the beginning of Aldringen's military career in central Europe. Most of the papers are correspondence with Gallas and Colloredo in the period of the Mantuan War and of Wallenstein's increasing interest in northwestern Germany (1626), and will therefore be discussed later. But the first of the three boxes contains information about the so-called Spanish Regiment of 1620.[93]

The Episcopal Library at Litoměřice, under the administration of the local State Archive, was founded by Emmanuel Waldstein, and its contents are complemented by the holdings of the former Waldstein of Duchov Library, now at Mnichovo Hradiště. The Waldstein and Šlejnic manuscripts in the Episcopal Library include many from the years 1618–20: the MSS in the section *Bohemica* contain transcriptions ascribed to Slavata, and the call-number I Q 42 13 contains pamphlets from the year 1620. Similar in character is the Castle Library at Rychnov (the 'Kolovrat Library'), particularly in its sections XVII and

XVIII. Work in this library is facilitated by good catalogues in the National Museum at Prague.

The *Kolovrat Family Archive* (Kolovrat-Libštejnský), now in the State Archive at Zámrsk, contains the not very extensive correspondence of Zdeněk Lev Libštejnský-Kolovrat, one of the few Bohemian officers who served the Emperor. In 1619 Zdeněk was captured at Vodňany and imprisoned in the White Tower at Prague. He later emigrated to Saxony and in 1621 took part in the siege of Tábor. His correspondence about Spanish officers in the garrison at Budweis is preserved in the Roudnice Archive (call-number B 236) in the State Archive at Žitenice.[94] Also there is the *Family Archive of Colloredo-Mansfeld of Opočno*, mainly the papers of Rudolph Colloredo, which also concerns the 1630s. For the period of the Bohemian War there are about thirteen important transcripts from the Vienna Military Archive (the sections *Wiener Hofkriegsrat*, *Innerösterreichische Hofkriegsrat*, *Prager Hofkriegsrat*), which concern the career of Rudolph Colloredo; he originally commanded an infantry platoon in Friuli (1618), then from August 1618 an infantry regiment which patrolled the Lower Austrian border against the Hungarians. The rest of this collection will be decribed below.[95] The third collection in the State Archive at Zámrsk, the *Piccolomini Family Archive*, contains only a few documents dealing with Ottavio Piccolomini in these years (group VI, nos. 10,221ff; VIII, nos. 16,430ff.), and is more important for the Wallenstein period and for the end of the war.

The *Waldstein Family Archive*, in the State Archive at Mnichovo Hradiště, will likewise be discussed later. For the period of the Bohemian War the most important section here is the 'Manuscript Section', containing registers of the Estates' army for 1620. Other such military documents formerly located here have been transferred to the State Central Archive at Prague, but for the years after 1625 they are still at Mnichovo Hradiště. The section 'Waldsteiniana' once contained the correspondence of Adam Waldstein for 1618–19, but this has been transferred elsewhere (36 documents from fasc. XII). Copies of Adam's correspondence are in fasc. V (Correspondence with Ferdinand II, 1617–20). The section 'Autographs' has important documents from the Anhalt Chancery; fragments from the Estates' Chancery from the period of the Rebellion which seem to have interested Albrecht Wallenstein; papers from Buquoy's military chancery; and some of the correspondence of F. K. Khevenhüller. In the second part of this section ('Autographs II') there is a collection from the papers of Maximilian of Bavaria, beginning in 1620, twenty letters of Cardinal Khlesl, Mathias' adviser, and letters from the Ambassador Oñate to F. Khevenhüller. Also here are letters from Oñate to Buquoy from 1619–20 and letters from Marradas, beginning in 1619. There are also some papers of members of the Directorate, chiefly Wenceslas of Roupov (letters sent in 1618 to Christian of Anhalt).[96]

State Archive, branch at Český Krumlov: here, in the Schwarzenberg Family Archive, is the correspondence of Adam von Schwarzenberg, the Brandenburg Ambassador in Vienna, from 1611.[97]

The *District and Municipal Archive at České Budějovice* contains a collection of 'Militaria' with some documents concerning Buquoy and Marradas in 1619–21, and a German register for the collection 'Thirty Years' War' in the Buquoy Archive, now in the State Archive at Třeboň, which was described above.

Of the sources in Słovakia the most important are the official and private correspondence of Thurzo and Pálffy. The *State Archive at Bytča* contains the family correspondence of Imrich Thurzo (1598–1621), son of the Palatine George Thurzo, who took part in the Bohemian War as a military commander and a diplomat for Gabriel Bethlen. This correspondence, which forms the section T.K. (*Thurzo korespondence*) covers the period 1619–21 and concerns developments in Bohemia, some details of the activities of Dampierre and Buquoy, the siege of Vienna in 1619, the Cossack contingent under Drugeth (1620) used against Bethlen, etc.[98]

The *Pálffy Family Archive* in the State Central Archive, Bratislava, is difficult to work with because it has not yet been determined how much of the material in the original catalogue (*Elenchus Novus . . . per Andream Eördögh, 1624*) has been preserved. There are documents concerning the Turkish Wars, belonging to Nicholas Pálffy, documents from the series *Publico-Politica* bý Stephen Pálffy (1616, call-number 1 4 II), and his correspondence (from 1618), some of it with his cousin Paul (from 1620). The Pálffy papers are more valuable for the period after 1622.[99]

THE BOHEMIAN WAR AND RELATIONS BETWEEN THE EUROPEAN EAST AND WEST

The title of this section requires some explanation. In the first place, it cannot be stressed enough that the meaning of the terms 'east' and 'west' is not only geographical but also economic and social. This is shown graphically, though superficially, by the seventeenth-century map of *Europe, Recently Described*, by William Blaeuw, which in its time was perhaps the most accessible source of geographical knowledge for Europeans.[100] In Blaeuw's projection 'Russia' and 'Muscovy' are located in the northeast of the European continent, not in the east. The distortion springs from the viewpoint of the author, a Dutch cartographer presenting a picture of Europe in conformity with the preconceptions of his customers in Amsterdam or Middelburg.

In the seventeenth century 'Europe' was no more than a geographical expression. It did not form a political unity: on the one hand, 'Christian Solidarity' had expired; on the other, a conception of the 'World' had arisen during the sixteenth century in which the 'chief enemies of Christian Europe', the Turks, had a place along with their enemies to the east led by Abbasid Persia, and which also included the further-flung lands of the East and West Indies.[101] In the sixteenth century the horizons of the maritime powers were extended so far that the creation of coalitions was envisaged which would transcend the boundaries of Europe.[102] This was demonstrated most clearly in a paper delivered in Stockholm by the Soviet historian B. F. Porshnev.[103]

The fact that a capitalist economy developed most quickly in the northern part of the Netherlands and in England should not lead us to identify these regions with 'western Europe' as a whole. Neither can the conflicts of the Thirty Years' War be reduced to episodes in a conflict between the west and the east. The progressive social forces in the northern provinces of the Netherlands owed their economic strength precisely to their profitable commercial relations with eastern Europe.[104]

Today we consider 'The Thirty Years' War' in new terms. Most historians have looked at the conflict between 1618 and 1648 primarily as a 'central European' or a 'German' conflict, whose remarkable feature was that its original 'religious' character gradually transformed itself into a 'political' one. This was the view of Friedrich Schiller, and it has proved remarkably durable. Modern historians, without exaggerating or ignoring the rôle of religion and political ideologies, see the conflict as far wider than simply 'central European'.[105]

Historians of the last decade speak with justification of an 'Italian' period of the Thirty Years' War (the period of the War of Mantua), of the connection between the War of Smolensk and the struggle of Sweden and her allies with the Habsburgs, and finally of the relationship between the Thirty Years' War and the Eighty Years' War between the Netherlands and Spain.[106]

Studies of the 'Bohemian War', that is the conflict from 1618 to

1620, convince us even further that the 'Thirty Years' War' must be understood in broader terms than those of a military and diplomatic conflict. The history of the 'Bohemian question', the struggle of the Bohemian Estates against the feudal and Catholic programme of the Habsburgs, shows vividly that the tension and conflict grew out of the complicated economic and social situation that prevailed in the period of transition from feudalism to capitalism.[107] The Thirty Years' War then, as a whole, was a political conflict which sprang from the inner tensions of a complex economic and social situation: that is the thesis and also the assumption of this section.

The questions raised by so drastic a broadening of the theme cannot be solved straight away. There have been far fewer exploratory studies in economic and social history than in military or political history. The social situation is particularly unclear, but it is now generally accepted that the struggle of the Netherlands against Spain created a kind of society and a kind of state organization that were new in Europe. That is why the 'Dutch' question joined the 'Turkish' question as one of the chief problems of European society at that time.[108]

In the case of the Dutch struggle with Spain we may certainly speak of a conflict between a predominantly bourgeois society and one that was predominantly feudal. Elsewhere the lines are not so clearly marked. In most European countries at the beginning of the seventeenth century we also find a latent conflict between the classes in feudal society.

This section will deal first with the Bohemian Rebellion and the viewpoints of its political leaders. The following parts will consider the penetration into central Europe of the power of the anti-Habsburg coalition, the result of contacts between opponents of the Habsburgs in the west and the east of Europe, particularly in the years when fundamental changes were occurring or were imminent in the military conflict and in relations between European states.

The first phase of the Thirty Years' War is the so-called Bohemian War (1618–20). It takes its name from the rebellion of the Bohemian Estates against the Habsburgs, begun in May 1618 with the defenestration of Prague, the outbreak of violence between representatives of the Bohemian nobility and the representatives of the Emperor Mathias. The background of the outbreak of hostilities is complex, but it may be said in general that it involved a contest for power springing from the whole course of Bohemian economic and social evolution in the sixteenth century. From the end of the sixteenth century the Habsburgs ruled in the Bohemian Crownlands with the help of a small 'Spanish' faction of Catholic noblemen at the Prague court. The character of this government and its organization was alien to the country; its economic measures were, from the viewpoint of the towns, disastrous. Agricultural production offered several possibilities for progressive development: before 1618, for instance, there was discussion of the respective merits of direct exploitation and leasing at rent. The economic position of the minor nobility, holders of small or medium-sized estates, was poor. The only kind of economic activity that could be made to pay was large-scale production of finished or semi-finished articles – beer, wine, malt, flax, or yarn. Most of the wealthier noblemen lacked the means of investment, and the smaller nobles, restricted to the production of grain, were frequently forced to sell some of their land, and often invested their ready cash in loans to the Estates or the King. This led to the political radicalization of the lesser nobility and a majority of the greater nobility, who from the end of the sixteenth century were pushed into opposition to the régime, whose feudal-Catholic programme conflicted with the Hussite and Reformed-Humanist tradition of the country.[109]

From 1604 Habsburg politics entered a period of crisis whose results were the 'Fratricidal War of the House of Habsburg' and the Estates' rebellion of 1608–9. In their struggle against the Emperor Rudolph, the Estates in all the provinces ruled by the Habsburgs began to join together. Thus there arose the Confederation of the Austrian, Hungarian and Moravian Estates, and the Bohemian–Silesian Confederation. A union of the two confederations, however, was not achieved, and it was impossible to overcome the particularism of each of the provinces. There remained, furthermore, the serious deficiency that all the political action between 1605 and 1609 took place without the participation of the towns and the peasants. The 'freedom of the Estates' did not mean 'Swiss' freedom, that is the freedom of the peasants.[110]

Possessed of a decisive programme, the Estates strengthened their position by a series of legal acts (the Letter of Majesty of Rudolph II). But the adroit policies of the 'Spanish' party, supported by the Nuncio and the Spanish Ambassador, prevented a decisive victory of the Estates. The Habsburgs' first attempt at strong action, mounted by Rudolph II with the help of mercenary troops, ended in failure. But in 1615 the Habsburgs, this time Mathias, achieved a great success by postponing the Estates' right to consent to taxation for five years and by getting them to take over some of the Imperial debt. Two years later

Spanish diplomacy succeeded in concluding the Oñate Agreement by which the Austrian and Spanish Habsburgs agreed to support a single candidate after the death of the heirless Mathias. This was to be Ferdinand, the Archduke of Styria, who was also accepted as the successor to the Bohemian throne at the Diet of 1617. This represented a decisive success because Ferdinand of Styria stood for a programme of recatholicization and absolutism.[111] Thus encouraged, members of the Spanish party in Vienna, the seat of Mathias' Court, moved sharply against their opponents in the winter of 1617–18 and also gained control of the administration of the royal towns in Bohemia.

To the members of the Estates' opposition there was one course of action which had proved its effectiveness as early as 1605–9 and in 1611: armed rebellion. The Bohemian War, then, was provoked by the breakdown of a certain balance of power which had prevailed between the monarch and the Estates after 1609. The whole action was prepared by a handful of the high nobility, but it was joined *en masse* by the lesser nobility, often also by the Catholics among them, and more reluctantly by the towns as well. The initiative of the popular masses in the movement was purposely damped down by the Estates; they were given religious slogans, so effective in the land of Hus. From the very beginning the Estates viewed their rebellion against the Habsburgs as part of a great European conflict which was to end Habsburg power and remove the danger that Europe would be ruled by a Spanish-Catholic 'universal' monarchy. In this picture of things there was no place for the conception of the rebellion as a popular movement (which would threaten the traditional feudal structure of society), or as a religious war. The action, therefore, was presented to the foreign public as an essentially political one, directed against 'evil counsellors' rather than against Mathias himself. This was the thesis of the first *Bohemian Apology*, written even before the defenestration.[112]

Since the Estates assumed that their rebellion would attract foreign help, they embarked right from the start on an extensive campaign of diplomacy. Its character was consistent until the election of Frederick of the Palatinate as King of Bohemia in August 1619. In 1618–19 the Estates pursued two ways to gain allies and widen the conflict – both of which had proved useful in the past.

The first was the attempt to resuscitate and enlarge alliances of the Estates. In the summer of 1618 the Estates obtained aid without much difficulty from the Silesian Estates, on the basis of the confederation agreement. They were joined by the Estates of Upper and Lower

Lusatia. In the autumn the army of this Bohemian–Silesian–Lusatian confederation blocked the first invasion of the Imperial army into eastern Bohemia, which had been made possible by the neutrality of Moravia. Moravia was not won over to the confederation until the spring of 1619. In June 1619, the Bohemian–Moravian army, which enjoyed the sympathy of the Protestant Estates of Upper and Lower Austria, was able to threaten Vienna itself. The Upper and Lower Austrian Estates joined the Bohemian Confederation during the July 1619 meeting of the Bohemian Diet. Thus, the lands of the Austrian Habsburgs (with the exception of Hungary, with which negotiations were being conducted) were transformed in the Bohemian Confederation (*Confederatio Bohemica*) into a union of Estates' oligarchies, bound together by the person of an elected king. The programme of the Confederation, obviously modelled on the Dutch example, was the work of the leaders of the conservative rebellion. In contrast to the Netherlands, the Bohemian Confederation was firmly in the hands of the nobility, and only included the burghers as inferior partners. There was never any question of extending it to include the mass of unfree peasants. On the whole it evolved too slowly to become a serious threat to the Habsburgs; and because of its narrow social base it was incapable of taking the lead in a life and death struggle.[113]

The second possibility included negotiations with older anti-Habsburg groups and attempts to influence public opinion in western Europe by political propaganda, and here they did not miss a single opportunity. But the situation in the spring of 1619 was not very favourable for Bohemia. The United Netherlands, on whom the Bohemians chiefly relied, had concluded a truce with Spain, to run until 1621. Its army under Maurice of Orange-Nassau faced Spinola's Spanish troops, and from 1617 the quarrel between the Arminians and the Gomarists had bordered on civil war. Until the spring of 1619 – that is, until the final victory of the Stadholder Maurice over Oldenbarnevelt – the Dutch could offer no more than verbal encouragement.[114] The allies of the Dutch – Sweden, the German Protestant Union under Frederick of the Palatinate, and the Duke of Savoy Charles Emmanuel – did not possess enough forces to make the substantial contribution that was so badly needed, especially in the first months of the Rebellion. The only gain was one infantry regiment, which Mansfeld had originally recruited for Charles Emmanuel of Savoy to continue the war against Spain. Mansfeld's troops arrived in Bohemia in the autumn of 1618 and at the end of the year captured Pilsen.[115]

Charles Emmanuel supposed that by sending Mansfeld's regiment to Bohemia he would at once rid himself of an unpleasant financial burden and place in his debt the English King James I, father-in-law of Frederick of the Palatinate, whose close relations with the Bohemian rebels were no secret. But James I was horrified rather than pleased by his son-in-law's Bohemian interests, nor did he follow with pleasure the negotiations for an entente with the Dutch States General. He saw himself rather in the rôle of mediator, settling the issues between the Habsburgs and their opponents:[116] this despite the fact that his ambassadors – Herbert in Paris and Dudley Carleton at The Hague, supported the Bohemian rebels. Official English policy in 1618–19 was limited to inevitably unsuccessful mediation.

James' position was shared by his brother-in-law Christian IV of Denmark and by most of the German Lutheran princes led by Johann Georg of Saxony. And even the Protestant Union, reasoning that in Bohemia the conflict was not entirely a religious one, limited itself to benevolent neutrality. Neither Frederick of the Palatinate nor his chief counsellor Christian of Anhalt could change the situation. Even Frederick himself officially supported mediation until the death of Mathias on 20 March 1619. Mathias' death also deprived the English mission led by Doncaster, who followed the court of Ferdinand of Styria like a phantom, of all its significance.[117]

With Ferdinand, known for his bigotry and his dependence on the clergy, no agreement was possible. The uselessness of attempts at reconciliation was also admitted by Mathias, who, of course, could rely on his Spanish and Belgian relatives for support. Archduke Albert, favouring immediate war with the United Netherlands, was a particularly strong supporter of Vienna from the very beginning of the conflict and maintained that everything was at stake in Bohemia.[118] The Imperial campaign of 1618 was made possible only by the aid offered by Albert and the Spanish Ambassador Oñate. Those who advocated taking up the Bohemian challenge with determination only survived the critical period with help from the Netherlands – critical until it was possible to win Madrid over to the idea of decisive action even at substantial cost. In the years 1618–19 the struggle against the Bohemians was only maintained by the forces mobilized by the Viennese members of the 'Spanish' party and their friends abroad. Besides Archduke Albert they included the warlike Spanish viceroys in Milan and Naples, the Polish Catholic branch of the Wasas and the papal Curia which was slowly resuscitating the Catholic League in Southern Germany.[119]

The spring of 1619 ended the period in which both sides were biding their time and arming themselves. Events on the battlefields demanded incisive diplomatic action, because the situation had changed radically. Thurn's Bohemian–Moravian army was forced to return quickly to Bohemia, where the Imperial General Buquoy with reinforcements from the Netherlands had unexpectedly defeated Mansfeld and thrown Prague into confusion. Only reinforcements from Austria and the first troops from the United Netherlands restored the balance of forces in southern Bohemia and neutralized the threat to Moravia. But it was impossible to prevent the German princes at Frankfurt from recognizing Ferdinand's Bohemian electoral vote, thereby granting him recognition as King of Bohemia. In spite of the protests of the Bohemian envoys Ferdinand, with the consent of the Lutheran princes, was elected Emperor on 28 August 1619.

This did not prevent the supporters of the Palatine prince from staging a real coup at the Diet of the Bohemian Crown at Prague, where they succeeded in pushing through the dethronement of Ferdinand, a new constitution for the Confederation, and finally, on 26 August 1619, the election of Frederick of the Palatinate as King of Bohemia. Not everyone supported these measures. In The Hague it was said that in Prague there were people who would have preferred some middle way, that the Palatinate should, to be sure, send them aid, but not their monarch as well. Sir Dudley Carleton wrote from The Hague that

> it is doubtful whether the Bohemians and their allies would follow the example of these [the Dutch] provinces, or of the Swiss, by forming a union of cantons... And I have all the more support for my view from reading the letters of some of the Directors, written shortly before the election of the Palatine Prince. I find in their breasts not so much arrogance, but that they were thinking of how to unite in confederation with this state [the United Netherlands] and the Hanseatic cities...[120]

Such 'republican' views of the Confederation were shared by some of the bourgeois officials of the Bohemian Chancery, led by the Director Peter Milner of Milhaus, but they could not get them accepted by the Diet. Neither, of course, were the Savoyard or Saxon candidates accepted. This meant that Charles Emmanuel disappeared from the ranks of Bohemia's allies, and that Johann Georg of Saxony even moved toward a rapprochement with the Emperor. Dudley Carleton accurately foresaw that the Bohemians would now have to acquiesce in the Palatine dynastic policy: 'Now they have chosen a King they must chiefly address themselves to Kings and absolute Princes.'[121]

This meant throwing out the whole existing conception of the Rebellion as a political conflict between the Estates and the monarch. The Palatine diplomats now had their hands full trying to create the impression that their master, in making his bid for the Bohemian Crown, was not seeking simply to satisfy his ambition but was trying to secure the safety of the Protestant religion. This profession did not prove particularly convincing, and although Maurice of Orange-Nassau, the new ruler in the Netherlands, favoured aiding the Bohemian cause, the prudent States General made such aid dependent upon collaboration with the English. But Anglo-Dutch relations were not improving; the negotiations in London were not progressing, and what was worse, it became obvious that King James did not agree with his son-in-law's decision to accept the Bohemian Crown.

So once again time was lost, and the new king was unable to turn the tide of the battle with his own forces. The Protestant Union also held back, and so apart from the Netherlands Bohemia's only ally in the autumn of 1619 was the Transylvanian Prince Gabriel Bethlen, with whom the Bohemian Estates had been negotiating for an alliance ever since the spring. But the 'Transylvanian Mithridates' had his own troubles. In Transylvania, dependent upon the Turks, he relied on the towns and the heyducks, warlike peasants in the border regions. Transylvania was a buffer state between the Habsburg part of Hungary and Turkish-controlled territory. Bethlen aimed to increase his power, preferably by gaining the rest of Hungary (that is Upper Hungary). This territory, however, was ruled by magnates, and the Upper Hungarian towns, though they supported him, were unable to offer him sufficient means to carry out such an ambitious policy: Bethlen lacked money and adequate infantry and artillery.[122]

At first glance the situation in the autumn of 1619 seemed propitious: only the Alpine lands, without Upper and Lower Austria, remained faithful to Ferdinand. But the Palatine kingdom did not rest on secure foundations. Frederick owed the Bohemian throne to a small group of noblemen, and to these he had to turn over the government of the country. His government was paid for once again by the towns and the bourgeoisie on to whom the burden of taxation was shifted; there was no sympathy between them and the new government. Frederick himself had no use for the Hussite tradition, and his religious policies were dictated by a narrow Calvinism which exacerbated the people, who now regarded his armies as the same sort of threatening marauders as the Imperial forces. The peasants, who had taken part in the rebellion against the Emperor in 1618, were now convinced as well that there was little to choose between the opposing armies. The social basis of the Palatine kingdom was certainly no wider than that of the Estates' government; on the contrary, it was steadily and visibly contracting.

The economic weakness and social narrowness of the Prague government ensured the failure of the autumn campaign of the Bohemian and Hungarian forces against Vienna. In Poland the troops recruited by Drugeth of Humenné turned against eastern Slovakia and forced Bethlen to interrupt his Austrian operations. In any case his taste for war had slackened when he learned of the financial difficulties facing his Bohemian allies. At the beginning of January 1620, following the example of Frederick, he had himself elected 'Prince' in Hungary and gave his blessing to the conclusion of an alliance between Bohemia and Hungary, which was signed on 15 January. But at the beginning of February he signed a truce with Ferdinand II, to run until September. Although the truce did not embrace the Hungarian Estates, it was nevertheless a hard blow for the Bohemian camp. It was intensified by the failure of the Protestant Union to deliver any financial aid, and, except for the Netherlands, none of the friends of the new king raised a finger in defence of the Bohemian cause.

By the time the derisive title 'Winter King' was first applied to Frederick in the propaganda of the period, the initiative in the conflict had clearly passed to the Habsburg–Catholic coalition. On 8 October 1619, in an agreement signed at Munich, it was joined by Maximilian of Bavaria and the Catholic League who agreed to recruit an army of 30,000 troops by the spring of the following year.[123] The alliance between the Habsburgs and the League had not only the blessing of Pope Paul V Borghese, but also his financial support. To be sure, this did not amount to very much, but it was more than the Netherlands supplied to the Bohemians – often sluggish monthly instalments of 50,000 florins. The example of the Curia was followed by the Medici Duke of Tuscany, and finally Philip III of Spain joined in supplying aid to his Viennese relatives. Archduke Albert and Ferdinand's Ambassador Khevenhüller successfully extracted a grant from Madrid amounting to 1,600,000 Spanish crowns for the military actions planned for the following spring. Most of this money was placed at the disposal of the Spanish General in the Netherlands, Spinola, for use, not against the Dutch, but against the Palatine possessions of the King of Bohemia.[124] Thus in the winter of 1619–20, when not one European power openly engaged itself on the side of the Bohemians and their new king, three armies were being prepared against them: Spinola's in the Spanish Netherlands, that of the League under Maximilian of Bavaria, and Buquoy's in Lower Austria. Against the Bohemians stood not a potential but a very real and powerful coalition, reaching from the Atlantic and Mediterranean coasts of Spain to the Baltic shores of Poland, for the Polish King Sigismund III was also prepared to assist the Habsburgs. It was only because of the opposition of his own Estates that this aid was limited to the recruitment of auxiliary troops which later laid waste Moravia and Austria.[125]

The League and the Habsburgs gained an unexpected ally in Johann Georg of Saxony, who at the meeting of the Princes of the Empire at Mühlhausen on 21 March 1620 joined the enemies of the Bohemians and was entrusted with the 'execution' of the Diet's edict in Lusatia and Silesia. The aid granted the Bohemians by Johann Georg's long-time enemy Johann Ernst of Saxe-Weimar amounted to little. Finally the Protestant Union, which had agreed to defend the Palatinate, fell away from the Bohemians. With the help of French and English mediators the leaders of the Union signed a treaty at Ulm on 3 July 1620, which effectively 'neutralized' the territory of the Empire. In reality this meant that the Palatinate remained open to attack from Spinola's Spanish troops and Bohemia was exposed to attack from the Emperor, the League, and the Elector of Saxony.[126]

As the United Netherlands and James I of England were unable to agree on a common policy, this betrayal by the Union and Saxony set the seal on Bohemia's isolation. Though the English Ambassador at The Hague could not detect any connection between the defence of Bohemia and quarrels over the East Indies spice trade, whaling operations off Greenland, and fishing rights off the Scottish and Icelandic coasts, these issues in the end proved insurmountable. In the spring of 1620 the Dutch sent two regiments of infantry and one of cavalry to Bohemia; at the beginning of the summer one infantry regiment arrived from England. That was all. For England and the Netherlands the Rhineland was of more immediate concern than Bohemia, and when the danger of an invasion of the Palatinate became apparent all their forces were of course concentrated there. English policy was to sacrifice Bohemia as long as the Palatinate was in danger. The Dutch States General, to be sure, suggested a diversion – an attack against Spain, both at sea and in Germany – but none of this was acceptable to James I. So the Bohemians were left to their fate.[127]

In Bohemia, meanwhile, the situation steadily worsened. Most of the towns withdrew from the struggle, and the peasants took revenge on their tormentors, the troops of both armies. In the spring of 1620 the peasants around Prague and Tábor rose up against Dutch soldiers. Peasants from the Tábor region, following a white and red flag, offered their support against the enemy if the Estates would free them 'from fealty to the barons and declare us free men'. But none of the barons of the Estates' camp was willing to negotiate with them. Only J. E. Tschernembl suggested in the War Council that 'the serfs be freed and serfdom abolished. . . . Common people will then be willing to fight for their country.' Tschernembl was convinced that the 'common people' would fight better than armies of mercenaries, but his words elicited no more response than the offers of the peasants.[128]

The result of this situation was that in the summer and autumn of 1620 Prague was cut off from the west by peasant uprisings. Foreign observers, the Dutchman van Mario, the Venetian Carlo Antonini and the Englishman Francis Nethersole, all agreed that the response of the 'wretched peasants' was not to be wondered at.[129]

The peasant uprisings, the dissatisfaction of the townspeople, the exploitation by the great noblemen and the impoverishment of the lesser nobility, all added up to a doubtful recommendation for Bohemia in her search for allies. The Swedish agent Ruthgersius warned his master, Gustavus Adolphus, against alliance with the Bohemians. The Swedish King was not interested so much in Bohemia as in Silesia, where he hoped to acquire an important power base in his wars against the Poles.

In this way the 'Bohemian question' came to be raised in the negotiations between Sweden and Muscovy. The Bohemians urged Gustavus Adolphus quickly to conclude an alliance with Muscovy, for such an alliance would be of great help to the Bohemian state. The Swedes should ask Moscow to warn the Poles against interference in the conflict between Bohemia and the Emperor.[130] The Bohemian diplomats had a broad European perspective and tried to use every opportunity for the creation of a European coalition against the Habsburgs, but they failed. Even from Sweden they only gained a bit of artillery, which in any case never arrived on the Bohemian battlefields.

At the end of July 1620, the army of Maximilian of Bavaria entered Upper Austria and within a few days established control. Maximilian's army joined the Imperial forces under Buquoy and in the beginning of September – at the same time that Spinola began his Rhine offensive against the Palatinate – the united armies entered Bohemia. Plans were not entirely clear; therefore there was no march directly on Prague. They were joined by Imperial troops who had been investing Budweis and by fresh troops from Bavaria. At Rakovník the Imperial forces waited for news of Johann Georg's entry into Lusatia, then on 8 November 1620, in a battle outside Prague, they defeated the Bohemian army, whose leaders had not expected a major engagement so close to the approach of winter. They had contingency plans for continuing the struggle from Silesia under the leadership of Frederick of the Palatinate.[131]

These plans, obviously arising from the hope that the end of the truce between the Netherlands and Spain would lead to a generalization of the conflict and therefore a situation more favourable for Bohemia, dissolved into dreams during the winter of 1620–1. The rebellion against the Habsburgs led by the Bohemian Estates collapsed. In the spring of 1621 the States General received their ally Frederick of the Palatinate in The Hague, but he was only accompanied by a nucleus of his court. The Bohemian War was at an end, even though in Bohemia itself garrisons loyal to Frederick held out until 1622. The 'Bohemian question', the struggle for the existence of the Bohemian state and ultimately even the Bohemian people, continued to be waged, though in new and different forms.

The Bohemian War ended with the victory of the Habsburg coalition which showed itself able to mobilize and deploy its forces more effectively. The coalition was homogeneous and the anti-Habsburg camp was not. The anti-Habsburg coalition existed mainly on paper in the writings of contemporary propagandists; it never constituted a firm unit. This does not mean that the conception of it held by the Bohemians was in itself impossible. In the economic and social situation that prevailed, however, this coalition could not be formed before the summer of 1619, and by this time prospects for a military victory over the Habsburgs were minute. The advantage gained by the Habsburgs in 1619 could not be equalled by their opponents. Thus, the struggle for Bohemia and the Palatinate was contained as a localized conflict and ended in the victory of that camp which was able most quickly and thoroughly to mobilize its resources.

3

The Dutch period of conflict 1621–5

PROBLEMS AND SOURCES

This period of the war, which used to be called the War of the Palatinate, was investigated by A. Gindely,[1] J. Goll,[2] and later chiefly by O. Odložilík.[3]

The work of the Moravian historian František Hrubý has helped to form a new picture of the period. His first book, *The Collapse of the Bohemian Uprising in Moravia,*[4] was followed by the excellent biography of Ladislav Velen of Žerotín, mentioned above, and by his edition of *Moravian Correspondence and Documents 1620–1636* (volume I, 1620–1624).[5] The collection *Albrecht Wallenstein and Bohemia after the White Mountain*, also mentioned above, contains studies of various aspects of the situation in the Bohemian lands after 1620. E. Nohejlová-Prátová has explored questions of the currency in those critical years,[6] and V. Pešák has worked on taxation in the same period.[7] V. Líva's edition contains source material for military actions,[8] and T. V. Bílek has studied the confiscations.[9]

On the basis of materials in the State Archive at Weimar, I have investigated the policies of the dukes of Saxe-Weimar.[10] I have also explored the rôle of Spanish forces in actions against Bethlen, Mansfeld and the rebels,[11] and Dutch attempts to form a new anti-Habsburg coalition under Danish or Swedish leadership.[12] I have also published in collaboration with Miroslav Hroch a study of the general aspects of the 'Bohemian question' in the early period of the Thirty Years' War.[13]

V. Fialová has studied the continuation of the war in Moravia,[14] and has also published a close study of an important source, the *Holešov Chronicle 1615–1645.*[15] František Dostál has studied the Wallachian uprising, both in a monograph and in a number of articles in the journal *Valašsko.*[16]

The Palatinate is covered chiefly in F. H. Schubert's studies of

Frederick's government-in-exile in the Netherlands[17] and in his biography of the Palatine diplomat Camerarius.[18]

Romolo Quazza and A. Pfister have followed events in the Valtelline and the beginnings of French interest in northern Italy.[19] B. Badura, in his work mentioned above, has explained the connections between the struggle over the Valtelline and the Bohemian question.

The beginnings of interest on the part of the Danish King Christian IV in intervention in central Europe have been discussed by T. Christiansen, who points out that this was concentrated chiefly in northwestern Germany, the region of Lower Saxony.[20]

Modern Hungarian historians have devoted a good deal of attention to the policy of Gabriel Bethlen, who was trapped by the economic and social situation of Transylvania and Upper Hungary on the one hand and the political vacuum between Turkey and Vienna on the other. In these studies appears the Imperial Colonel Wallenstein, who played a quite significant if rather dubious rôle, particularly in the campaign of 1623. Sufficient attention has been given to the rise of Albrecht Wallenstein, most recently in two biographies of his banker and financial adviser Jan de Witte, written by Karel Vít and E. Ernstberger.[21]

The whole period has been made much clearer by the work of František Hrubý and the studies by Otakar Odložilík. It cannot be said, however, that the reasons for the quick collapse of the Estates' Rebellion in Bohemia and Moravia, as well as in Silesia and Lusatia, are entirely clear. The rôle of The Hague court of Frederick of the Palatinate, vacillating between attempts at greater diplomatic and military activity and willingness to fall into line behind the policies of James I of England, is likewise far from clear. The close relations between Frederick and the Stadholder Maurice of Orange-Nassau and his representative Frederick Hendrik have been overlooked. The question of the disappearance of Christian of Anhalt and Hohenlohe, both of whom were in key positions in the Palatine régime in Bohemia, from the ranks of Frederick's advisers has been similarly neglected.

More detailed studies have pointed out the significance of the activities of the émigré group at Berlin and the influence of former Bohemian rebels in the circle around Gabriel Bethlen. Odložilík's biography of Heinrich von Thurn indicated the unrealized possibilities that lie in this direction.

For reasons mentioned above, the sources which are available today consist almost entirely of papers revealing the military and diplomatic activities of the Habsburg camp. They deal not only with events in

Bohemia and the Palatinate (in the most recent literature the term 'Bohemian–Palatine War' has become current), but with far wider horizons, with diplomatic activities extending to the edges of the continent – to England, Spain and elsewhere.

The sources for the period 1621–5 include many which have already been mentioned in connection with the Bohemian War: chiefly, the Buquoy Military Chancery (State Archive, Třeboň) and the 'Moravian Collection' of the State Archive at Brno – particularly the Dietrichstein Family Archive, containing Dietrichstein's correspondence for 1620–1 (f. 845–6), the 'Historical Archive', and the *Grosse Korrespondenz.*

The *Grosse Korrespondenz* contains fragments of the original archive of the Cardinal which were carried off to Stockholm by the Swedes. Subsequently they found their way to Vienna, thence to Prague. In 1959 the State Archive at Brno acquired eighteen boxes from this collection containing correspondence between 1621 and 1636. The collection includes original letters addressed to the Cardinal and drafts of his replies. The correspondence is richest for the years 1622–3, sketchy for the period 1624–6, then more complete until 1632. The most active of the Cardinal's correspondents were Guillermo Verdugo, Cardinals Aldobrandini and Barberini, J. F. Breiner, Nicholas Esterházy, R. Collalto, and Oñate – members of the 'Spanish' party at the Imperial court and members of the Roman Curia. Among those to whom the Cardinal wrote are Marradas, Karl von Liechtenstein, Karel of Žerotín the Elder, Adam Waldstein, Albrecht Wallenstein, Questenberg, and others. The collection has scarcely been touched by scholars.

The section 'Morava' in the 'Historical Archive' also contains rich materials for the years 1622–3. Here is Dietrichstein's correspondence with Ferdinand II, concerning the progress of the war in Moravia, and also the correspondence with the Court War Council. There is a great deal of material concerning the administration, with information about confiscations, trials, currency manipulation and appeals from the rebels. Documents from the year 1624 touch uprisings in the land (the Wallachians), the punishment of rebels and the difficult economic situation.[22]

The Dietrichstein correspondence continues, of course, in the former archepiscopal archive of Kroměříž (now in the State Archive at Olomouc). The correspondence of R. Collalto is continued in the State Archive, Brno, but most of it is from the period after 1625.

The State Archive branch at Žlutice also contains two important collections which begin in the preceding period: the Nostitz-Rieneck Family Archive and the Verdugo Family Archive.

The *Nostitz-Rieneck Archive* contains documents from about 1620. Item number DD 2 is a collection of Cardinal Dietrichstein's drafts for the period 1621–31, which augments the collection at Brno and Olomouc. In 1621 begins the correspondence with the Imperial court (call-number EE 2), from 1622 we find military affairs (SS 1) and papers of the Chamber (LL 2). There are papers from the embassy of Otto Nostitz at Dresden, 1622–5 (B 2) and those of Jiří Bořita of Martinic to Hungary, Bavaria, Frankfurt and Brandenburg (from 1624 to 1643, call-number NN 7). Papers of Pavel Michna of Vacínov concerning his activities in the Bohemian Chamber after 1625 have the call-number EE 3. This entire collection becomes important again for the 1640s.[23]

The *Verdugo Archive* begins with the personal papers of Guillermo Verdugo from 1611, but it is important only from 1620, the beginning of Verdugo's involvement in the Bohemian War. The correspondence of Christian of Anhalt the Younger with Verdugo from 1621 to 1627 is significant here because it documents the gradual enticement of the younger Anhalt, Verdugo's prisoner after the Battle of the White Mountain, and also of his father, to the Imperial side. There is also correspondence from 1623–8, when Verdugo commanded the Spanish troops in the Lower Palatinate. From the same period there are letters from Ambrosio Spinola to Verdugo (1626–7). The later period is covered by letters to Francisco Verdugo from Colonel Andrés de Contreras, concerning, among other things, the foundation of the Hibernian Monastery at Prague. The so-called Verdugo Papers concern property matters from 1633 to 1668; there are also letters from the stewards of the Verdugo estate of Doupov, from Baltasar Cicogna, the Jesuit Arriaga, and the Abbot Isidor de la Cruz in Prague. There is a striking quantity of material to illumine conflicts between the new lords and their peasants.

The State Archive at Děčín contains similar material in the papers of Rudolph Thun (d. 1636), in the *Thun-Hohenstein Archive.* From 1622–5 Rudolph Thun received news of the war, particularly from German and Alpine battlefields. The State Archive at Český Krumlov possesses, in the *Schwarzenberg Family Archive,* the papers of Georg Ludwig von Schwarzenberg, dealing with his embassy to the League (1616) and his missions to the Spanish Netherlands and England (1622–3), to Spain (1624), and to the Archduke Leopold in Strasbourg

(1625) for the recruitment of Spanish soldiers.[24] Much in these missions was very important: in Madrid, for example, Schwarzenberg sounded out the Spanish response to the prospect of a marriage between the Prince of Wales and the Infanta. The Eggenberg collection contains no documents touching on the activities of Johann Ulrich. These are to be found in the Wallenstein Collection in the State Archive at Mnichovo Hradiště.

The *Waldstein Archive* is now divided into the following sections: I. 'Documents' (*Listiny*), II. 'Manuscripts' (*Rukopisy*), III. 'Autographs', IV. 'Wallensteiniana', V. 'The Doksy Section' (*Dokská manipulace*), VI. 'The Prague Section' (*Pražská manipulace*), and VII. 'Maps and Plans'. Sources for the history of the Thirty Years' War are distributed unevenly among these sections. The collection is composed essentially of the papers of members of the Waldstein family who took part in the war (chiefly Albrecht Wallenstein, Adam and Max Waldstein), and of documents collected by members of the family – for example Emmanuel Ernst, Bishop of Litoměřice, or Ernest Charles, who at the end of the last century bought many autographs, often of doubtful origin.

The papers of Albrecht Wallenstein begin with his first generalship, and therefore belong to the period after 1625. Albrecht Wallenstein's most important *privilegia* were first kept at Jičín, then from 1628 at Hrubá Skála. His heir, Maximilian Waldstein, tried to retain what he could of the generalissimo's property. This included Hrubá Skála (1636), together with most of its legal muniments and *privilegia*, a collection which became the core of the family archive. To this were added the papers of Maximilian and his father Adam. Their papers were kept in the Wallenstein Palace at Prague into the eighteenth century, then transferred to Duchcov. But by 1841 they were in the possession of the branch of the family at Mnichovo Hradiště, and they were adroitly employed by Christian Waldstein in his quarrel with Vienna over the return of property confiscated from Wallenstein's heirs. Only after the end of the Second World War were all the family papers brought together at Mnichovo Hradiště.

Section I ('Documents') contains *privilegia* and some papers of Albrecht Wallenstein; section II ('Manuscripts') includes an unfortunately only partially preserved diary of Adam Waldstein which is similar to the journals of Zdeněk Lobkowitz, though the decade between 1618 and 1628 is missing. The parts which survive, moreover, betray evidence of self-censorship on the part of this diffident member of the Habsburg party and steadfast proponent of conciliation. Section IV

('Wallensteiniana') originally contained sixteen folio volumes of original documents and transcriptions, collected chiefly for genealogical purposes by Bishop Emmanuel Ernst of Waldstein, the founder of the Episcopal Library at Litoměřice, which was described above. The first of these volumes contains only copies of documents from section I, the second materials for the biography of Albrecht Wallenstein; the third volume concerns the landed property of Adam Waldstein (who took great pains with the management of his property after 1621); the fourth volume contains some interesting documents concerning the beginnings of the generalissimo's career. The fifth volume includes copies of the correspondence of Adam Waldstein with Ferdinand II from 1617 to 1620; the sixth contains correspondence of Ferdinand II with Albrecht Wallenstein from 1628 to 1633 and papers relating to the Duchy of Friedland. The seventh volume has been lost; the eighth concerns military affairs; the ninth volume contains papers about the division of the Smiřický estates (1622). The tenth and eleventh volumes consist of miscellanea about the General. Part of the twelfth volume has been lost, and the remainder contains documents from 1663–4. The thirteenth, fourteenth and fifteenth volumes contain papers relating to sales and exchanges of the estates of Albrecht Wallenstein. The sixteenth volume contains records of the Jičín Chamber.

Section V, ('The Doksy Section') is the most extensive part of the archive, and after the First World War it was housed in the castle of Doksy. It contains sixteen original documents concerning Wallenstein's appointments, instructions given by Wallenstein in 1625, decrees concerning the principality of Mecklenburg, and correspondence of Albrecht with Maximilian of Bavaria from 1624 to 1633. There are also transcriptions from various Bohemian and foreign archives, notably from the Harrach Archive in Vienna. Further, there are transcriptions of correspondence of Adam Waldstein from the period of the Rebellion and originals of his correspondence with Karel of Žerotín the Elder from 1631 to 1635. The military papers include reports of the Swedish campaigns during the war.

The interesting Autograph Collection (section III) was gathered at the end of the last century by Ernest Charles Waldstein with the help of Dr E. Schebek. Materials from the Family Archives of Khevenhüller, Piccolomini and others were acquired from dealers in Vienna and Berlin. The Collection is divided into four series: series I contains nine groups ('Emperors and Princes', 'Statesmen from the Imperial Lands and the Imperial Camp', 'The Imperial and League Armies', 'The Swedish Army', 'The Danish Army', 'Other Armies', 'Protestant

Clergy', 'Catholic Clergy', and 'Other Participants'). Together the first series represents about 1,300 documents, all of which were once preserved in other collections (for example, about a fifth of these documents came from the Military Chancery of Ottavio Piccolomini of Náchod). The number of documents from the Anhalt Chancery is slightly smaller. Other documents were acquired from the Buquoy Archive, from the remnants of the Estates' Chancery, and the Khevenhüller registry; and finally there are some documents from the Imperial Free Cities. Series II contains 1,700 documents arranged alphabetically by author. The archive of F. K. Khevenhüller contributes about a third of the series. In addition there are papers of Maximilian of Bavaria and letters of Johann Ulrich von Eggenberg, Oñate, Piccolomini, Pappenheim, Questenberg, and autographs of Albrecht Wallenstein from the years 1619 to 1634 (95 documents). Swedish autographs form a separate group, containing papers of Axel Oxenstierna, L. Torstensson, Erskein, and others. Series III is a small collection of about 270 documents dealing primarily with the Austrian provinces before the war. But there are also important pieces from Piccolomini's correspondence, mainly from 1633–4, and a letter from Mansfeld to Christian of Anhalt written in 1618 regarding the Directorate. Series IV is Schebek's collection, consisting chiefly of documents from the Piccolomini Archive relevant to Wallenstein's fall in 1634.[25]

The State Archive at Mnichovo Hradiště also possesses a manuscript, 'Diarium', by Johann Putz von Adlersturm (author of the anti-Wallenstein tract *Chaos perduellionis*), which begins with Putz's arrival in Bohemia in 1622.

The *Schlick Family Archive* in the State Archive at Zámrsk contains papers of Heinrich Schlick, later President of the Court War Council, beginning in 1622. The most important part of the collection belongs to the Wallenstein period, after 1625, and to the period when Schlick, as President of the War Council, had copies made of all important official documents to guide him in the Council meetings.[26] This collection, therefore, will be mentioned more than once in the following pages.

Slovak collections relevant to these years include the Thurzo and Pálffy Archives both of which have been introduced above. The *Illésházy Family Archive* (at Nitra) was collected as early as 1667, and its most important part is the correspondence of Stephen, Caspar and George Illésházy. Work here, however, is hampered by poor organization; some of the original material, moreover, was removed to the Budapest Archive in the last century. The chief subject of the correspondence is the Estates' rebellion against the Habsburgs led by George Rákóczy and F. Vesselényi.[27]

There is also documentation for the Estates' Rebellion in the Bratislava Municipal Archive. The Kremnica Municipal Archive contains documents, calendars, correspondence, and also minutes of the representatives of central Slovakian mining towns from the 1560s and after. The Archive of Banská Bystrica contains an interesting *Registrum alterum archivalium ab anno 1611–1630*. Finally, the Levoča Municipal Archive possesses several valuable sets of documents: in its section XIV are minutes of the meetings of the five Upper Hungarian towns Košice, Levoča, Prešov, Solivar and Bardejov; the same section also contains reports of the Town Council from 1619 to 1625 and ordnance reports from 1610 to 1621, while section XVI is composed of fragments of several family archives, including that of Drugeth of Humenné.[28]

It may be concluded from this survey that the documentary evidence available concerning this period of the Thirty Years' War, when repeated fighting took place on Bohemian and Slovakian territory even though the focus of the conflict had shifted to western Europe, is of sufficient volume and significance to lead to perceptible modifications of the traditional interpretation of the period. The military registers afford a view of the struggle for the Palatinate and of the conflict between Spain and the United Netherlands (who bore the brunt of the effort against the Habsburgs), and the diplomatic correspondence available here enables us to trace the Dutch attempts to form an extensive alliance.

THE SPANIARDS IN BOHEMIA AND MORAVIA

The years 1621–5 represent an important transitional period in the history of the Thirty Years' War whose significance has only relatively recently been appreciated by historians. E. A. Beller, who wrote a brief survey of the politico-military conflict for the fourth volume of the *New Cambridge Modern History*, characterized this period as a time in which the leaders of both camps, Ferdinand II and Frederick of the Palatinate, searched for new allies.[29] In essence, therefore, he repeated the conclusion reached as early as 1882 by Anton Gindely in his survey of the Thirty Years' War.[30] It is interesting to note that the fourth volume in the Cambridge series bears the title *The Decline of Spain and the Thirty Years' War*.

In the same volume H. R. Trevor-Roper described Spain's relations with the rest of Europe in the years 1598–1621. He took careful note of Spain's interest in Central Europe, where in 1617 Zúñiga and Oñate were successful in having Ferdinand of Styria recognized as successor to the Emperor Mathias, in return for which the Austrian Habsburgs were willing to cede Alsatia and the Tyrol. But from 1617, when Zúñiga after his return from Prague became the leading member of the *Consejo de Estado*, the 'War party' came to power in Madrid. This also included Spanish viceroys and ambassadors elsewhere: Osuna in Naples, Bedmar in Venice, Feria in Milan, Oñate in Vienna. In the view of these makers of Spanish policy it was time to discard the notion of the *Pax Hispanica*, and even to abandon attempts to renew the Twelve Years' Truce with the Dutch States General in 1621. Count Gondomar, Spanish Ambassador in England, Carlos Coloma, Viceroy in Cambrai, and Baltasar de Zúñiga in Madrid, all began to take the position that the Truce should not be extended. Coloma and Zúñiga, as good Castilians, were in favour of destroying the Netherlands with an offensive by Spinola's army. Gondomar, on the other hand, favoured an invasion of England and hoped to renew the old plans for the *Empresa de Inglaterra*. At the same time he was willing to effect radical structural changes in the organization and administration of the Spanish Empire, and in this he came quite close to the ideas of the *Arbitristas* of the Economic Council (*Consejo de Hacienda*), who pointed to the desperate condition of the Castilian finances and recommended fundamental reforms. They were against renewing the war with the Dutch, and for a time in 1621 their arguments prevailed. But when Philip III and the Archduke Albert in Brussels both suddenly died, the commercial interests in the West and East Indies – members of the Council for Portugal and the Council for India – accepted the views of Coloma and Zúñiga: 'Thus the merging of the wars – the war in Bohemia and the war of the Netherlands – was to engender the worst of all European wars: the Thirty Years' War, in which the European supremacy of Spain would founder'.[31]

According to the Groningen historian E. H. Kossman, the decisive factor at this point was the Marquis de Bedmar, Cardinal de la Cueva. De la Cueva had been transferred to the Netherlands in 1618 after leaving Venice under suspicion of having plotted a coup against the Signoria. Now, after the death of the Archduke Albert, he became the ruler of the Spanish Netherlands. De la Cueva dominated Albert's widow the Infanta Isabella Clara, just as her nephew Philip IV was dominated by Baltasar de Zúñiga and his nephew Olivares. After 1621 the United Netherlands merely tried to defend themselves against

Spanish superiority; after 1624 they received financial and diplomatic aid from France; then in 1629 they began to take the offensive.[32] The collection of the Algemeen Rijksarchief at The Hague is not very rich for the 1620s (the Orange-Nassau Archive is not normally open to scholars), and information about the resolutions of the Estates General is very scarce. Still it is possible to find sufficient evidence that the Stadholders Maurice and Frederick Hendrik, representatives of the Orangist dynastic policy and heirs of the aggressive Gomarists of the crisis period before 1619, understood the necessity to take the offensive in defending the Netherlands, and in 1621–3 they were not without success.[33]

All this was indicated earlier by Gindely in the fourth volume of his *Geschichte des böhmischen Aufstandes*, by B. Mendl in his article about Frederick of the Palatinate, and by František Hrubý in his biography of Ladislav Velen of Žerotín. Otakar Odložilík used chiefly the Palatine documents now at Munich and the Brandenburg papers at Merseburg for his books about the Bohemian émigrés after the Battle of the White Mountain.[34] Unfortunately these works have largely escaped the notice of non-Czech historians. Thus after the Second World War F. H. Schubert of the University of Frankfurt studied the same materials without being aware of Odložilík's work. Schubert's study of the Netherlands during the Thirty Years' War is marked by a rare understanding for the symbiosis between politics and society, and it presents the view that the Netherlands represented a new socio-political element in international relations.[35] His study of 'Political Protestantism', whose chief representative he considers to have been Frederick of the Palatinate (who after 1621 resided at The Hague or at Rhenen), shows how the policy of the Palatine government-in-exile changed. Originally it had been aggressive, on the pattern formulated by Christian of Anhalt, but pursuing essentially dynastic aims. After 1622 a confessionally motivated policy prevailed whose spokesman was Camerarius, though later it returned to a more dynastically oriented line under the courtier–diplomat Russdorf.[36] But in all its forms the policy of the Palatine government-in-exile used the Dutch Stadholders Maurice and Frederick Hendrik to test the reaction of the other European powers to truly radical policies.

J. H. Elliott used the *Hacienda* collection in the Archivo General de Simancas to elucidate the tragic situation into which the Spanish Empire and its real ruler, the Conde Duque Olivares, fell after 1622. Spain became involved in a conflict for which the army of Flanders alone demanded an increase of expenditure from one and a half million ducats to three and a half millions, while the total expenditure of the government reached the astronomical figure of eight millions per annum. The war necessitated the implementation of reforms which had been put off in the past but which for lack of money were now impossible to realize.[37]

Some Spanish historians of this period have restated the traditional defence of the 'Imperial' policy articulated by Gondomar, Osuna and others.[38] Others have attempted to revise some of the traditional interpretations. The essentially personal approach of the first group is shared by the American historian Charles Howard Carter, whose book on the *Secret Diplomacy of the Habsburgs* has been noted earlier. Though it is supposed to extend to 1625, Carter's work in fact concludes with the failure of the Pecquius mission. J. Reglá points to the crucial year 1621 as the end of Spanish hegemony and the beginning of the seventeenth-century crisis in Spain. In his view 'Spanish troops fought at the side of Ferdinand II from the beginning of the conflict in Bohemia, where they contributed to the victory at the White Mountain. But large-scale military intervention in this war came only with the reign of Philip IV.'[39] In his seminar at the University of Valencia José Maria Jover began a large-scale project in which three of his young associates – Carmen Calatayud, María del Carmen Calvo and Rafael Ródenas Vilar – were to investigate Spanish policy during the Thirty Years' War. María del Carmen Calvo's book on Spanish foreign policy in the era of Gustavus Adolphus (1630–5) appeared in 1964; Ródenas Vilar published his work on Spain's European policy between 1624 and 1630 in 1967; while Carmen Calatayud's research on the beginnings of the Spanish intervention has not yet appeared.[40] For central Europe Ródenas relied primarily on Gindely's brief history of Germany, and he combined sources from Simancas with documents from Munich. His conclusion is that Spinola's attack on the Lower Palatinate and the advance by the Prince of Feria, Governor of Milan, into the Valtelline, constituted the first armed intervention. The second intervention took place at almost the same time: Dutch contingents advanced into the Lower Palatinate to prevent the Spaniards from controlling the Rhine route, after the Valtelline had already given them control of the Alpine passes.[41] Between 1621 and 1624 Spinola tried in vain to destroy the United Netherlands in a 'lightning war' (*guerra relámpago*). This was chiefly because the pillars of political power – the Castilian nobility and clergy, as well as the burghers of the Flemish towns – did not consider the war against the United Provinces to be crucial. It was only Portuguese entrepreneurs who were willing to finance campaigns in

Flanders, but that was not enough. And once the 'lightning war' ended in failure, the whole affair was lost for Madrid.[42]

In contrast with earlier Spanish historians, Reglá, Jover and Ródenas Vilar give first place to the power struggle – the campaign to destroy the 'Carthage' on the shores of the Zuider Zee – and de-emphasize the religious aspect, whose special rôle, however, cannot be doubted.[43] The economic and political aspects also predominate in J. H. Elliott's book about the revolt in Catalonia. Elliott's sources from the *Hacienda* collection of the Simancas Archive show how the economic position of the Spanish monarchy worsened. Commerce with America declined, and in the year 1620, instead of the two million ducats in silver which had once been the usual annual cargo of the fleet, only 800,000 silver ducats arrived.[44]

When in August 1618 news arrived of the revolt in Bohemia, the *Válido* Lerma requested the Economic Council to send funds to Germany and Italy. The President of the Council refused, giving as his reason the fact that normal sources of income had dried up, and that the whole royal *hacienda* was already deeply in debt. But Philip III replied that the present needs were so important that the Economic Council must find the money for them, for Germany could not be evacuated.[45] A few months later the Economic Council was joined in its opposition by the Council for Castile, which on 1 February 1619 submitted its famous *consulta* expressing the apprehensions of the *Arbítristas.* Even though these opinions had been well publicized in the tract of Fernández Navarrete, they had no influence upon Lerma or his successor the Duke de Uceda.[46] But the *consultas* of the Council of State for 1621, which should contain justifications either for extending the Twelve Years' Truce or else for renewing the war, have not survived, so that the arguments advanced by Trevor-Roper, although they are logical, remain unsubstantiated. In the end, of course, Olivares had to find the funds to continue the war in the Netherlands, just as Lerma had had to find money for intervention against the Bohemians, because in 1621 as in 1618 political arguments prevailed over economic ones.[47]

This glance at problems that have only recently been approached shows that for the period 1621–5 many questions remain unanswered. But now there appears to be no serious objection to viewing the Thirty Years' War as a politico-military conflict between two models of politics and society, represented respectively by Spain and the United Netherlands.[48] If the Bohemian War can be described as a localized conflict of a general character, then in 1621 the Netherlands became the open organizer of all opposition against the European hegemony of the Spanish and Austrian Habsburgs, against the 'Austracism' of the contemporary pamphleteers. This does not, of course, mean that all differences of opinion have been swept away. There is not yet a satisfactory study of the general tendencies and the structural aspects of Dutch foreign policy in the first half of the seventeenth century, which could be placed beside M. A. M. Franken's work on the second half of the century.[49]

As long as there is no published study of Spanish intervention in the Thirty Years' War before 1624, it must remain an open question whether this intervention really began in 1618, as Reglá concludes, or only after 1621, or not until 1624, with the Franco-Spanish conflict over the Valtelline, as Ródenas Vilar's argument maintains. After the publication of papers from Buquoy's military chancery in the second volume of the *Documenta Bohemica*, there can be no doubt that Spanish aid and Spanish credit, channelled not directly from Madrid but instead through the Ambassador Oñate at Vienna and the Archduke Albert at Brussels, had already saved the Habsburgs in central Europe by the autumn of 1618.[50]

The papers published in the second volume of *Documenta Bohemica* can be supplemented by material contained in the Archivo General de Simancas (much of which is available in transcript in the Prague State Central Archive)[51] and also, of course, by documents in the Austrian State Archive at Vienna.[52] One indication of the Europe-wide character of the conflict from its very beginning is the fact that it immediately preoccupied most of the European governments. This indicates a further reason why the historian's task today is far more difficult than was that of his predecessors, who selected only partial or incomplete materials.

Just as Spanish policy cannot be fully explained entirely on the basis of documents from the Archivo General de Simancas and the National Library at Madrid,[53] so also a more limited problem such as the question of the beginning and duration of Spanish military intervention can only be solved with the help of a much wider selection of source material than has been consulted so far.

A concrete indication of the extent of Spanish intervention at the end of 1620 is given by an index of the Imperial army (*Lista Kayserlicher Kriegs-Armada*).[54] The army's titular commander was the Emperor Ferdinand II, but it was actually directed by the Army Council (*Hofkriegs-Rat*) headed by Johann Caspar Stadion. One of its members was Henri Duval Dampierre, who had been transferred from the Spanish Netherlands. The first of the generals listed is Ambrosio Spinola, 'Imperial Lieutenant-General and the Spanish King's Captain-General in the Netherlands'. Among the field-marshals are: Charles Bonaventure Longueval Buquoy, the actual Commander of the Imperial forces; the Commander of the League army Johann Tserclaes de Tilly; and M. A. Althan. Among the lieutenant-generals (*Generälen-Veldt-Wachtmeister*) are Dampierre; Hieronymo Caraffa, 'Marquess of Montenegro and General of the Spanish Crown'; Carlo Marquis di Spinelli, 'Spanish General'.[55]

The infantry was divided into 'German' (*Auff teutschem Fuss*) and 'Spanish' sections (*Auff hispanischem Fuss*). There were six regiments, or rather large units, of Spanish infantry; a *brigata* of Italian troops led by Spinola arrived in Bohemia from Naples in the autumn of 1619 and numbered thirty-one companies. Lieutenant-Colonel Hennin de Bournonville led Buquoy's brigade of fifteen companies of Walloon troops which arrived in 1619 from the Spanish Netherlands. Lieutenant-Colonel Edward Geraldin commanded Buquoy's second brigade of fifteen companies of Walloon and Irish troops, which similarly arrived in the summer of 1619. Colonel Guillermo Verdugo commanded a regiment of Walloon troops whose fifteen companies arrived in the autumn of 1619 from Naples. Two further regiments had been supplied earlier. Colonel Maurice de Créange (Kriechinger) led a Spanish regiment of five companies, which had originally been supplied by Oñate to Ferdinand of Styria for his conflict with the Venetians; in 1618 this regiment was transferred to Bohemia; and lastly the regiment of Otto Fugger with seven companies of Walloon troops was in Vienna in 1619. In 1620 the Index places it in Lower Austria and notes its composition as Spanish. It is more likely that it was organized on the Spanish pattern and paid by the Spanish war treasury. In these six regiments there were altogether eighty-eight companies, or about 18,000 infantrymen, while the 'German' infantry numbered only seventy-eight companies.

One company of Spanish infantry was led by Ferdinand Corratti, who was also in Bohemia in 1620. The company of Upper German troops stationed at Budweis was led by one of the few Bohemian noblemen in the Imperial service, Zdeněk Kolovrat-Libštejnský, and it was financed at least partly from Spanish sources. Altogether, then, Spain financed ninety infantry companies, or more than half the infantry that the Emperor had at his disposal.[56]

But this was not all. Of the five cavalry regiments, four were composed of Spaniards or Walloons. As early as 1618 the former commander of the Emperor Rudolph II's bodyguard, Don Baltasar de Marradas, commanded a regiment of Spanish cavalry of ten companies. His second-in-command was Captain Don Felipe de Areyzaga, and the regiment was in the field in Bohemia. Albrecht Wallenstein, with the help of the Archduke Albert, recruited two cavalry regiments in the Spanish Netherlands in 1619 (altogether twenty Walloon companies) which were sent to fight against the Bohemians. The first regiment was commanded by Lieutenant-Colonel Pierre de la Motte, the second by Lieutenant-Colonel Torquato Conti. Maximilian von Liechtenstein led ten companies of Walloon cavalrymen, who from 1619 fought in Moravia or along the Moravian frontier.[57]

An arquebusier regiment, led by Pietro di Medici (serving under Dampierre) had arrived in Bohemia earlier. This regiment, sometimes called the 'Florentine' because it was paid by the Duke of Tuscany, had five companies, composed partly of Walloons, partly of Germans. Walloons made up the five companies of the arquebusier regiments of Colonel Gauchier de Marchan who arrived in the summer of 1619 from Flanders. Finally, Buquoy's bodyguard (*Leibguardia*) was made up of a Walloon company under the command of Lieutenant-Colonel Laguy.

The Bohemian campaign and the Battle of the White Mountain caused some casualties among the Spanish regiments and their commanders. Dampierre was killed before the gates of Pressburg; Colonel Jean de la Croix and Lieutenant-Colonel Ferdinand Coratti fell at the Battle of the White Mountain.[58]

There can be no doubt that the Spanish military intervention in central Europe was of the greatest significance. The Spaniards supplied the Austrian Habsburgs with the contingents which under Dampierre and Buquoy moved against the forces of the Bohemian Estates in the autumn of 1618. They reinforced Buquoy's bridgehead in southern Bohemia around Budweis, and from the winter of 1619–20 they ensured the absolute numerical superiority of the Imperial army over the army of the Bohemian Estates and their allies.[59]

Just how important the Spanish effort was can be seen from a table showing the numbers of Imperial companies in the years 1619–25, derived from the Indexes for the individual years in the Wallenstein Military Chancery.[60]

In the beginning, in 1618, the government in Vienna had at its disposal only two infantry and two cavalry regiments, which had been transferred on Oñate's recommendation from Istria. In 1619 there began a steady stream of Spanish reinforcement, with the transfer of

	1619	*1620*	*1621*	*1622*	*1623*	*1624*	*1625*
Infantry regiments (no. of companies)	100	180	162	161	176	127	150
Cuirassier regiments (no. of companies)	32	45	64	72	56	47	51
Arquebusiers	56	69	156	112	24	24	101
Dragoons						10	26
Chevaux-legers, Croats, Cossacks	20	*c.* 4,500 cav. troops	4,000 troops	2,700 troops	7 companies		12 companies

contingents from Naples, Milan and Flanders. In 1620 the 'Spanish' contingents represented at least a half of the entire Imperial army.

It remains to scrutinize the extent of Spanish intervention in the years 1621–5. Here, besides the Buquoy chancery, we also have the papers of other members of the 'Spanish party', some of them first printed in František Hrubý's pioneering edition and now also in the third volume of the *Documenta Bohemica.*

The table (pp. 82–3) shows that the greater part of the Spanish infantry moved from Bohemia into Moravia in the winter of 1620–1 and thence to Hungary. After Buquoy's death the army came under the command of Caraccioli, then from 1622, of Caraffa, and during the year 1622 it was moved into the Palatinate.[61] Until 1624 one regiment of Walloon infantry under Guillermo Verdugo remained in central Europe. Three of the five cavalry regiments composed of Spaniards (Marradas) or Walloons (the Wallenstein regiments) remained in central Europe until 1625. During the year 1622, after the peace treaty with Bethlen, the contingents were transferred to the Empire, then in 1623 they were quickly returned to Moravia. Some contingents were transferred to the service of the League or of the Archduke Leopold, or were returned to the Spanish command in Flanders. The last remnants were dissolved by Wallenstein's military reform of 1625. At that time most of the contingents which interest us were transferred to the Netherlands for the siege of Breda. After the exit of Caraccioli and Caraffa, Baltasar de Marradas became their Supreme Imperial Commander. Marradas, who came from Valencia, acquired a large complex of estates around Hluboká in southern Bohemia, from which he observed with envy the brilliant rise of his fortunate rival Albrecht Wallenstein. Here also, with the other 'Spaniards' – members of the pro-Spanish clique among the Imperial generals – he intrigued for Wallenstein's downfall in the beginning of 1634.[62] Don Martin de Huerta enjoyed a central European career similar to Marradas', though

The extent of Spanish intervention, 1621–5

	1620	*1621*	*1622*	*1623*	*1624*	*1625*
Spinelli's Neapolitan *brigata*	31 companies (Bohemia)	Moravia	Caraffa	Moravia	–	–
Buquoy–Hennin Walloon infantry	15 comp. Bohemia	Caraccioli, 1,200 t.	Moravia	–	–	–
Buquoy–Geraldin Walloon–Irish infantry	15 comp. Bohemia	–	1,000 troops (Moravia)	–	–	–
Verdugo, Walloon infantry	15 comp. Bohemia	1,200 t. (Moravia)	–	–	Moravia	Palatinate (?)
Creange, Spanish infantry	5 comp. Bohemia	8 comp. Lower Aust.	–	–	–	–
Fugger, Walloon infantry	7 comp. Lower Austria	7 comp. Hungarian frontier	Moravia	–	–	–
Aldobrandini, papal infantry	–	10 comp. Moravia	10 comp. Moravia	–	–	–
Z. Kolovrat	1 comp. Budweis	1 comp. Budweis	1 comp. Budweis	2 comp. Budweis	1 comp. Budweis	(expanded into regiment)
F. Carrati, Sp. infantry	1 comp. Bohemia	–	–	–	–	–
Liechtenstein Walloon cuirassiers	10 companies Moravia	5 comp. Moravia	–	–	–	–
Marradas–Areyzaga Sp. cuirassiers (after 1623, Huerta)	10 comp. Bohemia	6 comp. Hungary	6 comp. (Nové Zamky)	6 comp. Moravia, Silesia	6 comp. Silesia	6 comp. Silesia
Wallenstein–La Motte Walloon cuirassiers	10 comp. Bohemia	10 comp. Hungary	10 comp. Empire	10 comp. Empire	10 comp. Empire	6 comp. Empire
Wallenstein–Conti Walloon cuirassiers	10 comp. Bohemia	10 comp. Hungary	5 comp. Moravia	5 comp. Moravia	5 comp. Moravia	2 comp. Moravia

	1620	*1621*	*1622*	*1623*	*1624*	*1625*
Dampierre–Medici Walloon arquebusiers	5 comp. Bohemia	5 comp. Hungary	–	–	–	1 comp. (?) Bohemia
Areyzaga Walloon arquebusiers (later Spanish and Walloon)	–	5 comp. Alsace	5 comp. Alsace	5 comp. Bohemia	5 comp. Bohemia	5 comp. Empire
Buquoy, Walloon bodyguard	1 comp. Bohemia	1 comp. Hungary	–	–	–	–
Aldobrandini arquebusiers	5 comp. Hungary	10 comp. Hungary	5 comp. Hungary	–	–	–
Des Fours arquebusiers	5 comp. Hungarian frontier	–	–	–	–	10 comp. with League in the Empire
Coronini arquebusiers	1 comp. Empire	–	–	–	5 comp. Netherlands	5 comp. Netherlands
Montecuccoli arquebusiers	5 comp. Bohemia	10 comp. Hungary	10 comp. Hungary	–	–	1 comp. Moravia
M. de Huerta arquebusiers	–	1 comp. Bohemia	–	–	–	–
Saxe-Lauenburg arquebusiers (from 1621 cuirassiers)	5 comp. Moravia	10 comp. Lower Palatinate	10 comp. Palatinate	–	–	10 comp. Empire
Gauchier Walloon arquebusiers	5 comp. Bohemia	Moravia	–	–	–	–
Strozzi Walloon arquebusiers (in Bohemia from 1619)	–	–	1 comp. Bohemia	1 comp. Bohemia	6 comp. Empire	5 comp. Netherlands

on a much smaller scale, and there were other Spanish officers who received Bohemian estates as part of their reward.

One of them was Colonel Paradis de Echaide, Commander of Schauenburg's infantry regiment, which fought in Bohemia, Austria, Alsace (1621–4), then in 1625 moved to Italy and entered the service of Spain. This regiment was composed of German infantrymen, as was the Nassau regiment, though it also contained soldiers from the Netherlands. In 1625 this regiment took part in the siege of Breda. The cavalry regiment of Adolph Duke of Holstein ended finally in the Netherlands as well. The table, though it is limited to the former 'Spanish' contingents of 1620, shows clearly how the composition of the regiments changed, and how brief their existence sometimes was.

It may be concluded that, although the policies of the Spanish and Austrian Habsburgs were seriously at odds in many ways between 1621 and 1625, Madrid still kept its interest focused on events in central Europe. Without Spanish help the threats to Vienna in 1621 and 1623 would have been far more difficult for the Austrian Habsburgs to deal with. These were ventures which at times stood on the threshold of success. If the representatives of the 'Spanish party', who after 1620 directed the administration of Bohemia and Moravia, managed to prevail in the end, they were helped to a considerable extent by Spanish diplomatic support. We know this from the correspondence of the Moravian Governor Cardinal Dietrichstein. The correspondence of the Bohemian Supreme Chancellor Zdeněk Vojtěch Lobkowitz is unfortunately only fragmentary and does not reveal whether Lobkowitz identified himself with the policies of Spain to the same extent as Dietrichstein. The latter, to be sure, was in constant conflict with the Spanish commanders who were destroying the country, but he spoke of the King of Spain as 'Our King'. Whether this attitude was shared by Lobkowitz is difficult to determine: he was certainly better informed than Dietrichstein about the conflicts between the policies of Vienna and Madrid, and from the materials in his library we may surmise that he shared the fears of the *Arbítristas* for the fate of the Spanish Empire.[63]

In Bohemia the chief stage of the preceding period of the conflict, the anti-Habsburg opposition, had not yet been completely crushed: the last garrisons in southern Bohemia held out until February and May 1623 (Třeboň and Zvíkov), and Glatz capitulated only in October. In 1621 the Margrave Johann Georg of Jägerndorf conducted a diversion in Moravia whose aim was to take either Pressburg or Vienna with the help of Gabriel Bethlen, Duke of Transylvania. Thanks to some of the émigré Bohemian nobleman and the rebellious Moravian Wallachians, the eastern half of Moravia slipped from Imperial control. But the campaign failed to realize its ultimate goal, and on 6 January 1622, Bethlen was obliged to sign the Peace of Nikolsburg. The course of the campaign, which was aided by Bathyány's revolt in Hungary, is clarified by material from the chanceries of Ferdinand II, Dietrichstein and Collalto. Bethlen also threatened Moravia in his later campaign of 1623–4, which was a result of contacts between Bethlen, Constantinople and the Netherlands. Some of the Bohemian émigrés also tried to involve themselves in this diplomatic activity, so that it was Heinrich von Thurn, for example, who conducted the negotiations in Constantinople.[64] The political results of this campaign, in which Turks, Tartars and Hungarians participated, were, in spite of a few minor military successes, practically nil.

The military aspect of the conflict in the Bohemian lands can be traced quite easily in the materials collected in the *Documenta Bohemica*, volume III – particularly the placement of the armies: at the beginning of this phase of the war there were three – those of the Emperor, the League, and Spain. It is easy to trace the transfer of part of the Spanish forces to the Empire, but more difficult to find documentation for the army of the League in 1622. In 1624 there was a decline in the number of soldiers in central Europe, and the contingents financed by Spain were shifted from Bohemia to the main battlefields of the war in the Netherlands and the Valtelline. This transfer was completed in the beginning of 1625, when, however, some of the contingents were returned to Bohemia and Moravia, to be incorporated into Wallenstein's first great army.

There is also important evidence of political aims (and the means that were sought to accomplish them) in the varied mass of letters and reports from a network of informants both official and private. Depending upon their authors' position and access to information, they may contain important facts or merely testimony of personal hopes and fears. Thus Cardinal Dietrichstein was regularly supplied with information by Amaro Mendez Feijóo, by Giulio Cesare Massa, by the Spanish secretary in Venice Andrea Irless, and by the secretary of the Duke of Feria at Milan, Roque de Ayerbe. Collalto received important information from his brother-in-law Khevenhüller at Madrid, and his private informant, the Venetian postmaster Niccolo Rossi, sent him news from Constantinople of relations between the Porte and Persia and of the negotiations with Bethlen. The Supreme

Chancellor in Prague Zdeněk Lobkowitz had an informant in Paris who sent news of Graubünden, still the object of careful attention from Spain, and also of France, which was steadily gaining significance in the conflict (though the Franco-Dutch coalition only materialized in 1624). The Valtelline was the chief theme in the reports of Giuliano Medici, who also reported the activities of the Duke of Savoy, of Feria and Venice. French ambassadors at Rome conducted negotiations about the Valtelline as early as 1621. Collalto himself supplied reports – sometimes brief, sometimes more thorough, but consistently interesting – of conditions in the Habsburg lands, in Hungary, and in the Empire.

In 1622 Baron Somogyi sent a revealing and significant report from Brussels, which became a very important centre of activity after the expiration of the Twelve Years' Truce between Spain and the United Netherlands.[65] Ferdinand II sent Georg Ludwig von Schwarzenberg as ambassador to the Infanta at Brussels, and he dispatched Otto von Nostitz, the German Vice-Chancellor in Bohemia, as ambassador to the court of Johann Georg at Dresden. Schwarzenberg also sent reports to F. K. Khevenhüller of his negotiations with Gondomar and Buckingham in London. Khevenhüller for his part received information as well from Herman von Questenberg and Maximilian of Bavaria about the negotiations with Olivares. After the resumption of hostilities between Spain and the United Netherlands, information appeared regularly in Somogyi's reports about the struggle between Spinola and Maurice of Orange-Nassau, from the conquest of Jülich to the siege of Bergen-op-Zoom. There was also news of the recruitment of Scots and Irishmen to serve against the Dutch.

With Tilly's victories at Wimpfen and Höchst the military fate of the Palatinale was sealed. The documents contain reflections of King James' attempt to arrange a marriage between the Prince of Wales and the Infanta. There are reports on the assembly at Regensburg in 1623 and the withdrawal of Frederick's title of Elector, as well as on Spanish opposition to the plans of Maximilian of Bavaria,[66] which of course were supported by the Infanta. Ferdinand II also urges Schwarzenberg to co-operate with Spinola and Cardinal de la Cueva in a plan to capture a part of the army of the Dutch States General. Since Mansfeld entered the service of the Signoria, there is news of the alliance of Venice, Savoy and France and of the conflicting interests of Venice and Spain in the Valtelline.

For the year 1624 there are significant reports from Maximilian of Bavaria to Khevenhüller concerning Venice's negotiations with France,

Holland, the Turks and Gabriel Bethlen. Ferdinand of Bavaria also reports on the meeting of the princes and on plans for an alliance which was also to include England after her break with Spain. From Constantinople come reports from Lustrier, former Canon of Olomouc Cathedral, of relations between Bethlen and Zigmund Báthory and their position *vis à vis* the Ottoman Empire. The diplomatic negotiations were intensive and complex. Ferdinand II sends Schwarzenberg via Milan to Madrid, where he is to meet with Olivares; he entrusts the peace negotiations in Hungary to Adam Bořita of Martinic; and he dispatches Otto von Nostitz to Johann Georg of Saxony. Because of a possible Swedish intervention in the conflict, Axel Oxenstierna expresses interest in the peace treaty between Poland and Denmark.

The activities of the informants continued, of course, into the first half of the year 1625: Althan's mission to Buda provided reports explaining the background of Bethlen's actions in 1625–6; from the north came news of a probable alliance between Sweden and Denmark. In Dresden Otto von Nostitz was to emphasize the importance of a united defence against the Anglo-Dutch coalition which was being joined by Denmark and France. Nostitz also transmitted James's assurances that he wished to avoid the use of force.

Perhaps the most important fact to emerge from the relations and reports is that there was a marked difference in the plans and policies of the two branches of the Habsburg family, and that the divergence appeared as early as 1622–3. This is emphasized by the beginnings of an independent policy on the part of Maximilian of Bavaria and his brother Ferdinand, the Prince Archbishop of Cologne. The differences were also evident in the military field: Ferdinand II, to be sure, agreed to the recruitment of soldiers in his lands for the army of the Spanish Viceroy in Milan, but the implication of Archduke Leopold's note to the Marquess of Valdifuentes concerning the withdrawal of Schauenburg's regiment is clear: since Alsace was to remain unprotected, the Marquess and the ministers of the Spanish King must take the blame if something should go wrong there.

Since the Spanish military commanders sent voluminous reports from the battlefields, the documents contain much material concerning the campaign in the Empire. Thus we are informed of the day-to-day situation in the Palatinate (by Verdugo), in the Spanish Netherlands (by Spinelli), and in Italy (by Caracciola).

Other documents in this printed edition throw light on the rivalry between the governors of Bohemia and Moravia, Liechtenstein and Dietrichstein, as well as on the quarrel between these two and the military commanders who were plundering the land. Finally there are documents illustrating Wallenstein's rise, the enmity he incurred from Slavata, Collalto, and Martinic, and the animosity that all of them felt toward Marradas.

THE BEGINNING OF THE SECOND PHASE OF THE CONFLICT

When, in the spring of 1621, the Twelve Years' Truce expired and military action was resumed, the Dutch Republic was far from having solved its internal political tensions and problems. After the death of Oldenbarnevelt in 1619 a veritable witch hunt was instituted against Remonstrants or Arminians. It dwindled with time, however, for the Republic and its rulers were occupied by other troubles, involving foreign policy, the economy and, more immediately, the situation on the borders of the Republic. The economic prospects were not bright: the economic crisis which affected various regions of Europe in 1621 made itself felt in the Netherlands as well. The West Indies Company, whose foundation became a bone of contention between the Republic and Spain, as well as among factions of the Regents (the Dutch ruling class) began to operate in 1621. For the time being, however, it cost much money and brought no return. The financial market was weak, and this had repercussions particularly in Amsterdam.[67]

Here, in 1621, the Burgomaster Pauw, the great opponent of Oldenbarnevelt, fell from power. Oldenbarnevelt was succeeded in 1620 as Grand Pensionary (*raadspensionaris*) by Anthonie Duyck, whose power and competence were far more limited than his predecessor's. With Duyck's succession there began the period of the great influence of Prince Maurice of Orange-Nassau and his faction upon foreign policy. Maurice and his chief adviser, Aerssens van Sommelsdijk, relied chiefly upon alliance with England, of which Oldenbarnevelt – with good reason as it turned out – had always been mistrustful.

The first years of the renewed struggle against the Spaniards – a struggle which Prince Maurice had foreseen and which at least from 1618 he had considered inevitable – were not years of unqualified success. With the defeat on the White Mountain central Europe had lost its significance for the Dutch. As early as the end of 1620 the Palatinate was far more important to them than Bohemia. The Dutch, of course, appreciated the importance of the fact that their 'hereditary enemy' Spain was occupied deep in the heart of the continent. But they did not attach overriding importance either to the resistance of their own troops in Bohemia, who held out until the autumn of 1622, or to the enduring attempts to come to an agreement with the English on the formation of a workable coalition against the Habsburgs.

In 1620 the States General had to admit the failure of their hopes that the Palatine–Bohemian–Hungarian Confederation would tie up the strength of the Habsburgs in central Europe. Furthermore, the German Protestant Union, where Dutch interests were represented by Comenius' friend Brederode, ingloriously collapsed. The Upper Palatinate, to be sure, was still defended by Mansfeld's troops, which arrived from western Bohemia, but neither English nor Dutch reinforcements could guarantee the safety of the Lower Palatinate against the Spanish threat.

Protestant policy-making in the grand style, as it had been conducted from Frederick's accession until the Battle of the White Mountain, expired at his miniature court at The Hague. There was no hope of overcoming the differences which separated England from the Netherlands, Denmark from Sweden, Brandenburg and Saxe-Weimar from the Elector of Saxony and other Lutheran princes. Of the group which had advised Frederick to accept the Bohemian Crown in 1619, Christian of Anhalt – the advocate of adventuresome power politics – had disappeared. There still remained L. Camerarius, the brothers Christoph and Achatius von Dohna, Plessen, and Solms. But those who were effective at The Hague were those who disagreed with the 'Bohemian adventure' – J. J. von Russdorf, A. Pawell, Lingelsheim. Camerarius was the advocate of a broad coalition based on a 'common cause' (*causa communis*), while Pawell instead pursued dynastic politics (*causa Palatina*).[68] But how could an alliance for a common cause be realized when James of England precisely in 1621 was trying to persuade his son-in-law to give up his claims to the Bohemian Crown and instead defend the Palatinate? Furthermore, because as a result Frederick himself held back, collaboration with the Dutch, with Frederick's former vassals and present representatives in Bohemia, Moravia and Silesia, and with Gabriel Bethlen, was at best only half-hearted. Thus in 1621 there was no chance of achieving military co-ordination on the battlefields of western and central Europe. The Dutch had written off central Europe several months before Bethlen's truce with the Emperor, which eliminated him from the anti-Habsburg camp. In the autumn of 1621 the army of Maximilian of Bavaria occupied the Upper Palatinate, from which Mansfeld and his veterans withdrew into the Rhine Valley. At about the same time Spinola occupied Jülich and at the beginning of 1622 was threatening the last of Frederick's holdings in the Lower Palatinate.

At the beginning of 1622 James also became convinced that the Spaniards did not intend to restore Frederick to the Palatinate, and he therefore declared himself in favour of military action designed to clear the Spaniards out of that territory. Frederick thus set out secretly from The Hague with an entourage which included Bohemians and Moravians, crossed French territory, and arrived in the Palatinate where Mansfeld was waiting together with the armies of the Margrave of Baden and Christian von Halberstadt, both paid for by the Dutch. The Dutch had also contributed 50,000 florins toward the journey of Frederick and his entourage.[69] In April Mansfeld achieved a certain success against the armies of the Imperial allies, led by Tilly, but the tables were turned when Tilly defeated the Margrave of Baden at Wimpfen and Christian von Halberstadt at Höchst. Then, together with the Spaniards and the forces of Archduke Leopold, Tilly began to put pressure on Mansfeld.

At this decisive moment English diplomacy once again intervened inauspiciously. King James, fearing that Frederick's conduct might endanger his plans for marriage between Charles, Prince of Wales, and the Spanish Infanta, requested his son-in-law to withdraw from the conflict.[70] Frederick actually did withdraw to Sedan before the opening of the Spanish offensive against the Palatinate. In September 1622, the Palatine capital Heidelberg fell, and soon afterwards it was the turn of the last Palatine fortresses in the Rhine Valley. The struggle for the Palatinate was already decided when Frederick returned to The Hague in a state of despondency. More than one of the Bohemians in his entourage remained in the Palatinate or at Sedan.[71]

But the situation was also serious in the Netherlands. Spinola's forces were besieging the fortress of Bergen-op-Zoom, saved only by the arrival of Mansfeld's troops who had courageously fought their way out of the Palatinate through Alsace and the Spanish Netherlands.

Unfortunately only a few documents for the year 1622 have been preserved at The Hague which might have helped us to clarify the policies of the States General and their attitude to Frederick and his party. But from the following winter, we can follow closely the feverish activity of Dutch diplomacy, now thoroughly aware of the significance of the loss of Bohemia which had enabled the Spaniards to withdraw their forces from central Europe. Since the orientation toward England had proved fruitless, Maurice of Orange-Nassau was obliged to return to Oldenbarnevelt's policy and solicit aid from France. In 1622 the group supporting war 'in the grand style' lost Christian of Anhalt, who now sought a path to conciliation with the Emperor. No explanation for his unexpected defection emerges either from the correspondence of Frederick of the Palatinate or from the papers of Camerarius. But Anhalt's correspondence and that of his son, who had been taken prisoner at the Battle of the White Mountain, with the younger Anhalt's captor Verdugo, show how both were gradually won over to the other side.[72]

The opinions of those who still favoured a continuation of the struggle also underwent modification. For instance Camerarius, under pressure of the realities of the situation, looked for ways to form a coalition whose aims would be political rather than religious. The States General conducted delicate negotiations with several central German principalities, through the mediation of Abraham Richter, the agent of the German Protestant princes at The Hague. Chief among the objects of Dutch attention was Saxe-Weimar, whose prince, Johann Ernst, had long maintained close ties with the Netherlands. In January 1623 the States General received Bethlen's envoy Ehrenfried von Berbisdorf, who reported a new plan of action against Vienna for which Bethlen counted on co-ordinated action in western and central Europe and also on the help of the Turks. Negotiations on the last point were being conducted in Constantinople by H. M. von Thurn.[73] Bethlen's partners were to be Mansfeld, who with Dutch money was to recruit a new army in Friesland, and Christian von Halberstadt, who was to do the same in Lower Saxony. Frederick of the Palatinate, who at the Imperial Diet at Regensburg in February 1623 was deprived of his electoral dignity, was also prompted to personal intervention in the conflict. But once again he was effectively blocked by English diplomacy which in the face of all previous experience was renewing attempts to arrange a marriage between Prince Charles and the Spanish Infanta. Only when the Prince's adventurous journey to Madrid ended in fiasco and a definitive parting of ways between England and Spain did the situation become more favourable for a joint Anglo-Dutch effort. By then, however, it was already autumn – too late to plan and execute any substantial military action. Christian von Halberstadt, who according to the plan was to join with Bethlen's forces, was instead pushed to the west by Tilly, then defeated by him at Stadtlohn at the beginning of August. Bethlen called in vain for Dutch help against the House of Austria and the perfidious Spaniards. He received only vague promises and a hint that for the States General 'bellum navale', sea war with Spain, took precedence.[74] In any case, Bethlen soon afterwards concluded a truce by which he deserted his allies in Moravia. Mansfeld disbanded his army and entered the service of Venice, which together with Savoy and with French aid was attempting to create a common front against Spanish hegemony in northern Italy. In the spring of the following year (1627) Count Thurn also followed Mansfeld's example. Their plans were carefully observed from Strasbourg, then from Basel, by the Dutch diplomat Brederode.[75]

Bethlen, however, did not consider the situation to be hopeless. From Berlin Ladislav Velen of Žerotín sent to him at Banská Bystrica his confidant Jan Adam of Víckov, a mortal enemy of Wallenstein. Ladislav Velen of Žerotín had been the Captain-General of Moravia during the Rebellion and from 1621 to 1623 had remained close to Frederick of the Palatinate. On 8 January 1624 Jan Adam of Víckov presented his credentials and offered his services for a new plan of action; he returned to Berlin, whence together with Heinrich Mathias von Thurn he left for The Hague. On 6 March Víckov was received by the States General and presented Bethlen's offer of a treaty of alliance and a continuation of the struggle. The States General commended Bethlen's zeal and thoroughly approved the idea of a new confederation, to include Bohemians and Moravians, against the forces of the Spanish King. They promised substantial aid ('groote assistentie') against Spain, however, only if Anglo-Dutch relations improved and the West Indies Company overcame its current most serious crisis.[76] Víckov received from these 'generous lords' the gift of a golden chain and medal worth 1,200 florins, but to Bethlen he brought, besides empty Dutch promises, only a letter from Frederick of the Palatinate, dated 2 April 1624. Víckov's mission did nothing to alter the general ruin of Bethlen's campaign. The centre of Bohemian émigré politics shifted now from The Hague to Berlin and the court of the Elector of Brandenburg George William, Frederick's brother-in-law. According to Imperial agents, Víckov passed through Berlin between Hungary and the Netherlands no less than three times before the spring of 1625. And it may be assumed that it was he who brought to The Hague those pieces of correspondence which are still preserved there.

The diplomatic negotiations between Transylvania, Venice, northern and western Europe lasted through 1624. In June 1624, an alliance was finally concluded between the United Netherlands and France, somewhat relieving the situation on the southern border, where Spinola had penetrated as far as Breda. On the other hand, the French alliance meant that Dutch warships took part in the siege of the Huguenot stronghold La Rochelle, an action which naturally hardly aroused the enthusiasm of the Dutch pastors who rightly saw in this clause of the treaty a betrayal of their fellow-Protestants. The previous year they had initiated a new wave of persecution against the Remonstrants, following an unsuccessful attempt to assassinate Prince Maurice. The sons of Oldenbarnevelt were involved in the plot, and the blame, in spite of their protests, was laid on all Remonstrants.

Prince Maurice died on 23 April 1625, and was succeeded by his half-brother Frederick Hendrik, the son of William I of Orange and Louise de Coligny. At his brother's insistence, Frederick Hendrik married Amalia of Solms, lady-in-waiting to Elizabeth of Bohemia, whom Amalia had accompanied to Bohemia. The new Stadholder was unable to prevent the fall of Breda, which surrendered to Spinola's forces on 5 July 1625. This represented a great prestige victory for Spain, celebrated in the famous painting by Velasquez ('Las Lanzas'). But in the second half of 1625 the anti-Habsburg coalition, striven for ever since 1618, had just come into existence. The States General promised Bethlen a subsidy as early as May 1625, when they also began negotiations with 'the Kings, our friends' – that is the English, Danish and Swedish monarchs – for the opening of hostilities against the Habsburgs, whom they hoped to tie up both in Germany and Italy.[77]

In the end the coalition, concluded at the beginning of December 1625, failed to bring together all these monarchs, because the interests of Denmark and Sweden could not be reconciled. Besides the United Netherlands it included England, the Lower Saxon Circle, and the Kingdom of Denmark–Norway. It also included the 'King of Bohemia and Prince of the Palatinate' Frederick, but not Gabriel Bethlen. Negotiations with the latter were still being conducted, and at the same time opinion in Constantinople was being sounded to determine how the Turks would view a European-wide coalition directed against the Habsburgs. Bethlen wanted first to conclude treaties of alliance with the Prince of Brandenburg and with Sweden, by which he would offer to participate in a struggle both against Poland, the ally of the 'treacherous House of Austria', and against the 'Spanish universal monarchy'. Bethlen promised the Swedish King, Gustavus Adolphus, Silesia and Bohemia, and undertook to bring in Muscovy against the Poles. He also declared that he would break with the Turks, and requested allied help in removing them from Hungary.[78]

The realities turned out to be far more modest. When Transylvania was admitted to the Hague Coalition, the negotiations were conducted by Bethlen's envoy Quadt, a personal acquaintance of Comenius, and were limited to the question of alliance with Denmark.

War aims, too, were now viewed in a more sober light. Under pressure from the Dutch Regents and the City of London, the goals of the Coalition were framed in most cautious terms. A secret clause of the Hague Treaty spoke of the return of the Palatinate to Frederick, but made no mention of Bohemia. Frederick himself was probably informed of this, but his followers were not – particularly those in Berlin and even in Bohemia and Moravia, who looked forward to 1626 as the year of hope.

4

The Danish intervention and the attempts at the formation of a grand coalition

PROBLEMS AND SOURCES

In the period 1625–30 the destruction of old Bohemia was completed by an administrative coup embodied in the Renewed Constitution (*Verneuerte Landesordnung, Obnovené zřízení zemské*). In this revolutionary change a part was played by Albrecht Wallenstein who, more by management than by military action contributed to averting the ruin which threatened the Habsburg dynasty. Modern historians have quite legitimately focused on the problem of intervention in central Europe by Denmark and the Coalition in 1626–7, on Spanish 'maritime' plans in northern Germany, and finally on the 'Italian period' of the Thirty Years' War – the conflict over Mantua.

In the 1930s the Wallenstein question was the subject of controversy between Josef Pekař, who saw Wallenstein as a 'timorous traitor and foolish intriguer',[1] and Heinrich von Srbik, who regarded the Generalissimo as an idealistic fighter for a united Germany.[2] A. Ernstberger has assessed Wallenstein's greatness as an entrepreneur.[3] In an article 'Zur Problematik des Dreissigjährigen Krieges und der Wallensteinfrage'[4] I have attempted to bring together the various aspects of the problem.[5] The basic book now is *Wallenstein* by Golo Mann. M. Hroch has investigated Wallenstein's government in Mecklenburg[6] and questions of European trade during the war.[7] Our knowledge of Wallenstein's economic activities has been enlarged considerably by two important unpublished dissertations of the Charles University at Prague: K. Vít's work on Jan de Witte and his fall, and K. Stanka's study of mining and manufacture at Raspenava.

My study 'Moravia and Relations between Eastern and Western Europe, 1626–7'[8] is based on Moravian sources, on the correspondence of Georg Ernst of Saxe-Weimar (State Archive at Weimar), and on the Mitzlaff papers (Royal Archive, Copenhagen). It also follows up the work by František Roubík,[9] based on materials in Wallenstein's War

Chancery in the State Central Archive at Prague. Military action in Moravia in 1626–7 and the general situation there is covered by the second volume of František Hrubý's edition of *Moravian Correspondence and Documents, 1625–36*,[10] and by Vlasta Fialová's and František Dostál's studies of the Wallachian uprisings, which were cited earlier. B. Indra has described the popular movements in eastern Moravian towns in the period of the 'Wallachian War'.[11] The earlier solid work on peasant uprisings in Upper Austria by F. Stieve[12] has been followed in recent years by a history of Austrian Protestantism by Grete Mecenseffy[13] and a dissertation by the East German historian R. F. Schmiedt.[14]

Quite a lot has been written about the Danish-Norwegian state and the government of Christian IV; its aim has been chiefly to assess the historical function of Christian's régime. Particular emphasis has been placed on the rise of Denmark to the status of a great power, and on the significance of the Sound and its tolls for commerce between eastern and western Europe. New ground was broken in this area by M. Hroch's studies exploring the connections between the war and the economy in the Baltic region.[15] On the basis of this analysis we can now assess the Spanish–Dutch conflict, of which little account has been taken so far.

The significance of the plans for building up an Imperial naval force in the Baltic[16] one sign of a renewed Spanish expansionism) is recognized by Spanish historians and by the English historian J. H. Elliott.[17] The second wing of this front was northern Italy, where Spanish intervention brought about a protracted conflict with revived French power. The centre of the front against the Spanish onslaught was held in this period, too, by the Netherlands, whose position has been examined by C. R. Boxer. An important analysis of Dutch foreign policy may be found in the work of M. A. M. Franken.[18] This, of course, does not come close to explaining everything. Until now the interest of Dutch historians has centred on spectacular successes – for example Piet Heyn's capture of the Spanish treasure ships off Cuba in 1628. The Dutch successes at sea have tended to obscure the significance of the United Netherlands as a military power which during the latter part of the 1620s gradually forced the Spaniards back to the present-day frontier with Belgium. The study of Dutch internal politics in this period thus has its special pertinence, as does the analysis of sporadic Dutch intervention in central European battlefields during these years – for instance, in the campaign of 1626–7.[19]

Hans Sturmberger is the most recent historian to deal with the

Renewed Constitution for Bohemia and Moravia and with the problem of whether it signified a victory for monarchical absolutism in Bohemia and in the Habsburg multi-national empire.[20] The Bohemian emigration, which reached its zenith in 1627–8, was first examined by T. V. Bílek and B. Jelínek, later by Eduard Winter, the author of a broadly conceived study of Bohemian and Slovakian emigration to Germany in the seventeenth and eighteenth centuries.[21] Unfortunately, there have been no similar studies of Bohemian émigrés who found refuge in Poland (Leszno), in Hungary (in the territory of western Slovakia), or further afield (the Netherlands, for example). But the importance of this emigration and its internal system of communication has been revealed notably in research on the life and work of Comenius, the greatest of the émigrés after the Battle of the White Mountain.[22] It now seems that we shall have to modify our conception of the significance of Comenius' political activities and his relations with the Netherlands and The Hague court of Frederick of the Palatinate, and bear in mind that his first contacts with the country where he died were made through the mediation of the Palatine court.[23]

In general it must be said that the 'Danish' period of the Thirty Years' War has not been so thoroughly examined as the preceding and following stages – the Bohemian War and the Swedish War. This deficiency can undoubtedly be largely corrected with the help of materials in Czechoslovak archives and libraries, which for some problems – for instance the Wallenstein question – are of decisive importance.

Czechoslovak archives and libraries contain a large volume of so-far untouched material for the period 1625–30. This can be divided into several categories.

The first place belongs to sources relevant to Wallenstein's activities in the period of his so-called First Generalship, whose importance was emphasized by A. Ernstberger in his biography of Wallenstein's banker Jan de Witte, and by František Roubík in his pioneering work on Wallenstein and the campaign of 1626–7.[24] This group of documents is preserved in the first and larger section of the Wallenstein War Chancery, now in the State Central Archive at Prague, and in the section 'Wallensteiniana' in the State Archive at Mnichovo Hradiště. Only the papers of Rambold Collalto in the State Archive at Brno can be ranked with these collections of Wallensteiniana.

On the other hand, Wallenstein's subordinates – Aldringen, Piccolomini, Schlick, Gallas – remain definitely in the background as far as their papers for this period are concerned. The chief reason for this is that in 1634 all of them tried to destroy any compromising material which might connect them with the 'traitor'; many papers, too, were lost when some of the generals' families became extinct.

An exception is the group of sources for one important question – the 'Mantuan War', considered by Italian historians (in particular Romolo Quazza) as the 'Italian Phase' of the Thirty Years' War.[25] There is a simple reason why so much material has been preserved for this particular problem. When they were sent to conquer Mantua, Wallenstein's generals quarrelled over the spoils, and the legal actions over the *spartimento* dragged on for decades. Documents from the chanceries of Collalto (State Archive at Brno), Mathias Gallas and Johann Aldringen (State Archive, Děčín), as well as the correspondence of Schlick and Piccolomini, of course extend well beyond the year 1630.

Other sources help to explain Spain's maritime plans, Wallenstein's circumspect position on the Baltic, and his final break with some of the Spanish policy-makers. This diplomatic game, once understood only from the partial material used by F. Mareš, is further elucidated by the contents of Wallenstein's chancery and also by the valuable diplomatic correspondence of G. L. von Schwarzenberg and Khevenhüller, the Imperial envoy in Madrid (State Archive at Český Krumlov).[26]

Wallenstein's opponents, who belonged to the 'Spanish' party at the Imperial court – Slavata, Martinic and Michna, as well as Verdugo and Marradas – preserved their papers only in part. Marradas' correspondence is widely scattered; Slavata's papers are located chiefly in the State Archive at Jindřichův Hradec; letters of Martinic and Michna are in the Autograph Collection of the State Archive at Mnichovo Hradiště and the State Archive at Klatovy and its branch at Žlutice.

The collections of other archives and libraries are not so extensive. In the State Archive at Děčín are the papers of Rudolph Thun, and the State Archive at Jindřichův Hradec contains the papers of Wallenstein's quartermaster (supply officer) Humprecht Černín. Silesian documents concerning the confiscation of the estates belonging to noblemen who joined the Danes have been used in a study by J. Zukal.[27] The Wallenstein Collection in the State Archive at Mnichovo Hradiště contains documents from all parts of Europe. Military material in Slovak archives serves only to complement this rich and important collection.

The Wallenstein chancery

As far as we can tell, only four chanceries issued papers in Wallenstein's name: the court chanceries of the principalities of Friedland, Sagan, and Mecklenburg, and Wallenstein's personal and military chancery. The last, for our purposes the most important, began as a personal chancery in about 1622; from that time it preserved documents emanating from Wallenstein's military and entrepreneurial activities. When he was named generalissimo in 1625 it was reorganized but continued to perform the same functions.[28]

From that time its history can be traced in some detail. The chancery was not particularly large. In 1625 it was headed by M. Burckmeister, and in Hungary by Baltasar Thiel; in 1630 its *registrator* was L. Möring, who was later succeeded by Baltasar Wesselius and Dr Heinrich Nieman. In 1630, when it reached its greatest size, the chancery employed nine secretaries, one postmaster and six messengers. Among the secretaries were some Bohemians: in 1625 Daníel Třebický and Jan Počátecký. Wallenstein's chancery was organized roughly along the lines of the Royal Chancery, and its products, most of them various sorts of correspondence, imitated the forms used by the Royal Chancery. Wallenstein himself supervised the operation of his chancery, and it was he who was responsible for its organization in 1625, when it moved with him from Bohemia to northwestern Germany, then through Silesia and Moravia to Upper Hungary, and finally to the Baltic coast. After the conclusion of the Danish War it was transferred to southwestern Germany, and when Wallenstein was relieved of his command it was located at Memmingen.

Wallenstein, of course, had no plans to turn over the chancery to his successors or to the court at Vienna. In January, 1631, he transferred the 'Registratura' to Jičín, from where for reasons of safety it was deposited in the castle of Hrubá Skála as a part of the Wallenstein Family Archive. After Wallenstein's death the chancery and chamber were confiscated, and together with the military 'Registratura' from Hrubá Skála were transferred to the Viennese Hofkammer. In the second half of the seventeenth century it was moved to the Archive of the Bohemian Court Chamber, whence it found its way into the Archive of the 'Gubernium' during the eighteenth century. Here, in the 1830s all documents dealing with Wallenstein were classed under the heading 'Friedland' (call-number F67), which was divided into fifty-three subsections. Military documents were left in their original series. Drafts of letters to the Emperor are under F 67/49, and letters received from the Emperor under F 67/51; other correspondence is under F 67/42. Not all the documents have survived: the Wallenstein documents in the *Bohemica* of Jan Jeník z Bratřic indicate significant gaps.

At the end of 1631, when Wallenstein resumed his command, his personal chancery acquired a new military character and became the Chancery of the Military Staff, which accompanied the generalissimo on his campaigns. At the beginning of 1634 Wallenstein arrived in Pilsen. When he hurried to Eger on 22 February 1634, the chancery remained at Pilsen, where it was taken over by Caretto after Wallenstein's assassination. It was ransacked for proof of Wallenstein's treason, and the Emperor sent Wallmerode, counsellor of the Imperial Chancery, together with the former Wallenstein Chancery Director Wesselius, to Pilsen to arrange the documents and have them transported to Vienna. Thus the chancery arrived at Budweis, where a trial of the alleged traitors was held. The search for proof of Wallenstein's guilt, however, was fruitless, and the chancery therefore was not forwarded to Regensburg where the Imperial court had moved.

Thus the 'Registratura' remained forgotten in the attic of the Budweis Town Hall, from which it was eventually sent to Vienna in 1727, to be deposited in the Court Chancery. Here in 1842 a trunk full of documents was discovered in the cellar. The discovery aroused some interest, for at that time the Waldstein and Windischgrätz families were conducting a lawsuit for the return of property confiscated from Wallenstein.

The trunk contained documents from January 1633 to February 1634. A part of the 'Registratura' had remained unnoticed at Budweis where it was discovered in 1801, and ten years later, through the efforts of the Archduke Karl, it was deposited in the Military Archive at Vienna in the artificial collections *Feldakten* and *Feldarmee.* Originally this lot comprised 2,605 documents of which 500 were judged to be unimportant and destroyed. A part of the collection was turned over to the Court Library (now the National Library) and catalogued in the Autograph Collection, where it remains today.

Documents from the period of the First Generalship, therefore, remained in Bohemia – first in the Archive of the Lieutenant-Governor at Prague, then in the Archive of the Ministry of the Interior, now the State Central Archive. As a result of agreements reached between the Austrian and Czechoslovak governments this collection was enlarged by the addition of documents from the Haus-Hof-und Staatsarchiv at Vienna, but not from the Military Archive. Finally in 1939 some

Wallenstein documents which had been moved from Prague to Vienna during the Nazi occupation, were returned; at this time they were also joined by Wallenstein's army indexes, the *Kriegslisten*, which until then had been preserved in the castle library at Doksy. A few of the *Kriegslisten* remain in the State Archive at Mnichovo Hradiště. At present, therefore, about 17,000 of the 25,000 documents from Wallenstein's Military Chancery are located at Prague.

This extensive archive, until now divided into the four series mentioned above, includes written military orders, correspondence with the Imperial princes, Estates and cities, touching chiefly the quartering and supply of the army, and finally political correspondence. The first two groups of documents indicate the impact of the military conflict on various regions and are concerned mainly with logistical problems. The third, the political correspondence, contains a certain quantity of important material in cypher. We know, however, that matters of the greatest secrecy were never committed to paper: for example, Wallenstein's contact with Madrid was maintained entirely through confidants, chiefly Octavio Sforza, who was constantly travelling between Wallenstein's camp and Brussels or Madrid. The same holds true, up to a point, for Wallenstein's correspondence with the Emperor and with Tilly. It is useless, therefore, to expect to uncover correspondence with the Emperor's enemies. The real value of Wallenstein's military chancery lies in the materials which reveal the nature of military enterprise, explain tactics rather than strategy, and show the war as a day-to-day reality rather than the affair of great-power politics.

Interest has always focused chiefly on the correspondence from the period of the Second Generalship, which, therefore, has suffered the greatest losses. Hallwich published much from this part of the correspondence. On the other hand, the correspondence from the First Generalship has remained far less disturbed – even by modern scholars.

The *State Archive at Mnichovo Hradiště*, in its section 'Wallensteiniana', contains transcripts of correspondence with Ferdinand from 1628 to 1633. There are also records of Wallenstein's financial requests for the year 1628. In the so-called 'Prague Section' are transcripts of patents of 1628–4. The 'Doksy Section' includes a valuable collection of sixteen letters of appointment issued to Wallenstein (his appointment as Generalissimo and Admiral of the Atlantic and Baltic Seas), Imperial instructions for the army command of 1625, decrees dealing with the transfer of Mecklenburg to Wallenstein in 1629, and important correspondence between Wallenstein and Maximilian of Bavaria between 1624 and 1633. There are also transcripts here from domestic and foreign archives, particularly the Harrach Archive at Vienna. In the collection 'Autographs I' are valuable materials from the Anhalt Chancery and from central German cities; in Sections v and vi are autographs of Danish officers. 'Autographs II' contains letters from Maximilian of Bavaria from 1620–9, with news of diplomatic negotiations and of the military situation; also letters of Maximilian's brother Ferdinand, the Archbishop of Cologne, from 1622–9; an account of Khevenhüller's expenses for the year 1628 as Imperial Ambassador at Madrid; letters from Olivares beginning in 1623, from J. L. von Schwarzenberg in 1622, Herman von Questenberg in the period 1622–7, and Johann Werdenberg in 1628–36. Some of these letters are addressed to Wallenstein, and there are also various types of notes from Wallenstein. There is a noteworthy letter from Pappenheim at Stillingen describing the siege of Magdeburg in December 1630.[29]

The Collalto Family Archive

The only collection that can compete with the Wallenstein materials at Prague and Mnichovo Hradiště is the Collalto Family Archive, in the State Archive at Brno (call-number G 169; formerly F 16, Brtnice).[30] Its core is the correspondence of Rambald Collalto, which is divided into three groups. The first is correspondence received, the second his drafts, and the third the correspondence of other prominent figures. Each of these groups is unfortunately organized according to the social position of the correspondents.

Among the correspondence received are confidential letters from Ferdinand II (1626–30); letters from the German princes, and from Silesian and Italian princes; correspondence with the Court War Council (1613–29); letters from Colloredo, from Cardinal Dietrichstein (1616–30, altogether seventy-seven documents), Eggenberg, Gallas, Marradas, Montecuccoli, Piccolomini, Spinola, Tilly, Trautmannsdorf, and 320 letters from Albrecht Wallenstein, most of which have been published. After these important figures come members of the Church hierarchy, sub-commanders, officers, cities, and so forth.

Drafts of Collalto's own correspondence run to the year 1630. They include the text of letters sent to the Emperor (1625–30, particularly concerning the truce with the Turks and Gabriel Bethlen), to Wallenstein and Tilly, to Dietrichstein, Questenberg, Eggenberg and Werdenberg, to the Court War Council. This group also includes Collalto's report concerning the conflict in Hungary and a notebook *Conceptis aliquot responsiarum* ... of 1629.

The third group contains correspondence from Albrecht Wallenstein addressed chiefly to Italians (1616–20). Particularly noteworthy are a series of letters of 1629–30 dealing with the hostilities in Italy, the Mantua campaign. There is a similar though less extensive series concerning the war in Hungary (1625–30).

Smaller collections for the period 1625–30

Another prominent figure in this period and after was Wallenstein's collaborator Johann Aldringen, who died under mysterious circumstances in 1634. Aldringen, as we know from foreign sources,[31] was the generalissimo's confidant for negotiations with the Spanish agent de Roy in northwestern Germany and with Foppema van Aitzema, the Dutch agent at Hamburg and Altona. Unfortunately the *Family Archive of the Clary-Aldringens*, in the State Archive at Děčín, contains nothing relating to these negotiations. There are, however, documents concerning the Danish War (1626–9), dealing chiefly with northern Germany, and the Italian period of the War (1629–31 – mainly in the correspondence with Colloredo and Collalto and in the military notebooks). The Italian material is most valuable and concerns above all the 'spartimento' law suits with Gallas and Colloredo (boxes 32–34). There are also a number of documents, both originals and copies, from other family archives. The same State Archive also contains the *Clam-Gallas Family Archive*, with the 'Military Chancery' of Mathias Gallas, which, however, includes only nineteen documents for this period. But the box labelled 'Gallas–Aldringen Suit 1630–1668' (call-number XIX/21) contains material about the quarrel over the spoils of the Mantuan War. The third collection from Děčín is the *Thun-Hohenstein Family Archive.* The papers of Rudolph Thun (d. 1636) include records of his travel expenses at his entry into Wallenstein's army (1627) and an account of the siege of Stralsund (1628). There is a large quantity of uncatalogued material among the papers of Wolfgang Theodorich (d. 1642) concerning Italy and the South Tyrol in the years of the Mantuan War.

The Rhineland and the Palatinate are covered in the papers of Guillermo and Francisco Verdugo, preserved in the Verdugo Collection in the State Archive of Pilsen at Žlutice. This collection was surveyed in the preceding chapter. The Schlick and Colloredo-Mansfeld family archives in the State Archive at Zámrsk also extend into this period. The correspondence of Heinrich Schlick in particular continues, though its most important sections deal with the 1630s and 1640s.

The *Papers of Heřman Černín* (Czernin), Wallenstein's Quartermaster-General, in the State Archive at Jindřichův Hradec, occupy a special position. Most of them are stored in three boxes covering the years 1625–7, containing orders from Wallenstein, Černín's drafts of letters to German cities, reports from subordinate supply officers, supply lists (particularly of grain) from central and northern Germany. There are reports from Pavel Michna of Vacínov about grain contributions from Bohemia shipped along the Elbe to Dessau, and about military supplies during the forced march through Silesia to Hungary and back; there are also reports concerning individual regiments and companies. The second section of this collection is composed of bills and receipts, command lists, and finally, documents concerning the execution of orders issued by Černín from 1627. On the whole the material is valuable, and it reveals the economic condition of a significant part of Central Europe, with important information concerning prices and the organization of the army. It forms a counterpart to the papers of Johann Ernst, Duke of Saxe-Weimar in the State Archive at Weimar, which provides similar information about the Danish-Saxon army in the years 1625–7.[32]

The *Schwarzenberg Family Archive* in the State Archive at Český Krumlov contains the important correspondence of Georg Ludwig von Schwarzenberg for the years 1626–8, concerning the maritime policies of Wallenstein and Spain, relations between the Netherlands and the Hansa towns, and trade policies. This material has its counterpart in the Algemeen Rijksarchief at The Hague and in the papers of the Hansa towns, much of which is in the State Central Archive at Potsdam. Earlier scholars (such as F. Mareš) made only limited use of these materials, probably because of the language difficulties.[33]

The *Piccolomini Family Archive*, in the State Archive at Zámrsk, deals with the conflict between Spain and the Netherlands in its section XVIII of the correspondence of Ottavio Piccolomini. Related documents are also to be found in section VIII ('The Thirty Years' War'). Italian affairs after 1629 are covered by section XII, and Spanish policy in the 1620s by section XIII. In section IV ('Affairs of the Duchy of Amalfi') there is correspondence between Ascanio and Ottavio Piccolomini beginning in 1628, which contains reports of the Dutch–Spanish conflict and also information about Wallenstein. This collection, in spite of the losses it has suffered over the years, is still among the richest.[34]

The correspondence of Zdeněk Vojtěch Lobkowitz ends with his death in 1628 (call-number B 209–231, FA Lobkowicz-Roudnice, in the State Archive of Litoměřice at Žitenice). This correspondence, together with that of his wife Polyxena, is the prime source of information about the political intrigues at the court in Vienna.

Cardinal Dietrichstein, the Moravian counterpart to the Lobkowitzes, deposited his correspondence from these years in various places. In the 'Historical Archive' (Dietrichstein Family Archive, State Archive at Brno, call-number G-140, II 220–23) are documents concerning the administration of the province, chiefly during the tense year 1626. There is supplementary material in the 'Unbound Correspondence' in the State Archive at Olomouc (V.ü. 36–7).

In the State Archive at Opava this period is represented in the scanty collection of the Tax Office of the Principality of Troppau 1627–8, containing assessments which are important for the situation after the Danish occupation. Other collections are the 'Execution Commission 1629–1644' and 'Militaria'. It is therefore necessary to rely also on the material used in the two studies of the Silesian confiscations by Josef Zukal – particularly the Inquisition Acts of 1629.[35]

Of the Slovak materials, the Pálffy and Esterházy family archives contain papers pertinent to the period 1625–30. These were described earlier; they are, unfortunately, poorly organized, and any surprising discoveries are highly unlikely.

THE DANISH WAR IN MORAVIA AND HUNGARY 1626–7

In the register of the shoemakers' guild at Frýdek in Moravia we read two succinct entries which briefly indicate contemporary awareness of the connection between Moravia and the rest of Europe, between individuals and great political conflicts:

> The year 1618: At Prague the Bohemian lords commenced war against the Roman Emperor, when, on Wednesday after the Feast of the Holy Ghost, they threw three Imperial councellors out of a window, kindling a spark which then engulfed all Europe. – The year 1626: on Christmas Day, the Danish troops plundered the town of Frýdek and murdered eighty-two persons.[36]

Today, when the political relations between the east and the west of Europe in the period of the Thirty Years' War are so avidly studied,[37] we would do well to look at a study by Josef Macůrek. Forty years ago he pointed out the close connection between the so-called Bohemian question and relations between the eastern and western European powers.[38] Macůrek's work substantially overturned the old but tenacious thesis that the Thirty Years' War was a religious conflict which expanded to involve all of Europe.[39] On some points we can go further than Macůrek did in his original study of the Bohemian Rebellion and Poland. Today, for example, we have the record of the audience in 1620 of Frederick's envoy the Palatine Count Johann Casimir with the Swedish King Gustavus Adolphus. This demonstrates that the Bohemians, at the beginning of 1620, were well aware of the negotiations for an alliance between Sweden and Muscovy, and that such an alliance would serve the interests of the Bohemian rebellion against the Habsburgs. Prague would welcome its speedy conclusion and requested that Moscow be urged to issue a warning to the Poles to discourage them from intervening in the conflict between the Bohemian Estates and the Emperor. Frederick of the Palatinate was convinced that Moscow, too, would benefit from this arrangement by establishing a claim on English gratitude.[40]

Today we view the Thirty Years' War as a political conflict rooted in the tensions of the complex economic and social situation which prevailed throughout Europe in this period. Therefore, of course, we cannot accept the earlier notions of a changing character of the conflict. If the war was essentially European-wide, then the logical supposition must be that its international character appears in the relationship of the 'Bohemian question' to those European lands which were not yet drawn into the conflict. In this connection the example of the policies of the Danish–Norwegian Kingdom in the first phases of the Thirty Years' War, and particularly in the years 1626–7, is highly instructive.

At first glance the homeland of Prince Hamlet had little in common with the Bohemian lands at the beginning of the seventeenth century. The transition from feudalism to capitalism manifested itself in quite different ways in the two countries. Denmark was not one of the economically most advanced regions of Europe, which were the Netherlands, England and France.[41] Dutch and English commercial capital, operating in the fields of finance and production, was attempting to stifle competition from the Hansa towns in the Baltic. Taking into consideration the general European situation, we can now attempt to distinguish the different conditions that prevailed in the various parts of the Baltic regions. In Poland and Prussia, classic areas of the so-called 'second serfdom', economic tensions manifested themselves quite differently from in Jutland, Scania or Swedish Dalecarlia.[42] Christian IV's Kingdom of Denmark–Norway was economically by far the most advanced country in northern Europe at the beginning of the seventeenth century, and the so-called War of Kalmar (1611–13) demonstrated its superiority over Sweden. Between 1590 and 1620 the volume of commerce through the Sound reached its zenith: so, too, did the collection of tolls. At the same time the Danes received high prices for their agricultural produce, so that their financial position became increasingly firm. Since in Denmark as elsewhere inflation was beginning to be felt, Christian introduced economic policies which may be justifiably called mercantilist. Their aim was to remove the necessity of importing finished goods from abroad. Therefore the merchant navy was encouraged, commercial companies founded, monopolies granted, and foreign artisans welcomed. But the country lacked sufficient capital, and its middle class was feeble. The King could not count on support either from the artisans, whose guilds he had abolished, or from the domestic merchants. Therefore at the beginning of the seventeenth century those elements already existed which eventually overturned this propitious economic development. The all-powerful King, relying on foreign capital – chiefly on Dutch commercial capital – clashed with the feudal landlords, who were attempting to consolidate their power over the peasantry. It was of course not to the advantage of the United Netherlands to strengthen exclusively one of the competitors for the 'imperium maris Baltiči'; thus in 1613–14 they concluded an alliance with Sweden and the Hansa towns. With the help of Dutch capital and Dutch ships the Swedish infantry captured one position after another in the eastern Baltic and drew near to the mouth of the Vistula. Christian IV believed that he could assure Danish hegemony in the north by consolidating his position in the Duchy of Schleswig-Holstein, thus controlling the mouth of the Elbe and the Weser.[43]

It is true that Hungarian (*i.e.* central Slovakian) copper passed through the Sound, chiefly on its way to the Amsterdam market, and Astrid Friis has shown the continental proportions of this commerce. But the Sound was also traversed by Polish grain, Finnish timber, and Russian flax and hemp. Denmark was dependent on none of these articles and contented herself with the collection of passage dues. Danish economic interests in central Europe were negligible, and the reverse was also true. The reasons for this mutual lack of interest may be traced chiefly to the complicated situation in the Baltic region and in central Europe. In both regions the interests which came into conflict were those of potential antagonists, but not those of the two camps into which Europe was really divided. In the Baltic the Danes competed with Sweden and Muscovite Russia; England and the Netherlands both applied pressure, and France demonstrated a lively interest. The internal conflicts between these powers retreated into the background when it came to taking a position against the Sweden of the Vasas, or when the Spanish or Austrian Habsburgs wished to gain a foothold in the area. In central Europe political predominance was held by the Catholic–Feudal coalition of the Spanish and Austrian Habsburgs, allied with the 'Spain of the North', Poland.

It should not be forgotten that Moravia, and in particular the *Collegium Nordicum* at Olomouc, were to be the point of departure for the Counter-Reformation directed against Sweden and also against the Danish Kingdom.[44] Tycho Brahe was certainly not the type of émigré imagined in such vivid terms by the Swedish nobles in Poland.[45] Nor as far as is known, did trials against graduates of the Jesuit colleges at Braniewo and Olomouc come to be held in Denmark as they were in Sweden: in 1616 against Messenius, a year later Henrik Hammerus, in 1624 Göran Bähr, Zacharias Anthelius and Erick Nuirennius.[46] However, it is certain that in the last years of the sixteenth century and at the beginning of the seventeenth, the college at Olomouc numbered among its students eleven Danes, four Norwegians and several natives of Scania.

This shows that Moravia at this time was not quite so isolated from Northern Europe as is generally supposed. Of the two chief questions of European politics – the Dutch question and the Turkish question – the second undoubtedly concerned Moravia far more urgently, particularly after the hard experience of 1605; yet in 1618 the land hardly presented the aspect of a quiet backwater. This is borne out by (among other things) the attention given Moravia by west European publicists from the very beginning of the Bohemian Rebellion. Moravia became a focus of European public interest during the Estates' offensive, in the spring of 1619, when, after Thurn's intervention, her Estates joined the Rebellion.

This development preceded the diplomatic offensive of the Bohemian Estates, who in March 1619 sent their agents Herman Frenk and Elias Rozín of Javorník to The Hague and made written application to the Swedish and Danish monarchs for aid.[47] In both these letters the Estates emphasized that for them it was 'a necessary struggle in defence of political freedom'. They requested Gustavus Adolphus' intercession in The Hague and the Hansa towns, and that of Christian IV with the English King, his relative, and with the Dukes of Brunswick and Holstein. At first glance the situation seemed propitious: the two Scandinavian rulers had met shortly before at Halmstad where they discussed the Swedish suggestions for an alliance. At Halmstad, however, no mention was made of Bohemia, and Christian IV was not eager for a Danish–Swedish alliance, finding in it advantage only for Sweden in her conflict with Poland. It seems that it was only the Imperial Council which was willing to aid the Bohemians, at least financially, but its attitude changed with reports of the armament of the Spanish navy.[48] Christian himself was scarcely pleased with the prospect of defending for the Bohemian Estates those liberties of which he had so recently deprived the Danish Estates. A second Bohemian request for aid (13 July) and a letter of intercession from Frederick of the Palatinate (26 June) had the sole result that Christian began to use the danger to Bohemia as an argument to gain the support of the Estates of Lower Saxony. In a letter of 5 August 1619 Christian expressed to Frederick his sorrow at the troubles within the Empire and offered him a 'confidential communication' of news.[49]

When Christian's protests about the dangers in Bohemia failed to have any detectable effect upon the Lower Saxon Estates, he turned his attention once again to strengthening the Danish position at the mouth of the Elbe and the Weser. At this point he probably received the third and final letter from the Bohemian Estates, who on 19 December informed him that they had dethroned Ferdinand II and elected Frederick of the Palatinate. At the same time they asked for aid, both military and financial.[50] At the beginning of 1620 Christian is supposed to have sent a special envoy to Prague who was to determine whether the Bohemians had involved themselves in an armed revolt against the Emperor or in a legal defence of their privileges. At the same time Frederick's ambassadors at Copenhagen, George Duke of Lüneburg and Andreas Pawell (Paulsön) requested Christian's aid. Christian offered no financial help; on the other hand, he was willing to offer a certain measure of diplomatic assistance. The feelers that he sent out to England, to Johann Georg of Saxony, and to the court of the Archduke Albert at Brussels were however, unproductive.[51] Christian went so far as to submit to the Imperial Council a letter enquiring whether he should grant the aid requested by Bohemia and the Union. At the same time, of course, he proposed concrete measures against the Habsburgs and the Estates of the Lower Elbe. Since Christian IV was not accustomed to yield up his autonomy voluntarily, it is practically certain that he submitted his enquiry only because he knew that it would be denied and leave him blameless. And the Imperial Council, at a meeting held on 1/11 March 1620, did indeed refuse to extend aid to the Bohemians. In the Council's view the conflict was not a religious one, an impression that was reinforced by the ambiguous stance of the Union. An offer of assistance could be made only in the case of a justified war in defence of religious freedom.[52]

Thus in the spring of 1620 the Imperial ambassadors and the English envoy Sir Robert Anstruther assailed Christian's neutrality. His general position on the Bohemian 'Rebellion' remained basically unchanged. He recommended that Frederick come to terms with the Emperor, reminded the Duke of Saxony of his duty to his co-religionists, and satisfied King James at least partially by having 200,000 Reichsthalers entrusted to Anstruther for Frederick of the Palatinate.[53] This sum, paid to Frederick's commissioners at Bredstedt on 20 August 1620, represented the totality of the help that the Bohemians received from Denmark. As the Dutch merchant Govert Brasse shrewdly wrote to the States General from Copenhagen, there could be no question of more substantial aid until the Bohemian affair became a 'gemeene religionssaeke', a general conflict of a religious character.[54] Since it was not, the Imperial Council (on 25 August) again refused to grant aid to Bohemia. The Council was even reluctant to contribute to the sum of 200,000 thalers, though this amount actually represented Denmark's repayment of a loan from England.

Nevertheless, in The Hague and in London much was expected from the Danish intervention – if not for Bohemia, then at least for Frederick. News of the Bohemian defeat and of Spanish advances in the Rhenish Palatinate, which directly threatened the United Netherlands, led, in the winter of 1620–1, to a last Dutch diplomatic attempt to win over Christian IV for a coalition against the Habsburgs. Frederick's envoys Plessen and Camerarius were dispatched to Denmark and Sweden; Frederick himself wished to make the journey to Denmark. The Dutch had an envoy, Caspar van Vossbergen, at Copenhagen, and the Danes Jacob Uhlfeldt at The Hague. But the negotiations held in February and March 1621 at Segeberg, which were intended to result in the creation of an anti-Habsburg coalition, ended in failure, and the treaty of alliance between Denmark and the Netherlands remained unsigned.[55]

In April the Union capitulated to Spinola's forces in Germany, and on 12 May 1621 Christian IV advised Frederick that nothing could be achieved at that time 'armata manu', by force of arms.[56] His unsuccessful policies of mediation and neutrality towards Bohemia ended on this resigned note.

Fruitless attempts by Palatine and Dutch diplomacy to secure Christian IV for a coalition against the Habsburgs continued until 1624. In 1621 Christoph von Dohna had attempted to secure supporting action for Johann Georg von Jägerndorf and Gabriel Bethlen. In 1622 Camerarius was at Copenhagen, and the following year the former Bohemian Supreme Chancellor Wenceslas William of Roupov arrived there as well. But Christian remained unmoved even in the face of a Spanish military threat to Lower Saxony which, however, was something of an unknown quantity and, as it turned out, a poorly planned venture.[57] Not until the second half of 1623 did a more hopeful situation begin to emerge. Frederick's old emissaries Johann Ernst of Saxe-Weimar and Count Johann Casimir of the Palatinate renewed their activities in Germany. New hopes rested on the Netherlands which since the fall of the Palatinate had conducted a single-handed struggle against the power of Spain, and, after the collapse of plans for a Spanish marriage for the Prince of Wales, on England. In the winter of 1623–4 Sir Robert Anstruther's negotiations in Denmark assumed a more concrete form. In accordance with English policy Anstruther succeeded in securing Christian's agreement to the restitution of the Palatinate (though not the restitution of Bohemia) by emphasizing the growing threat to northwestern Germany represented by the League and the Spaniards, particularly in view of Sweden's withdrawal. Anglo-Dutch aims, then, were far more modest than the hopes of the Bohemian émigrés, who were concentrated at the miniature court of Frederick of the Palatinate at The Hague and to a lesser extent at the court of Johann Ernst of Saxe-Weimar. The reports of the latter's agent Abraham Richter show how closely Johann Ernst (who as early as 1620 had fought against the Emperor in Bohemia) was following the development of the situation.[58]

From February 1625 Johann Ernst negotiated for a commission in the Danish army, and at the end of the month, as a Danish colonel, he recruited a cavalry regiment at Hamburg whose fourteen Rittmeisters included two Bohemians, Slavata and Sekerka.[59] As commander of the Danish cavalry and quartermaster-general, Johann Ernst faced Tilly in Lower Saxony in the summer of 1625 and later stood against Wallenstein. In the autumn he participated in the siege of Hannover, begun before the formal conclusion of the anti-Habsburg coalition which included England, the United Netherlands, Christian IV of

Denmark, and Frederick of the Palatinate, and was signed at The Hague on 9 December 1625. The Hague Coalition represented the first attempt at the formation of a broad anti-Habsburg alliance; it was indirectly supported by France and was far removed from the conception of a 'Corpus evangelicorum' held perhaps by the Danish Royal Council in 1620 when they considered the conditions for a general conflict.[60] At The Hague, the motives were frankly those of power, and they were undoubtedly shared by Christian IV who longed to control the mouth of the Elbe and the Weser. The failure of the Coalition has led historians to overlook the fact that in 1625 this anti-Habsburg group was (with the exception of Frederick of the Palatinate, who represented nobody apart from the émigrés) a logical alliance of the most progressive western and northern European states. Of course, Sweden was absent, because her conditions for adherence were too stringent for the English. Actually it was his competition with Gustavus Adolphus more than rational considerations which drew Christian IV into the orbit of the Coalition, whose character was otherwise hardly to his taste.

Christian also sent a special ambassador to Gabriel Bethlen, whose actions he hoped to co-ordinate with the allied military offensive. Bethlen replied that such a struggle required thorough preparation, and that he wanted more precise guarantees from the allies before he planned any campaigns for the year 1626. He considered it essential to reach agreement on the specific nature of the proposed collaboration between the allied armies and his own contingents.[61] Bethlen's caution was amply justified in view of his past experience. Co-ordination of action on the battlefields of western and central Europe was not once realized throughout the whole period of the Thirty Years' War. The prospects for 1626, therefore, were not particularly bright, even leaving aside the fact that the interests of Christian's allies were not entirely compatible and in England's case even led to the sabotage of continental actions that had been agreed upon.

Mansfeld was named commander of the Coalition army; he was responsible primarily to the Dutch States General and Frederick of the Palatinate. Johann Ernst of Saxe-Weimar was one of the Danish generals, but it is interesting that in March 1626 he sent his confidant M. Streyff to London and Amsterdam to negotiate and gather information.[62] In the winter of 1626–7 Mansfeld's contingents joined the Danish troops under General Fuchs and Johann Ernst. The allied forces were to apply pressure to the League's forces under Tilly and the Imperial army under Wallenstein, and were to co-operate with an independent force under Christian von Halberstadt. In mid-February 1626 the allied army took Altmark, but on 25 April it was defeated at Dessau.[63] At the time of Christian von Halberstadt's death on 16 June it seemed that military actions would accomplish nothing. The tireless activity of the Transylvanian envoy Quadt, however, who emphasized the favourable situation that was developing in central Europe, met with success. For in May a great peasant uprising broke out in Upper Austria which must have placed a serious strain on the strength of the armies of the Emperor and the League. In these circumstances it was decided to create a diversion in Silesia whose execution was entrusted to Mansfeld and the Duke of Saxe-Weimar. Danish contingents under Johann Ernst left the region of Stendal on 24 June. Crossing the Elbe at Havelberg, they skirted Berlin on the north (Brandenburg, like Saxony, had not joined the Coalition), and in mid-July reached Frankfurt-an-der-Oder with Mansfeld. From Frankfurt the forces of Johann Ernst and Mansfeld proceeded separately. Together they passed Breslau, then Johann Ernst continued through Oppeln and Kosel and arrived at Oderberg on 12 August. Mansfeld meanwhile marched through Pština to Těšín.[64]

The Danish forces and Mansfeld's troops thus reached the frontier between Moravia and Hungary, and it was now necessary for the commanders to agree on further action. Their negotiations, conducted from 23 to 30 August, are reported in three documents. On 23 August Johann Ernst conferred with Mansfeld and concluded that (a) they should join their forces, and 'via Olomouc and Hradiště' should await Bethlen along the Hungarian frontier, but that (b) four companies of 'Blue' Danish infantry should meanwhile hold Opava and the remaining four Jägerndorf, while the 'Green' regiment was to hold Hradec, Wigstein and Fulnek; at the same time, (c) Opava and the other towns should be fortified for their own defence and so that they could serve as centres of supply and reinforcement.[65]

On 30 August the Duke of Saxe-Weimar at Lipník suggested to Mansfeld that they should discharge none of their troops, should exact contributions, and should proceed at once to the rendezvous with Bethlen. If Bethlen rejected the plan for a diversion in Moravia, Silesia, Bohemia or Germany, this was to be undertaken by an army under the command of Mansfeld. But if Mansfeld should wish to depart for Venice, his army and artillery would be taken over by Johann Ernst for Christian IV.[66] These articles were conveyed by Colonel Baudissin and Captain-General Žerotín to Mansfeld at Lukov, where, after a discussion of the merits of an attack on Vienna or a blockade of

Breslau, it was decided to execute the compromise plan put forward by the Duke of Saxe-Weimar.[67] The main force was to proceed to the rendezvous with Bethlen, but the rest of the Danish detachments were to consolidate their position in Silesia.

At the beginning of September the troops began their march along the left bank of the River Morava, passed Kroměříž and Hulín, and proceeded through Uherský Brod to Trenčín. The Commissar Samuel Jeschenius and Colonel Peblis were sent to Bethlen, who left Transylvania only at the end of August to travel through Debrecen into Upper Hungary. Since there was scant agreement between them, Mansfeld and the Duke of Saxe-Weimar negotiated separately with Bethlen. They quarrelled over the artillery left behind at Těšín with Mansfeld's garrison and over the use of the newly recruited detachments. These became all the more important when news arrived of the defeat of the main part of the Danish army left behind in Germany, which occurred on 27 August at Lutter: now, certainly, no help could be expected from that quarter.

The position of the Danish and Mansfeld's troops, which were now being closely watched by Wallenstein's army, became steadily more precarious. On 22 September Bethlen had only reached Filakovo. Turkish reinforcements were at Nográd, Wallenstein was at Nitra, Mansfeld and Johann Ernst at Nemecké Pravno, to which they moved from their earlier positions near the source of the Rivers Hron and Nitra. The worried generals turned to Bethlen for advice about what steps to take next. Bethlen suggested that they bring all their Silesian detachments through the Jablunka Pass. This satisfied neither Mansfeld nor Johann Ernst, who, on the contrary, requested Bethlen's aid for Silesia where the allied forces were commanded by Žerotín and Mitzlaff. Johann Ernst proposed that some of the Silesian detachments should conduct a raid into Bohemia and then move into the Upper Palatinate.[68]

This, of course, did not suit Bethlen at all. He therefore concentrated on a quick assembly of all the allied forces in the Hron Valley, which he was approaching by way of Sečany. On 29 September he requested reinforcements from the Danish contingents to oppose Wallenstein's army, which was advancing through Nové Zámky.[69] The next day Wallenstein's army stood face to face with Bethlen at Drégelypalánk on the River Ipel. Bethlen, who had not been reached by the Danish reinforcements, finally retreated towards Sečany on the night of 1 October without giving battle and urged Mansfeld to proceed to Lučenec.[70] But since Wallenstein himself was none too sure of his position, he, too, withdrew – to Nové Zámky. Both these diversionary manoeuvres meant the end of military operations, but on 1 October neither Wallenstein nor Bethlen was aware of this. Bethlen therefore sent repeated requests for a rendezvous with the allied armies under Johann Ernst and Mansfeld. They finally united on 15 October near Šahy-Tekov.

In the main camp at Tekov a series of acrimonious talks took place between Mansfeld and Johann Ernst, who attempted to convince Mansfeld of the folly of his decision to leave for Venice with only a small cavalry force.[71] The whole discussion, in which Colonels Peblis and Berbisdorf also participated, merely served to emphasize the irreconcilable views of the two generals. Mansfeld would hear nothing of the earlier agreement and would not consider shifting any of his troops to Silesia. Soon afterward, around 10 November 1626, Mansfeld set out for Venice, and during the march, on the night of 29 November, he died near Sarajevo in Bosnia.

The command of the remaining detachments was taken over by Johann Ernst. His chief concern was to come to an agreement with Bethlen about winter quarters and supplies for the troops who, like Wallenstein's army at Nové Zámky, Trnava and Hlohovec, were dying off. These negotiations were in no way easy, for the Duke was aware that from 9 November Bethlen had been negotiating with the Hungarian Palatine for a truce.[72] On 21 November Bethlen offered his uneasy ally winter quarters in Turkish-held territory. The detachments were to reach the Turks via Banská Štiavnica, Kríž-nad-Hronom, Handlová and Prievidza, after which they would be protected from attack by Imperial forces by Turkish troops waiting at Bojnice and Topolčany. Johann Ernst was to remain with his infantry at Martin, with his eight cavalry companies in nearby villages. Mansfeld's infantry was to be quartered at Zniev, and 1,600 cavalrymen under Commissar Straussberg and 2,000 infantry on the estates of the Zniev monastery.[73]

At the beginning of December 1626 further negotiations awaited Johann Ernst – this time only to ensure that Bethlen did not forget his allies during his negotiations for a truce with the Emperor. Bethlen for his part, swamped with complaints about the lack of discipline among the remnant of the Saxe-Weimar detachments, was chiefly interested in getting rid of what was left of the armies of his former allies. Johann Ernst negotiated at first through emissaries sent to Bethlen at Banská Štiavnica. In instructions of 3 December Johann Ernst protested vigorously against his unfaithful ally's negotiations with the enemy. In any case, he insisted that Bethlen assure the Saxe-Weimar detachments a safe-conduct out of Hungary. Should the Emperor refuse these terms, Bethlen was to provide them with a sufficient convoy as far as Olomouc. Bethlen was to pay for the artillery, munitions and footwear which he had received from Mansfeld, and repay the financial subsidy.[74]

In further meetings, Johann Ernst requested that Bethlen guarantee the withdrawal of his troops through Trenčín, Kroměříž, Jägerndorf, and Odra. Bethlen was to return a part of the arms given him by Mansfeld, to support the proposed Danish attack on Moravia and Bohemia. The raid into Bohemia was to be conducted in conjunction with an uprising of the Bohemians if this could be fomented.[75] Further points conveyed by Johann Ernst to Bethlen revealed more of the Duke's plans. In the first place, he hoped to spark off rebellion throughout Moravia. With help from the detachments at Opava and the Moravian Wallachians, it would be possible, in his view, to gain the adherence of the Moravian Estates. Johann Ernst's plan was to return to Silesia through the Jablunka Pass and Těšín; Bethlen was to help him by sending four to five thousand cavalrymen and some mounted musketeers to Valašské Meziříčí. The cavalry escort was to be provided by Bethlen even if it became evident that no uprising was imminent.[76] In any case Johann Ernst wished to retain Opava and its environs. Because he calculated that in the spring Bethlen would once more move against the Emperor, the detachments at Opava could at worst be transferred to Hungary. If Mansfeld should fail to arrive with reinforcements from Venice, the Danish detachments were to be taken over by Bethlen or else reserved for Christian in the event of a Silesian campaign.[77]

Johann Ernst's last papers, composed most likely on the way to Pukanec, attempted to salvage whatever was possible for Christian IV. Even now the situation was not hopeless, for it would be a simple matter to aid rebellious peasants in Bohemia and elsewhere.[78] Johann Ernst's plan sketched at Pukanec was never completely formulated. On 14 December 1626 the thirty-two year old general of the disintegrating army died at Martin. His chancery and what remained of his forces were taken over by the Danish commissar Joachim Mitzlaff, who also arranged the transfer of the Duke's remains to Opava.[79]

Meanwhile Mitzlaff, with the help of Ladislav Velen of Žerotín and other Moravian and Silesian noblemen, substantially strengthened the Danish position during the autumn of 1626. Besides Ladislav of Žerotín, his collaborators included the former commander of the Bohemian Estates' cavalry Jan of Bubna, Jan Adam of Víckov, the

Žerotíns of Meziříčí, and Václav Bítovský. Žerotín, far from idle during the winter months, attempted to fill his contingents by recruiting in the eastern Moravian and Silesian countryside. A 'List of All Officers', complete to June 1627, shows that in the nineteen cavalry and thirty infantry companies of the Danish army, Bohemians, Moravians and Silesians formed about a third of the command staff.[80] In the cavalry regiment under Baudissin they included the Captains Jan Bílavský, Adam Kinský, Jiří Gerštorf, and a certain Pflug; in the Holk regiment, Hans Eberhard Gerštorf; in the regiment of Lieutenant-Colonel Kaltenhofen, Captains Rudický and Oderský of Lideřov; in the Ubach regiment, Captain Jiří Sekerka of Sedčice, recruited at Hamburg. One of the new cavalry regiments was commanded by Lieutenant-Colonel Ondřej Kochtický of Kochtice, formerly the envoy of the Silesian Estates to Poland and a counsellor of Frederick of the Palatinate. His son Ondřej was a captain in the same regiment. In the 'Green' infantry regiment under Lieutenant-Colonel Schlammersdorf, Jan Záborský served as a captain: in Rantzow's 'Green' regiment were Captains Jiří Jan Soběhrd and Jan Jiří of Švamberk; in the 'Yellow' regiment of Lieutenant-Colonel Riese were Major Jaroslav Volf Štampach and Captains Jiří Rustorff and Jan Gerštorf; in Khon's regiment Captains Jan Jakub Thurn and Hans Štáblovský.

In Hungary the Saxe-Weimar detachments lost five officers: four resigned after the Hungarian campaign, and one apparently deserted. At the beginning of 1627 Mitzlaff had at most about 12,000 troops under his command. That battle with Wallenstein's army was unthinkable under these circumstances must have been clear to Mitzlaff. It is probable that he was at least partly carrying out the wishes of the late general, and that he had agreed to the recruitment of soldiers in Silesia, Moravia, and probably also in Bohemia. This explains why in the spring and summer of 1627 a series of peasant uprisings broke out in central and northeastern Bohemia, which were connected with the activities of Danish or Opava emissaries. Mitzlaff was still concerned with the defence of Opava in mid-June 1627.[81] Until July Mitzlaff, Žerotín and their associates waited in Opava for Bethlen's arrival. In the end Wallenstein was successful in blocking the retreat routes at the mouth of the Oder. After a senseless attempt to march into Hungary, the infantry and artillery surrendered; a part of the cavalry reached the Baltic with Mitzlaff and Kochtický. A number of the former Saxe-Weimar captains turned up several years later in the Swedish army.

The Danish occupation of the Silesian region around Opava,

Jägerndorf and Těšín along the Moravian border has, until now, been considered a rather unimportant episode in this period of the war. It interested Josef Zukal only as one of the causes of the Liechtenstein confiscations, František Hrubý as one stage of the activities of Ladislav Velen of Žerotín, and František Roubík as a stimulus for Wallenstein's military campaigns.[82] Nor have German and Danish historians accorded the Silesian episode the attention that I believe it merits in their treatment of the 'Danish' phase of the Thirty Years' War.[83]

For the history of the anti-Habsburg resistance and of popular uprisings, the 'regiment' of Danes and émigrés who were active around Opava for three-quarters of a year was of great significance. This, however, is not all. V. Fialová, B. Indra and František Dostál have shown that the struggle against the Habsburgs was by no means the exclusive affair of the émigrés and the Estates' resistance.[84]

We have seen that in the period of the Bohemian Estates' Rebellion Christian IV had little sympathy for, or interest in, Bohemia. There is no reason to suppose that his outlook had changed by 1626. In meetings with English diplomats and later at the conclusion of the treaty of alliance at The Hague, Bohemia was not a subject of discussion. Nevertheless Christian became the leader of the resistance forces of the anti-Habsburg coalition, and his army penetrated into the heart of central Europe. They became the allies of the Prince of Transylvania – but also of the Turks. Its generals aroused the indignation of such a condottiere as Mansfeld because they counted on the collaboration not only of rebellious noblemen, but also of townsmen, the peasants, and the Moravian Wallachians. Just as the struggle against Habsburg hegemony resulted inevitably from concrete circumstances, so the Danish King was inevitably forced into a situation which was distasteful to him.

The position of Danish policy toward the Bohemian struggle for independence enables us to test the validity of traditional views. Neither in 1618 nor in 1626–7 was this position determined by religious motives. On the contrary, the Bohemian War was generally considered – with the agreement of the Bohemians themselves – to be a political, not a religious, conflict. This of course meant that for the Protestant monarchs who ruled in Saxony, Denmark and England, the Bohemians were 'rebels' against the providence-established authority. The causes of the conflict were substantially the same in both these periods. Therefore both the Bohemian and the Danish Wars were conflicts which could have been Europe-wide, though both ended as localized conflicts. If the Bohemians, following the advice of the Danish Royal

Council and of James of England, had emphasized only the religious motivation of their rebellion, would things have turned out differently? The example of the Danish War suggests that this tactic would not have helped them in the least. The 'secularization' of political thought in the seventeenth century was already so far advanced that 'religious' wars were accepted by everyone for what they were: struggles for power. If anything met with defeat on the battlefields from Desava to Drégelypalánk it was the notion of an effective 'Corpus evangelicorum'.

In the years 1626–7 the focus of a conflict which for a while united both fundamental problems of Europe was shifted to Moravian, Silesian and Slovakian soil. These questions concerned the Turkish threat and the fate of the United Netherlands. The remnants of the former 'Dutch' regiment of Colonel Nijhoff, incorporated into Mansfeld's detachments, marched into Turkish territory around Nográd and Vác. The lamentable fate of some of its members, described by an English participant in the campaign, shows that the two problems could not yet be organically united.[85]

It is highly doubtful whether Gabriel Bethlen, Prince of Transylvania at one time elected King of Hungary, was a figure who could successfully have resolved the quarrels in a statesmanlike way. These quarrels had until now caused the anti-Habsburg coalition to ignore the problems presented by Turkish expansion and accept collaboration with them as a necessary evil. The previously unknown correspondence of Gabriel Bethlen with Mansfeld and Johann Ernst of Saxe-Weimar most decidedly does not support the high assessment which Bethlen has received from the contemporary Hungarian historians P. Pach-Zsigmond and T. Wittman.[86] It seems that this judgement will have to be revised, because we now have substantially more material for the study of Bethlen's policy than was available to Gindely and Szekfü.[87]

And finally, in the conceptions of the European policy-makers that were formulated at The Hague, what rôle was played by the Bohemian lands and the people who lived there – not only the nobility but also the townsmen and the unfree peasants? We have seen that the impulse for the military action came from the Transylvania envoy Quadt, who, in the interests of Bethlen, and probably within the framework of earlier negotiations, succeeded in bringing about the central European campaign of Mansfeld and Johann Ernst of Saxe-Weimar. Then in June 1626 military operations had shifted onto Habsburg territory, and plans existed for a union with Bethlen's forces for a 'diversionary action' against Vienna.

In August of the same year Mansfeld was apparently thinking more seriously about an attack on Vienna; on the other hand his partner Johann Ernst favoured a union with Bethlen's troops (Bethlen was not yet anywhere near), to be followed by actions in Moravia, then in Bohemia and Germany, in order to operate together with the other forces of the coalition. This plan became completely impracticable with the defeat of the Danish main army near Lutter at the end of the month.

In September, when the forces of Saxe-Weimar and Mansfeld, the Turkish forces, and Bethlen's army all finally joined in what is now southern Slovakia, Bethlen advocated the evacuation of positions in Silesia and joint action in Hungary against Wallenstein. Since the Imperial forces were close by, Bethlen's views were nothing more than a reflection of his immediate apprehensions. It appears, however, that Mansfeld was steadily coming round to Bethlen's viewpoint. Both certainly foresaw that hostilities would cease during the winter months – the customary procedure – probably on the basis of an armistice; that Bethlen could formally assume command of the Danish–Mansfeld troops, particularly the infantry and artillery of which he had always been short; and that in the spring of 1627, perhaps with Venetian aid, he would renew the war. This is probably the reason why the question of the withdrawal of troops from Silesia in October so sharply divided the two generals. The Duke of Saxe-Weimar, following his instructions, insisted that his detachments remain at the disposition of his monarch, Christian IV.

In the spirit of these considerations Mansfeld departed for Venice, and Bethlen opened negotiations for a truce. Bad weather which set in in October and November threatened to upset all existing plans. In both armies troops were dying, discipline (such as it was) was deteriorating, and the tormented peasants were beginning to turn against the soldiers.[88] Even in these circumstances Johann Ernst stood by his plan to launch a new offensive from Opava in the spring of 1627 with the assistance of Bethlen and the Venetians. This was in essence a return to the old plan of August, except that the unified attack on Bohemia was to be prepared by a popular uprising in Moravia – procured by an intelligent use of the complaints of the Estates and the unfree peasantry. At the end of 1626 Johann Ernst counted quite seriously on the imminence of peasant uprisings – perhaps remembering the aid he had already received from the Moravian Wallachians.

Nothing could have been further from the thoughts of the ruler of a small duchy and the commander of a monarchical army, who shrank from the idea of 'rebellion', than collaboration with the rebellious subjects of the Habsburg Emperor. Feudal-Catholic pressure had apparently shifted the position of the popular masses to one of resistance against the Habsburgs. And this is the reason why the Danes were surrounded by émigrés from the defeated Estates' society, and why they met with such sympathy from the people, a sympathy which, as we have seen in the example of Frýdek, they were not always clever enough to exploit. Nevertheless the inhabitants of Hranice and Vsetín helped the Danes, and the unfree peasants of Bohemia were willing to take up arms in their cause. Johann Ernst's plans, taken up by Commissar Mitzlaff, who himself cannot be said to have suffered from feudal prejudices, enable us better to understand the reports of the conspiratorial activities of Jan of Bubna, and of the participation of the Estates' opposition in the peasant uprisings in the Bohemian regions of Kouřim and Čáslav in the summer of 1627. It is noteworthy that alongside the petty noblemen who had been hard hit by the confiscations after the Battle of the White Mountain, the official source lists emissaries from Opava, and that the uprising, traditionally linked with Mathias Ulický, was led by the recruitment officers sent from Opava, Matouš Jiří of Těchenice and Michal Fridrich Christpeins.[89]

In the period when antagonisms involving all Europe were brought into confrontation on Moravian and Slovakian territory, the popular resistance to the Habsburg programme of feudal and Catholic reaction was so significant a factor that it could not be neglected by soldiers who had come in the service of foreign powers to fulfil tasks which had little in common with the fate of the Czech people.

5

The Swedish–Dutch period of the conflict 1630–5

PROBLEMS AND SOURCES

Recent contributions dealing with the period 1630–5 include works by Dieter Albrecht – particularly his concise monograph on the relations of Richelieu and Gustavus Adolphus with Germany[1] and the last section of his book *Die auswärtige Politik Maximilians von Bayern, 1618–1635.*[2] The biography of Olivares by G. Marañon,[3] still useful for Spanish policy, has recently been supplemented by A. Domínguez Ortiz[4] and F. Tomás Valiente.[5]

R. Quazza's monograph remains the authoritative assessment of the Mantuan War;[6] D. Albrecht[7] and A. Leman[8] have traced the continually shifting policy of the papal Curia.

Work on Wallenstein was reviewed in the previous chapter; to it must be added the standard military history of the Thirty Years' War by E. von Frauenholz.[9] Of the most recent publications, the study by Beladiez has been mentioned; new biographies of Wallenstein have been published by Golo Mann and Josef Janáček.

The background of Swedish history is supplied by the German version of Ingvar Andersson's *Schwedische Geschichte*[10] and the abridged English version of Eli F. Heckscher's classic *Economic History of Sweden.*[11] Nils Ahnlund's *Gustav Adolf, King of Sweden* is another classic of Swedish historiography.[12] Michael Roberts has written a remarkable biography of the Lion of the North, combining a straightforward presentation with the analysis of several particular themes.[13] He has also studied the earlier growth of Swedish power[14] and edited an important anthology of essays on seventeenth-century Swedish history.[15]

V. M. Alekseyev has compiled a bibliography of Soviet work on the War of Smolensk, that is the 'Russian Period' of the Thirty Years' War.[16] B. F. Porshnev sees in the War of Smolensk a facet of the struggle between Sweden and Russia on the one hand and the Habsburgs and Poland on the other. O. L. Vainstein, however, concludes that Muscovite Russia was simply continuing her earlier political tradition. Porshnev's thesis has also been criticized by A. S. Kan. Porshnev has further studied the Russian rôle in European politics throughout the period of the Thirty Years' War. His paper at the Eleventh International Congress of Historical Sciences at Stockholm in 1960 serves as an excellent introduction to the whole set of problems and is equipped with an extensive bibliography.[17]

Relatively little is known about the gradual withdrawal of the Netherlands from the conflict. Besides the book by C. R. Boxer already mentioned on Dutch naval power and the first part of the dissertation, also mentioned above, by M. A. M. Franken, Pieter Geyl's synthesis of Dutch history in the first half of the seventeenth century remains extremely useful.[18] An essentially traditional approach is also evident in Geyl's essay on the Stadholder Frederick Hendrik, printed in a collection of his studies in Dutch history.[19]

A second current of Dutch historiography was represented, until his death in 1962, by Jan Romein who carried on a long and unresolved debate with Geyl. The attempt at a Marxist interpretation of Dutch history, which he wrote with his wife Annie Romein-Verschoor (*De lage landen bij de zee* (1949)), was begun before the Second World War, but it served as an important stimulus for the postwar generation of Dutch historians. Romein's influence is evident in the second volume of the *History of the Eighty Years' War*, written with obvious barbs against the German occupation, by Jacob Presser.[20] Romein's influence is even more evident in the work of Ivo Schöffer.

France in the period of Richelieu's régime is covered concisely in V. L. Tapié's book on France under Louis XIII.[21] Here a different line is followed by the work of Robert Mandrou, who has collaborated in an important history of French civilization and has written a study of France in the seventeenth and eighteenth centuries which has opened new perspectives for further research and contains a remarkable bibliographical section.[22]

Austro-Spanish relations have been studied by the historian of Austrian Protestantism Grete Mecenseffy, who has helped to clarify the situation surrounding Wallenstein's fall and the Spanish intervention, culminating in the Battle of Nördlingen.[23] José M. Jover has analysed the public reaction to the Peace of Prague from the Spanish point of view.[24] A most perceptive account of the 'political crisis' of the Olivares régime and at the same time a highly critical judgement on Spanish intervention in central Europe are contained in the sections written by Juan Reglá for the handbook of Spanish history mentioned above, *Introducción a la historia de España* which also reviews modern literature on the subject. Among the works dealing with Spanish intellectual history in the seventeenth century, particularly the tragic period of the 1630s, that of J. A. Maravall on seventeenth-century Spanish political philosophy should be mentioned.[25]

The most dramatic episode of the period 1630–5 was the fall of Wallenstein. The century-old association of Wallenstein's end with Schiller's drama meant that the Schiller centennial in the mid-1950s led to a renewal of interest in Wallenstein. Besides the studies by myself and my former students M. Hroch and K. Stanka only Frank Wollman among Czech historians has worked on Wallenstein. German-speaking historians, on the other hand, have contributed more: A. Ernstberger's study of Wallenstein and his banker Jan de Witte and H. von Srbik's newly revised study of Wallenstein's fall have already been mentioned. More favourable evaluations of Wallenstein are made in a number of East German literary-historical studies: J. R. Becher, *Denn er ist unser, Friedrich Schiller* (Berlin 1955); A. Abusch, *Schiller* (Berlin 1955). The only truly penetrating consideration has come from Thomas Mann (*Versuch über Wallenstein* (Berlin 1955)). It is precisely for these problems that the archives can offer much new material. Golo Mann's great biography, cited above, is now – at least until the appearance of volume v of the *Documenta Bohemica*, the starting-point for any further research.

For the period 1630–5, too, the sources in the Bohemian archives form the documentary basis for research into the European significance of Wallenstein and his policies. The section of Wallenstein's military chancery preserved at Prague is, to be sure, somewhat less important than that at Vienna, but other documents relevant to Wallenstein at Prague and Mnichovo Hradiště form a rich body of material that is indispensable for the solution of questions which historians have not yet begun to investigate. This is true both of army administration and of Wallenstein's activities as a military entrepreneur. As far as questions of high policy are concerned, we must begin by realizing that the most important negotiations, in the seventeenth century as in the twentieth, were not committed to paper, and that much important material was scattered after Wallenstein's death in February 1634. But even so it has been possible to identify some important documents among the correspondence of the people surrounding Wallenstein and also in several artificial collections.

Since most of Wallenstein's estates became the recompense granted to those who betrayed him, Wallensteiniana can now be found among the papers of Ottavio Piccolomini, Heinrich Schlick, Mathias Gallas, as well as Thun, Morzin, Colloredo; also significant is the correspondence of Cardinal Dietrichstein, Vilém Slavata and Karel of Žerotín. Of the direct participants in the Wallenstein tragedy, the papers of such figures as Cardinal Harrach and Johann Putz von Adlersthurm, author of the curious *Diarium et itinerarium*, have been preserved. And finally, for the question of Wallenstein's actual supporters in 1634, there is the important manuscript collection in the State Archive at Brno which contains material showing the repercussions of the so-called Troppau Rebellion of the spring of 1634.

The fascinating personality of the generalissimo gave rise to pamphlets and books, collections of leaflets and pictures. This can be seen from the collection 'Bellum Tricennale' in the Castle Library at Mnichovo Hradiště, the collection of prints at the castle of Český Šternberk, and museum collections at Prague and Cheb. There is pictorial documentation in the gallery in the castle of Duchcov (Dux) in the Great Hall of the Wallenstein Palace at Prague, and in the castles of Mnichovo Hradiště, Friedland, Náchod and Opočno.

The basic collection remains the Wallenstein Chancery in the State Central Archive at Prague, which was described in the preceding chapter.

However, future research will probably rely more heavily on Wallensteiniana preserved in various collections of the *Prague State Archive branch at Mnichovo Hradiště.* The Waldstein Family Archive contains, in its section I, Imperial *privilegia* and other documents. Section II ('Manuscripts') contains the journal of Adam Waldstein, extant for the years 1629, 1631, 1633 and 1634. The entries which would probably have been most interesting to us have been torn out, probably by the author himself. Here, too, is a document describing the punishment of the participants in the Estates' Rebellion, a transcript of reports of Jaroslav Rašín, a history of Albrecht Wallenstein written by J. Stentzsch with the assistance of V. Červenka, and materials for a biography of the generalissimo collected at the beginning of the nineteenth century. This section also contains the diary of Johann Putz von Adlersthurm, originally borrowed from abroad by the Waldstein archivist Dr J. Bergl when he identified Putz as the author of the pamphlet *Chaos Perduellionis.*[26]

Section IV of the Family Archive ('Wallensteiniana') contains a collection of diplomatic documents, transcripts from various sources, and in the fourth volume some interesting pieces of the correspondence of Adam Waldstein (for example a letter to Ferdinand II from 1633). The sixth volume contains copies of Ferdinand's letters to the generalissimo in the period 1628–33. There are a copy of Rašín's report and transcripts of the *Registratura* of the Jičín Chamber for the year 1631. The eighth volume of this section contains transcriptions of various documents and memorials, for example expert testimony relative to Wallenstein's replacement as commander by the Archduke Ferdinand. Volume XII contains documents about the institution of Imperial commissioners for the Duchy of Friedland in 1634 and drafts of letters received by the generalissimo in 1633 from the Bohemian Land administration. Section V of the Family Archive ('Prague Section') contains, as was mentioned earlier, Wallenstein's patents of title, and also copies of correspondence, for example with Maximilian of Bavaria, which run until 1633.[27] Here, too, are the originals of letters from Adam Waldstein to Karel of Žerotín between 1631 and 1635.

In series II of the Autograph Collection are letters of Johann Ulrich von Eggenberg (1621–34), Khevenhüller's letters to Ferdinand II and to Olivares. Holographs of J. L. von Schwarzenberg and J. Werdenberg reach into this period. There is also a unique letter from one Juan Diego de Putz, giving news of Wallenstein from Brussels. There are also some noteworthy Swedish autographs, for instance fifteen items of the correspondence of Axel Oxenstierna (1617–35), an important treaty between the Swedish Crown and three regions of the Imperial Knighthood, concluded at Heilbronn in 1633, and some papers of Gustavus Adolphus. Series III of this collection contains pieces of correspondence from the chancery of Ottavio Piccolomini, particularly from the years 1633–4, among them an interesting letter of February 1634 from Baltasar de Marradas to Piccolomini containing news of steps taken against the generalissimo which Piccolomini himself forwarded to his own correspondents in March. The liquidation of the Wallenstein 'plot' is also the subject of letters of Ernest de Suys and Gerhard von Questenberg. Series IV of the Autographs Collection contains correspondence of Piccolomini, chiefly from the year 1634. There are also letters of Mathias Gallas from February and March 1634, from Pilsen; letters of Marradas, Aldringen, F. Diodati, and other Imperial commanders.

An interesting supplement to all this are manuscripts preserved as an appendix to the *Bohemica* of Jan Jeník z Bratřic, now in the Library of the National Museum at Prague, chiefly in series II of the collection

'Waldstein Bohemica'. Among these interesting documents are a remarkable commentary by Jeník concerning Pelcl's biography and a manuscript discovered in 1786 in the monastery at Sedlec – 'Description of the Life and Heroic Deeds of Albrecht Count of Waldstein, Prince of Friedland...'. Jeník appended often ironical comments to the memorial verses. He saw Wallenstein as a traitor, not against the Emperor, but rather 'a traitor to his distressed country', a 'misshapen son of his Fatherland' and the tyrannical suppressor of peasant uprisings.[28]

After the State Archive at Mnichovo Hradiště, the most important depository for this period is the *State Archive at Litoměřice branch at Děčín.* In the *Clam-Gallas Family Archive* the most extensive section is the Military Chancery of Mathias Gallas, which has four boxes for the years 1631–4, about 600 to 700 documents. Also noteworthy are two boxes of private correspondence organized alphabetically by correspondents (1632–47), and one box of documents concerning the quarrels over the division of the Mantuan plunder ('Gallas–Aldringen Suit, 1630–1668').[29]

The Gallas Collection is supplemented by that of the Aldringens. The *Clary-Aldringen Family Archive* possesses in the papers of Johann Aldringen documents already mentioned on the Italian period of the Thirty Years' War (box 24), and with the Swedish period and the conflicts in Germany and Switzerland (October, 1633), news of the Battles of Breitenfeld and Lützen, and letters from Gallas, Wallenstein and Piccolomini.

The third significant collection from Děčín is composed of the papers of Rudolf Thun (d. 1636), in the *Thun-Hohenstein Family Archive.* The documents in Thun's military chancery (about 900 pieces for the years 1630–4, boxes 2–5) contain reports of military actions in northern Germany, Bohemia, and again in Germany. The other sections (for example 'Domain of Děčín') contain documents connected with the Saxon and Swedish invasions of Bohemia which are similar to materials in other archives. They are of a local character and would serve chiefly for the clarification of military actions and the study of their results.

A third major repository of documentation for this period is the *State Archive at Zámrsk* which possesses Wallensteiniana and other sources for the period in several collections:

The *Morzin Family Archive*, formerly at Vrchlabí, contains the papers of Rudolf and Paul Morzin, covering the years 1631–8. The *Piccolomini Family Archive* contains, among the papers of Ottavio Piccolomini in section IV ('Affairs of the Duchy of Amalfi') some reports of Wallenstein from Italy, and in section VI some generally meagre material concerning relations between Piccolomini and Wallenstein. Because some of the documents have apparently been destroyed and others stolen, the general picture is certainly distorted. Section VIII ('The Thirty Years' War') contains Wallensteiniana, correspondence with Spaniards, with the Imperial court and with other generals, news of the Battle of Lützen, of peace negotiations with Saxony, of negotiations for Ottavio's entry into the service of Spain (nos. 16, 430–28, 011). In the *Schlick Family Archive* the papers of Heinrich Schlick contain valuable material – copies of documents for Schlick's own use in conducting the affairs of the Court War Council, as well as his correspondence. Among the copies are decrees, rescripts and letters of Ferdinand II and Ferdinand III, reports to the Emperor, and correspondence received by court offices from agents at home and abroad, including Swedish generals and Chancellor Oxenstierna. Here, too, are copies of Albrecht Wallenstein's correspondence for the years 1629–1633. Heinrich Schlick's correspondence includes letters and reports for the Court War Council beginning in 1628, correspondence with the Emperor beginning in 1630, and reports from the battlefields beginning in 1632. 'Wallensteiniana' contains orders relative to quartering and supply beginning in 1632, Wallenstein's reports to the Emperor from 1632, transcriptions from the meeting of the colonels at Pilsen in 1634, the custody of Wallenstein's plate, and news of the removal of Wallenstein's followers in Silesia, including a copy of the death sentence delivered against Johann Ulrich Schaffgotsch in 1635.[30] The most important materials are in boxes 6–8 (section III). There are unique documents dealing with the execution at Eger, from January and February 1634 (III, 6; III, 7; III, 16). This group of papers also apparently underwent censorship.

The final important collection at Zámrsk is the *Colloredo-Mansfeld Family Archive*, possessing sources for the Thirty Years' War in the papers of Rudolph Colloredo (d. 1657) and Jeronym (d. 1637), in boxes 1–8. In 1634 Rudolph Colloredo suppressed the rebellion in Silesia led by Schaffgotsch, joined the clique of generals who were responsible for Wallenstein's death, and became Field Marshal-Lieutenant, to the great exasperation of Marradas. Here too are copies from Viennese archives, particularly from the collection of the Court War Council (the first and thirteenth volumes of the so-called *Archivalische Erhebungen*, transcriptions 1ff.).

To the resources of these main archives in Bohemia relatively little can be added from other archives. The State Archive branch at

Žitenice contains the papers of Wenceslas Eusebius of Lobkowitz, whose career resembled that of Heinrich Schlick. 'Letters from the Imperial Army', running from 1633 to 1650, are richer for the later years. They are particularly significant after 1636 when Lobkowitz became a member of the Court War Council. There are documents of a similar nature in fascicle A 82 ('Miscellanea from the Time of the Thirty Years' War') and in Q 16/36 ('Reports of Events of the War, 1632–1638').

The State Archive branch at Žlutice contains in the Nostitz-Rieneck Family Archive the rest of Cardinal Dietrichstein's drafts, extending until 1631 (call-number DD 2), correspondence with the Court (EE 2), and papers of the Bohemian Court Chamber (EE 3, GG 9, LL 2). The papers from the diplomatic missions of Jiří Bořita of Martinic (1624–41, call-number NN 7) are also valuable.

The State Archive branch at Český Krumlov has the papers of Adam von Schwarzenberg concerning the foreign policy of Brandenburg and events in the war (Schwarzenberg Family Archive, fasc. 308–9; 318). The branch at Jindřichův Hradec contains the papers of Vilém Slavata which yield some important information about Wallenstein and his end (volume VI of the 'Drafts'). Other significant volumes of the 'Drafts' are numbers II–V, and VII–X, the last again containing documents concerning Albrecht Wallenstein. On the other hand, number 93 of volume X, Slavata's *Historical Writings*, is nothing more than a copy of the manuscript in the State Archive at Mnichovo Hradiště which has already been discussed. Slavata's drafts, particularly for the years 1630–8, are an immeasurably important though little used source. As the Supreme Chancellor of Bohemia, a member of the State Privy Council and counsellor to Ferdinand II, Slavata was the recipient of truly first-hand information about the military conflict. His letters to the Supreme Burggrave Adam Waldstein, the High Steward Jaroslav Bořita of Martinic and the Chief Justice Hendrych of Kolovrat, contain much information about troop movements in the Bohemian lands as well as in Germany, Burgundy and Italy, and about the policies of the Austrian and Spanish Habsburgs and their enemies.[31]

Cardinal Dietrichstein continued to be the foremost representative of the old Court party in Moravia. His correspondence was described earlier. For the period 1630–5 the most important part of the Dietrichstein papers at Brno is the 'Historical Archive', section 'Morava'. Most plentifully represented here is Dietrichstein's correspondence with the Emperor, with Albrecht Wallenstein (particularly in 1632–3), with Marradas, and with A. Miniati, chiefly concerning the supply, payment and quartering of the army. The *Grosse Korrespondenz* ends for the most part in 1631; the year 1632 contains only a few pieces. For the year 1634 the Cardinal's drafts are of little significance. Some interesting documents have been preserved in the collections of the State Archive at Brno, for example a manuscript of the so-called 'Jesuit Chronicle of Opava' ('Rebellio Oppaviensis, 1634', Cerroni Collection).

THE WALLENSTEIN QUESTION

Who was Wallenstein? Idealist or egoist, traitor or statesman yearning for peace? That he was one of the outstanding participants in the Thirty Years' War cannot be doubted, nor that he was one of the most prominent commanders. He was also indisputably one of the foremost representatives of the Bohemian nobility, and probably the most ambiguous figure in central European politics before Bismarck.

More has been written about Wallenstein than about any other figure of the first half of the seventeenth century, not excluding Gustavus Adolphus of Sweden and Cardinal Richelieu. At the beginning of the fateful year 1634 a drama was performed in Madrid in which he was the central character. In 1639 came Henry Glapthorne's highly fantastical play. Jean-François Sarrasin was so fascinated by the generalissimo that he embarked on a biography, the *Conspiration de Walstein*. Galeazzo Gualdo Priorato published his biography of Wallenstein, in 1643.[32]

It would be useless to attempt to list the innumerable assessments of Wallenstein's career that have appeared since his death. The problems presented by his unique career, his rise to wealth and power, his grandiose dreams, his flirtations with treason and his near catastrophes, have fascinated all subsequent generations and have been solved by none.

Following J. H. Hagelgans, author of the first German portrait of Wallenstein (1640), Friedrich Schiller presented Wallenstein in his trilogy as a tragic hero moved by idealism. Soon afterwards he became the subject of debate among historians, who agreed at least on one point: that the generalissimo's character was extremely complex.[33] Leopold von Ranke first broke with the tradition in which Wallenstein was either hysterically condemned or uncritically idealized. In his *History of Wallenstein* Ranke reached the conclusion that Wallenstein was an egotistical but at the same time an idealistic seeker after peace.[34] From 1887 the Austrian public followed with mixed sympathies the quarrel between two leading historians, H. Hallwich, who saw in the generalissimo the forerunner of the contemporary movements 'Away from Rome' and 'Away from the Habsburgs', and Anton Gindely, who had his doubts about whether Wallenstein was actually a traitor.[35]

At the end of the last century Josef Pekař, one of Gindely's successors in the Chair of Austrian History in the Charles University at Prague, published a solid study of the last four years in the General's life. He concluded that the Wallenstein catastrophe was a tragedy for Bohemia rather than for Germany and that Wallenstein was certainly an egotistical traitor. His Viennese colleague, Heinrich von Srbik, wrote his book about Wallenstein's end primarily to refute Pekař's interpretation. Srbik acknowledged the failings of his hero's character but emphasized his idealism, his desire for peace, and his concern for the whole Empire, not just Bohemia.[36]

Since then the situation has completely changed. Besides the documents in the central archives at Vienna, traditionally used by historians, Wallenstein's military chancery has been discovered, and both its parts, preserved in Prague and Vienna, have been made available to scholars. Since 1945 the papers of his opponents have also become available for research: Piccolomini, Schlick, Gallas, Collalto, Slavata and others. On the basis of new sources František Roubík published his original study of Wallenstein's campaign in Slovakia in 1626 (1935), and Anton Ernstberger his books about Wallenstein and his banker Jan de Witte (1929ff). They have also served as the basis of more recent studies by M. Hroch, J. Kolman, K. Stanka and myself.[37] This flood of new material has made research into several quite new problems possible, but its sheer volume poses more than one problem of its own. The last decades have brought changes in traditional views both of the Thirty Years' War and of the seventeenth century in general. Both have come to be regarded as the formative period for modern European society. If we consider the Thirty Years' War as a phenomenon of continental proportions which profoundly influenced the history of international relations and the internal evolution of most European countries, we must logically reconsider the historical rôle played by one of its central figures. Wallenstein and his milieu present us with one of the most important and difficult problems in seventeenth-century history.

In 1608 a young nobleman from the retinue of Archduke Mathias called Albrecht of Valdštejn (Waldstein in German) asked the famous astronomer and astrologer Johann Kepler for a horoscope. Kepler replied:

I can truly say of this lord, that his mind is agile, active and far from tranquil. . .that he yearns for many things that he does not reveal outwardly. He will certainly be merciless, without brotherly or marital affection, respecting nobody, dedicated completely to himself and his own ambition. . . He will endeavour to attain many dignities and vast power – and thus he will attract many great and secret enemies, most of whom he will defeat. . . *Mercury* stands directly *in oppositio Jovis*, and it appears that he will have a special charm for many people and that he might become the head of a company of conspirators.

Reading these words, one wonders whether the future general or his subsequent biographers followed Kepler's horoscope more assiduously.[38]

Albrecht Wallenstein, as we shall call him from now on, was born in the village of Heřmanice in northeastern Bohemia on 14 September 1583 (old style). His father's family ranked among the most ancient of the Bohemian barons, and his mother's, the Smiřickýs, among the wealthiest. His grandfather George Waldstein had been a rebel and was punished for his part in the opposition to Ferdinand I in 1547. His three successive wives belonged to the most powerful noble families: Slavata, Žerotín and Lobkowitz. He had thirteen sons and six daughters, and his third son William, Albrecht's father, was lucky enough to inherit Heřmanice after the death of a childless uncle. William's wife, Lady Margaret of Smiřický, belonged to a family which had made a spectacular career during the previous century. The Smiřickýs had risen from their humble place in the knightly Estate to become powerful barons whose domains stretched from the outskirts of Prague to the Lusatian and Silesian frontier. They were the most astute estate managers in the realm and also the most progressive: they did not depend upon the labour service of their tenants nor even upon feudal rents, as did for example their neighbours in the northeast, the Trčkas of Lípa and the Kinskýs. Their tenants were at once the market for the commodities that their domains produced and the source of supply for the articles in which they traded – wheat and barley, or flax and linen in the mountains. They were hard bargainers, of course, but on the whole they were successful, and their peasants did not grumble.

William Waldstein did not attempt to emulate his father's ambitious political career; he was not rich enough. He died when Albrecht was twelve, having survived his wife by two years, and his son was sent to live with a relative of his mother's, Henry Slavata, at his castle of Košumberk. Slavata was a member of the Unity of the Brethren, and he had his own children, his nephew Vilém Slavata and probably

Albrecht as well, educated by teachers of this creed. In 1597 he sent Albrecht to the famous Lutheran school for young noblemen at Goldberg in Silesia.[39]

Wallenstein spent two years there which were remarkable for just one incident: a conflict with the townspeople who reviled him as a 'Picard', by which they meant Calvinist or member of the Brethren. In 1599 he left for the Academy at Altdorf near Nuremberg, a remarkable institution which attracted students and masters from all central Europe. Most of its professors were Germans, but there were also Italians, Swiss and French Calvinists, and disciples of the Leiden masters. The school was officially Lutheran, but it was as broadminded as its sponsor the City Council of Nuremberg, and its students included the future leaders of the Austrian and Bohemian opposition Georg Erasmus Tschernembl and Wenceslas William of Roupov. Unfortunately, Wallenstein can hardly have profited from his stay at Altdorf. In 1599 he came into repeated conflict with his surroundings: he wounded one of his servants, a local lad, and he fought with the burghers of Altdorf, for which he spent a few days in the municipal prison. Early in 1600, after a final disagreement with the school authorities, he left Altdorf to embark upon the customary grand tour of a hopeful young nobleman, of which we know only that it took him to France and Italy.[40]

The youthful Wallenstein did not reveal any more about himself in this period than he was to do in later years, and we can only sketch a rather informal picture of the influence he absorbed. We do not know whether he read much, but it is not likely – although he knew enough Italian to read (and imitate) Italian military treatises. He was able to speak Italian, and throughout his life he tried to live up to the tough and worldly standards of a *cortegiano*, even if they were already somewhat out of date. In fact, he always evinced great admiration for things Italian – Italian military theoreticians, Italian painters and architects, Italian fencing masters, as well as Italian comrades-at-arms, for which he was made to pay in the end. Thus, although his relatives were followers of the Protestant–Humanist 'model' of civilization that may be called 'Maritime', young Wallenstein was a decided adherent of the 'Mediterranean' model, though in his maturity he came to respect the achievements of the Dutch. He may have drunk like a Dutchman, but the abundant richness of his curses and epithets was decidedly Italian.

In 1602 this Czech Protestant landowner turned Italian *galantuomo* returned home to Heřmanice, evidently waiting for the opportunity to launch the career that he had been dreaming of. We know very little about him during the next several years. That he did not wish to remain in this godforsaken village is safe to assume, and in 1604 the Habsburg offensive against Bocskai's rebels in Upper Hungary gave him the chance to win fame on the battlefield. In October the 'crazy von Wallstein' had his life saved by Duke Carlo di Gonzaga-Nevers himself at Esztergom, and the next month he was nearly killed at the siege of Košice. His winter ride through the snow-covered Slovakian mountains in 1605 attracted a measure of attention. But, strangely enough, we have no word of him in the following summer, when Bocskai's troops were advancing into Moravia to threaten its second capital Brno. The Treaty of Vienna in June 1606, shortly after Wallenstein was commissioned a colonel in the army of the Moravian Estates, prevented him from distinguishing himself against Bocskai. But in the autumn, after the eruption of the quarrel between Rudolph II and Matthias, he found his way into the latter's army, perhaps through the good offices of his brother-in-law, the Moravian magnate Karel of Žerotín. He was appointed Mathias' chamberlain, and in 1608 he took part in the campaign against Prague.

Shortly afterwards he followed the example of his distant cousin and youthful companion at Košumberk Vilém Slavata and converted to Catholicism. In May 1609, perhaps through the mediation of the Fathers of the Jesuit College at Olomouc, where he might once have spent some time as a student, Wallenstein married Lady Lucretia Nekeš of Landek, widow of Arkleb of Víckov. The legend that Wallenstein's first wife was a wealthy old widow is only half true. She was born between 1582 and 1584 and was thus about the same age as her second husband, twenty-seven to twenty-nine. But she was indeed quite rich, having inherited the east Moravian domains of Rymice, Lukov and Vsetín from her father, her uncle and her first husband. In 1609 she accepted Albrecht as co-proprietor, and in 1610 she attempted to secure the rest of the property of her first husband's family. Her nephew Jan Adam of Víckov was foolish enough to give up his claim for the paltry sum of 8,000 florins, and protracted lawsuits ensued, especially with one of Jan Adam's cousins, Lady Bohunka, who later married Václav Bítovský of Bítov. Wallenstein never forgot these disputes, and fifteen years later he settled the score in an especially cruel way: after his victory in Silesia in 1627 Wallenstein singled out Václav Bítovský as his only prisoner to be sent to Brno to be tortured and eventually executed.[41]

His marriage to Lady Lucretia launched Wallenstein's career as a military entrepreneur. In 1611 he was one of the commanders of the Moravian contingents sent against the army of Leopold of Passau. In February he accompanied Mathias to the coronation at Prague as second-in-command of the Moravian cavalry. He spent the summer of 1612 in Italy, then joined the court of the Emperor Mathias. Lady Lucretia died in the spring of 1614, and Albrecht inherited all her property over the bitter protests of the Víckov family. Later in the year we find Wallenstein among the deputation sent by the Moravian Estates to the Archduke Ferdinand, and in 1615 he added the title of archducal chamberlain to his Imperial post. His health failed for the first time in 1615, and he convalesced at Rymice. But in 1617 he marched at the head of his own company of 200 cavalrymen to reinforce Archduke Ferdinand's siege of the Venetian fortress of Gradisca, where he fought beside the Spanish condottiere Baltasar de Marradas under Dampierre's command.

With the outbreak of the Bohemian Rebellion in 1618, the Moravian Diet appointed Wallenstein commander of an infantry regiment of 3,000 men, whose task was to safeguard the neutrality of the land. But he also concluded an agreement with Buquoy concerning the muster of a cuirassier regiment in the Spanish Netherlands for the sum of 40,000 florins, and he aided the defeated Dampierre by forwarding supplies. For all this Ferdinand conferred upon him the dignity of Imperial Colonel in March 1619. One month later his former comrade-at-arms in Hungary, Heinrich Mathias Count Thurn, began his march into Moravia. At the beginning of May, when the Moravian Estates joined the Bohemian rebellion, Colonel Wallenstein failed to persuade his regiment to desert, killed one of his subordinates and fled to Vienna with the Moravian treasury. He was declared a traitor, his property confiscated and turned over to Jan Adam of Víckov.[42]

From Vienna Wallenstein proceeded to Passau to assume command of a regiment which he brought to southern Bohemia to reinforce Buquoy's army, and on 10 June 1619 he contributed to the Imperial victory at Záblatí. He also participated in Dampierre's campaign in southern Moravia, and his regiment suffered heavy losses when the Imperial advance was stopped at Věstonice in August. The ranks were filled by recruits from the Rhineland, however, and upon recovering from another bout of ill health the following year, Wallenstein was able to resume command in time to take part in the Bohemian campaign led by Buquoy, Maximilian of Bavaria and Tilly. He was not present at the Battle of the White Mountain, however, for he was covering Mansfeld's troops in northwestern Bohemia, and in the next months he succeeded in pacifying nearly all of western Bohemia. His methods were efficient: he forbade plundering but exploited the resources of the towns to the fullest. It was quite a different story in Prague and throughout the rest of the country, where the victorious armies, especially the Walloon contingents from the Spanish Netherlands, behaved atrociously. Wallenstein's tactic was certainly not dictated by compassion for his countrymen. But he was not obliged to act greedily because he had more time than Buquoy, Marradas, Verdugo, Huerta and the other representatives of the Spanish party.

By this time Wallenstein had established his reputation as one of the most effective supporters of the Habsburgs. We know nothing of his convictions or motivations. Certainly he was pitiless and ambitious, but at the same time he was nobody's fool. He served the Emperor well, expected to be well rewarded, and saw to it that he was. In June 1621 he was only one of many servants of the Imperial cause who applied for recompense. None was more handsomely rewarded. Wallenstein was fortunate enough to be able to pose as heir to the Smiřický lands. Jan Albrecht Smiřický had been an acknowledged leader of the rising of 1618, but he died at the end of the year. His legitimate heir was a minor and an imbecile and also Wallenstein's distant cousin, so that the Colonel became first the guardian and very soon the owner of all the Smiřický property. The Smiřický lands were soon to form the nucleus of an enclave of about sixty domains, some of which Wallenstein received from the confiscations to defray the expenses of his two regiments. He proceeded so ruthlessly with the former proprietors and their families that the Bohemian Stadholders, his old colleagues Liechtenstein, Slavata and Martinic, loyalists like himself and just as greedy, were moved to compose a letter in December 1622 in which they urged him to behave more humanely.

At the end of 1621 Wallenstein was appointed military commander of Prague and therefore of all Bohemia. But he was effective in other ways as well. He excelled in obtaining credit for the Emperor, who, firmly in the Habsburg tradition, lacked financial sense and was perpetually without resources. When at the beginning of 1621 it became necessary to reimburse Buquoy to the extent of 600,000 thalers, it was Wallenstein who raised the sum with the help of the Dutch banker Jan de Witte and the Jewish merchant Bassevi, both of whom quickly became his invaluable collaborators. All three were members of a larger consortium consisting of members of the Spanish Court party at Vienna and Prague, which was empowered to issue a new coinage. They received a monopoly of the old currency, which they collected and sold to themselves as administrators of the mint. Then they issued debased currency, with which they proceeded to buy up confiscated property. Unfortunately, we do not know just how much they earned, but they did not all profit equally. In the first part of the fraudulent operation, the sale of the old coins to the mint, the Lieutenant-Governor Liechtenstein made a profit of 569 florins for every mark of silver delivered; Eggenberg, Ferdinand's chief adviser, received 448 florins; Wallenstein, however, received a mere 123 florins in exchange for a mark. The gigantic swindle helped to destroy the remains of the Estates' opposition and also to ruin Bohemia's economy for years to come. The scandal that it created led to the dissolution of the consortium in 1623.[43]

The state bankruptcy which was declared on 28 December 1623 coincided strangely with Wallenstein's second marriage to Isabella of Harrach, the daughter of an influential adviser of Ferdinand II. The same year he was promoted to the rank of *Oberste Wachtmeister* (corresponding more or less to that of Lieutenant-General), even though his part in the short-lived campaigns of 1621–3 against Bethlen Gábor was far from glorious. The Spaniard Marradas, who was attempting to emulate Wallenstein by constructing a complex of lands around his domain of Hluboká in southern Bohemia, was granted the same promotion at the same time.

At the end of 1622 Wallenstein became the head of the House of Waldstein of Friedland. The title came from the border domain which had been confiscated from the wealthy lords of Redern. In April 1623 he secured final title to the Smiřický lands in exchange for only 430,000 marks. In September he received the princely title. From 1623 Wallenstein was a close ally of his father-in-law Charles Harrach and J. U. von Eggenberg. When Eggenberg was granted the royal domain of Krumlov in southern Bohemia he automatically blocked further expansion of the Marradas property. Marradas, who regarded himself as the legitimate representative of the old Spanish Court party, was of course bitterly disappointed, and he became one of Wallenstein's earliest adversaries.[44]

In 1625 Friedland was established as a duchy, and it was virtually autonomous from an economic as well as an administrative point of view. Wallenstein was too clever to exploit his tenants as ruthlessly as he might have liked. The economic régime that had characterized the Smiřický domains before 1620 remained unchanged, and many of the old bailiffs continued in service even if their religious loyalties were doubtful. Of course, Wallenstein mobilized the economic activity of his subjects to the fullest, at first for the market, then later for the army. This does not mean that he was popular among the peasant population – his troops were used too often to quell disturbances in the countryside. But compared with the territory under the control of Huerta or Marradas, the Wallenstein lands were an island of order and harmony. And the chaos that prevailed in the rest of the land, abetted by the misrule of military commanders which threatened utterly to destroy the Bohemian economy, became the special target of Wallenstein's criticism. In the spring of 1622, acting as deputy for the absent Lieutenant-Governor Liechtenstein, Wallenstein enjoined the generals from imposing taxes, and this led to one of his earliest clashes with Marradas.[45]

In the spring of 1625 the anti-Habsburg coalition, including Mansfeld, Christian IV of Denmark and Bethlen Gábor, were preparing to launch an offensive. For a number of reasons Ferdinand II was going to have to act without the benefit of massive Spanish support, and it was in these circumstances that Wallenstein offered to raise an army of 30,000 men: twenty-one cavalry and six infantry regiments. As the troops began to gather in Germany in the region of Magdeburg during the summer, Wallenstein was within reach of his goal. He was no longer merely one of the Emperor's generals, he was going to become the generalissimo, the *capo* of the Imperial armies, which were entirely his own creation. The first phase of his campaign in 1626 ended in near catastrophe in Upper Hungary, and Wallenstein was saved by a truce between Bethlen and the Emperor. In the winter of 1626–7, however, he was able to reorganize his troops, and in the spring he moved into Silesia to block the retreat of the Danish army.[46]

By July Wallenstein was ready to embark upon the campaign that was to bring him to Jutland. Once Eggenberg's intervention mollified the German princes, who complained about the burden of supporting the Imperial armies, Wallenstein moved into Lower Saxony, with Tilly's support ejected the Danes from the Empire, and eventually pursued them into Jutland. At this point the balance of military and political superiority within the Imperial camp had clearly shifted from the Catholic League to the Emperor. Wallenstein occupied Mecklenburg and Pomerania, a potential naval base from which the Habsburgs might one day be able to strangle the Dutch Baltic trade. Olivares' old plan of establishing an *almirantazgo*, a vast shipping and commercial enterprise whose partners should include Spain, the Spanish Netherlands, the Hansa towns and Poland, was thus infused with new life.[47] Gabriel de Roy, the moving spirit behind this scheme, was appointed 'Commissary General of the Atlantic and Baltic Seas', while Wallenstein received the Duchy of Mecklenburg and was appointed 'General of the whole Imperial Armada as well as Admiral of the Atlantic and Baltic Seas'. This probably represented the pinnacle of his career. He was granted full authority for the recruitment of troops and for the appointment and promotion of all officers up to the rank of colonel. But during this time he was often quite ill. On 31 May 1628 he wrote out his will. Shortly before the members of his immediate family were raised to the ducal dignity, and he received the extraordinary Imperial privilege that his landed property might not be confiscated even in case of high treason.

The ambitious economic projects emanating from Madrid and Brussels greatly appealed to his imagination. He had already placed the entire administrative machinery of the Duchy of Friedland and its considerable productivity at the disposal of the army. His rural tenants and all his urban craftsmen were engaged in the gigantic task of supplying the needs of the army, which had reached unheard-of proportions. Although Spinola and the rest of the military theoreticians were convinced that an army which had reached 30,000 troops was only barely operational, Wallenstein thought nothing of bringing much higher numbers under his command. Within several weeks of mustering in 1625 he assembled about 24,000 men in the Egerland. But in September he had some 40,000 men under his command. In the summer of 1626 the Emperor agreed to a limit of 42,000, and in the autumn he raised it to 70,000. By 1627 Wallenstein's army reached the sensational figure of 100,000 troops. No European monarch had ever had such an army at his disposal. In 1628, however, the princes of the Catholic League requested a reduction. Some 13,000 troops were sent home, and a similar number were dispatched to Poland to aid Sigismund against the Swedes. But the numbers rose again, and in 1630 the army was about 95,000 strong.

On his way from Silesia to the Baltic coast in 1627, Wallenstein naïvely mistook the cargo-barges on the River Oder for ocean-going ships. Once he came into contact with the Hansa merchants and the Dutch in northern Germany, he began to appreciate the possibilities which the *almirantazgo* offered him and his prospective partners, whoever they might be. He was aware too that the project required a firm hold on a number of maritime bases. Collaboration with Sweden with its Dutch financial backing was out of the question, but the Hansa towns and Denmark might perhaps be won over. His own Duchy of Mecklenburg included two Hansa towns, Wismar and

Rostock, both of which accepted Imperial garrisons by the end of 1628. But Wallenstein's siege of Stralsund had to be lifted in August 1628. Throughout this period provisions, including uniforms and ammunition, were being forwarded from Friedland's capital of Jičín to Děčín, thence down the Elbe to Dessau. The iron-works at Raspenava and Friedland were producing arms, and a munitions factory was being constructed at Vrchlabí. The Elbe was to become the commercial artery linking Friedland with the European north.

In an effort to draw Denmark into the Habsburg orbit, Wallenstein persuaded the Emperor to grant Christian IV highly lenient terms, and the peace signed at Lübeck on 22 May 1629 meant the Danish withdrawal from Imperial affairs. The Spanish agent De Roy established himself at Glückstadt, the Danish port on the mouth of the Elbe, which a treaty with Spain envisaged as the headquarters of Spanish trade with the Baltic hinterlands, including Bohemia. The construction of an Imperial navy proceeded apace, and quite soon the Swedish and Dutch monopoly of the Baltic was endangered. If the Dutch and the French wished to continue their struggle with the Habsburgs, they were going to have to turn to Sweden instead of Denmark. Therefore in September 1629 the French mediated the truce of Altmark between Poland and Sweden, which freed Gustavus Adolphus for intervention in the Empire.

The Edict of Restitution, issued on 6 March 1629 after the triumphant termination of the Danish war, was regarded by most of the German states as the embodiment of the Habsburgs' absolutist schemes. The princes' resentment was inflamed by the high-handed treatment accorded some of their peers. The dukes of Mecklenburg, allies of the Danes, had been punished by having their patrimony awarded to the Imperial generalissimo as an Imperial fief, which placed him on an equal footing with the ancient dynasties. Since the Emperor's hugely magnified authority in the Empire rested upon the military and financial resources which Wallenstein had been able to raise, the opponents of Habsburg domination in the Empire logically directed their efforts towards undermining Wallenstein's position. And his novel logistical methods provided them with plausible arguments. He acted on the principle that the districts under his protection as well as the lands occupied by his army should contribute to the maintenance of his troops. Contributions were therefore levied in Catholic as well as in Protestant territories, whether allied, neutral or hostile.

The crisis came in the summer of 1630 during the Emperor's meeting with the Imperial Electors at Regensburg. Ferdinand needed their support for the Spanish war against the Netherlands and more immediately for the election of his eldest son as king of the Romans, heir-apparent to the Imperial Crown. The future Ferdinand III and the Imperial confessor Father Lamormain prejudiced the Emperor against Wallenstein, whose sacrifice they correctly perceived as the essential conditions of the Electors' co-operation. The final decision was accomplished by the *éminence grise* of the French delegation, Father Joseph. Richelieu's confidential agent found Maximilian of Bavaria especially responsive to his overtures, and after many weeks of haggling Ferdinand was obliged to yield to the Electors' demands. Wallenstein was dismissed on 13 August 1630, the Imperial army was placed under Tilly's command, and the Edict of Restitution was to be subjected to the scrutiny of the Imperial Diet.[48]

In return for all this, Ferdinand received absolutely nothing. The Electors flatly refused to supply either men or money against the Netherlands and France, and they even rejected the younger Ferdinand's candidature. Wallenstein and most of his generals withdrew into sullen isolation. His banker Jan de Witte was the immediate victim. He had invested so heavily in Wallenstein's military machinery that with the generalissimo's dismissal he faced bankruptcy, and he committed suicide in his palatial house in the Lesser Town of Prague on 11 September 1630. After divesting himself of Wallenstein, the Emperor proceeded to jeopardize his own position by refusing to appease the Protestant princes and the Imperial cities. The alliance between Sweden and Brandenburg posed a serious threat to Tilly's armies even though they had been strengthened by contingents released after the conclusion of the Mantuan war. The condition of the troops began to deteriorate once the flow of supplies from Wallenstein's Bohemian and Silesian magazines was halted. Communications with Silesia and Poland were interrupted by the Swedish advance into Brandenburg. To make matters worse, Tilly's lieutenant Pappenheim stormed the city of Magdeburg and utterly destroyed it, effectively ruining Tilly's whole plan of campaign. The unfortunate Imperial commander was forced to abandon the Duchy of Mecklenburg, and his attempt to retain the loyalty of Saxony by terror led directly to an alliance between the hesitant Elector Johann Georg and Sweden. Thus the Saxon Arnim, once Wallenstein's most capable general, was transferred to the service of Gustavus Adolphus.

After the Battle of Breitenfeld in September 1631, Tilly had to retreat southwards to the Bavarian frontier along the Danube, and the Saxon army marched into Silesia and Bohemia. On 15 November

Arnim occupied Prague, and hundreds of Bohemian émigrés followed in his train. But Gustavus did not follow the Saxons, as the Bohemian Protestants had expected. Instead he made his winter quarters in the Rhineland: Frankfurt became the seat of the Swedish Governor-General Oxenstierna, and the bishoprics of Bamberg and Würtzburg were organized into a Swedish fief as the Duchy of Franconia.

Wallenstein's allies in Vienna – Eggenberg, Harrach, Schlick, who had never given their consent to Wallenstein's dismissal in 1630, had been conducting a vigorous campaign in his favour, and he was recalled at the end of 1631. The Bohemian and Moravian exiles who were fighting against the Habsburgs had established tentative contacts with the former generalissimo as soon as the Swedes landed in Germany. Our only reports of these negotiations come from the mediators who survived the débâcle by selling themselves to the Viennese court, and their stories were later tampered with by Wallenstein's avowed enemies, particularly his distant cousin Vilém Slavata, whose sole ally for a long time was the maladroit and disgruntled Marradas. For this reason Wallenstein's talks with the émigrés and the King of Sweden are extremely difficult to interpret. Yet it is fairly obvious that there was scarcely any confidence between them, and the Saxon General Arnim, apparently Wallenstein's only confidant, was able to sabotage any rapprochement. We do not know whether Wallenstein really trusted the notoriously unreliable Saxons. But all the parties were masters of dissimulation, and the same mistrust characterized the later negotiations between Wallenstein and the Swedes through the mediation of the elderly Count Thurn.[49]

The Saxons allowed Wallenstein to re-occupy Prague at the end of May 1632, to the great distress of the Bohemian émigrés, who rightly considered themselves betrayed by their allies. In the middle of April Wallenstein took command of an army of 40,000 which had been raised in the Egerland. Within a short time he raised its strength to 70,000. The Emperor had no choice but to accept the Duke's conditions, and they were hard: an immediate subsidy of 400,000 guilders, the Silesian Duchy of Glogau in compensation for Mecklenburg, enfeoffment with all territories that might be confiscated in the course of operations, unrestricted authority in military matters, and full powers to conduct peace negotiations with Saxony, which however were to be submitted for Imperial approbation.

What Wallenstein proposed to accomplish with this unparalleled plenitude of power must remain a matter for conjecture. For the time being, at any rate, he was obliged to perform as a military commander rather than as a statesman. After clearing Bohemia of the Saxon troops, he led his army into the Upper Palatinate. Through the summer the Swedes and the Imperials faced each other in heavily fortified camps outside Nuremberg. The last Swedish attempt to dislodge Wallenstein failed on 3 September, and a fortnight later the armies separated. Gustavus moved into Bavaria, Wallenstein marched northwards towards Thuringia and Saxony. But since Gustavus could not afford to lose Saxony, he conducted a rapid march towards Leipzig. Wallenstein took up a defensive position near Lützen. On 16 November the Swedes attacked, but the outcome of the battle repeated the deadlock of Nuremberg. The Swedes had lost their king, but since Wallenstein hastily evacuated Saxony and thereby severely injured his reputation as a strategist, they regarded themselves as the victors.

The death of Gustavus Adolphus seemed to open the way to a general pacification. Johann Georg of Saxony and his north German allies were ready to begin negotiations with the Emperor, but they were out-manoeuvred by Oxenstierna's superior diplomacy, which succeeded in uniting the Protestant princes and cities in the Alliance of Heilbronn. The Swedish resolution to pursue an active policy and the massive intervention of the French nullified all the various peace proposals which emanated from Wallenstein's entourage during the summer of 1633. His army remained intact, but it was not to repeat its successes of 1628–30. The Viennese court was forced into a cautious attitude, and the Imperial Council went as far as to advocate a return to conciliatory religious policies in Germany. The Vice-Chancellor Strahlendorf even recommended that Wallenstein be entrusted with the general peace negotiations. Wallenstein doubtless realized the opportunities that lay before him. In January 1633 he renewed his secret talks with the Bohemian émigrés and the Saxons. But he also went further and sent a confidential agent to Oxenstierna, while Count William Kinský kept in close touch with Richelieu's envoy Feuquières at Dresden. By the end of June these conversations with France and Sweden appeared to have replaced earlier plans for co-operation with unpredictable Saxony. In September 1633 the great anti-Habsburg coalition was ready to negotiate with Wallenstein. At the beginning of October Arnim, fully authorized by Brandenburg and Saxony to sign a peace treaty, met with Wallenstein in Silesia, when the generalissimo suddenly threw part of his army into Saxony. Arnim and his Saxons hurriedly evacuated Silesia, and Wallenstein forced the remaining Swedish troops to submission at Steinau. By this time, certainly, nobody trusted Wallenstein. His victory at Steinau mollified the Imperial court somewhat, but his dismissal of the Swedish officers that he captured, among them many Bohemian émigrés, enraged it, and his enemies particularly welcomed the news that he had freed Count Thurn, one of the leaders of the Bohemian revolt of 1618.

At the same time Wallenstein openly challenged the Spanish party. His lieutenant, Field Marshal Aldringen, did arrive to relieve the Spaniards defending the fortresses of Breisach and Constance against the Swedes, but only against the generalissimo's express orders. In November the Swedish commander Bernhard of Weimar occupied Regensburg and penetrated Lower Bavaria as far as the Austrian frontier. In response to Maximilian of Bavaria's urgent entreaties for aid, Wallenstein marched his troops into the Upper Palatinate as far as the Swedish outposts, thence into the safety of Bohemia to make his winter headquarters at Pilsen, from which he did not stir in spite of the Emperor's repeated requests. Perhaps he wished to demonstrate his indispensability, or perhaps he intended to use his strategic position at Pilsen to continue his talks with the Swedes, the Saxons and the French. Whatever the real reasons for his extraordinary inaction at this crucial juncture, his fate was sealed by it.

In December, while Wallenstein's indications of readiness to conclude a secret convention with the Swedes and the French were being met with an unconcealed lack of trust, he was also rapidly losing his position in Vienna, where his old enemies were gaining the edge over Eggenberg. His generals, dissatisfied with their commander's tortuous negotiations, established contact with Marradas, whose seat at Hluboká became the centre of anti-Wallenstein intrigue. Piccolomini, whose advancement into the highest ranks of Wallenstein's army had been assured by Pappenheim's death at Lützen, spread the rumour among the officers that Wallenstein hoped to eject the Spaniards from Italy, while Marradas added that Wallenstein wished to deprive the Imperial Electors of their principalities.

By the end of December 1633 Eggenberg began to change his attitude. On 11 January 1634 Wallenstein summoned his senior officers to Pilsen and extracted from them an oath of unconditional allegiance to himself. Reports of this prompted the court to take the final step. On 24 January even Eggenberg consented to the Imperial decree which dismissed Wallenstein and offered amnesty to all the generals with the exception of Wallenstein and his closest collaborators Trčka and Kinský. The Emperor was still not certain how to settle Wallenstein's fate, but the Spanish Ambassador Oñate firmly opposed any half-hearted measures. Thus at the beginning of February the generals led by Gallas, Piccolomini, Aldringen and Marradas were in possession of the Imperial Decree of 24 January and were given an oral instruction to take the conspirators alive 'if possible', otherwise to 'execute them as convicted criminals'. On 18 February the Emperor issued a 'patent of proscription' which was immediately published. The command was turned over to Colloredo and the four generals mentioned above. Eggenberg's final intervention on Wallenstein's behalf on 20 February failed. Thus isolated, Wallenstein fled with 1,500 men from Pilsen to the frontier fortress of Eger. He appealed for help to Arnim and Bernhard of Weimar, but neither was eager to intervene. On 25 February 1634 Wallenstein's friends were assassinated during a banquet by a group of Scottish, Irish, English and German soldiers. The former generalissimo was stabbed to death in his bedroom.[50]

It is a remarkable and curious fact that Wallenstein's heirs never seriously attempted a 'rehabilitation' of their famous ancestor. This was true of the Waldstein-Wartenbergs and also of the Harrachs and Kaunitzes, who were closely related to his widow and daughter. Wallenstein's 'terra felix' disappeared after the Eger tragedy and passed into the hands of his assassins to become, like the rest of Bohemia, a 'terra deserta'. Wallenstein's twenty-four domains and fifty-five sub-fiefs, whose value was assessed at over nine million florins, were taken over by Gallas, Schlick, Putz von Adlersthurm and other fortune-seekers. The property of the Trčka family, estimated at four million florins, passed to the Piccolominis of Náchod and the Colloredos of Opočno. Similarly, the estates of William Kinský, assessed at 600,000 florins, were taken over by the Aldringens, Thurns and others.[51]

The 'military execution' at Eger threw all Europe into agitation and presented the authors of anti-Habsburg pamphlets with an unexpected trump card. Wallenstein's murder was a serious political mistake. Only a trial could have unearthed proof that he had conducted treasonable negotiations with the enemy. The Habsburgs' abandonment of legal procedures was interpreted as a reflection of the waning influence of the Spaniards (or the Jesuits) at the Imperial court at Vienna. The French blamed the Spanish Orator Count Oñate for Wallenstein's end and concluded that by this *acte sanglant* the Emperor had removed the only man capable of bringing peace to Europe.

But at the court, too, voices were raised in Wallenstein's defence – particularly later, when the most thorough searches had failed to turn up any firm evidence of his guilt. It is of course likely that such secret negotiations, if they took place, where not committed to paper; at the same time it is reasonable to expect that some written reference to them should turn up somewhere. The treacherous generals and colonels are likely to have destroyed documents which revealed their own activities in an unfavourable light, and one may confidently assume that any documents presenting evidence favourable to Wallenstein would have disappeared as well. The single witness to testify that Wallenstein wished to dethrone the Emperor was the unfortunate Colonel Schlief. But even he had only heard the story from William Kinský, who supposedly played no major rôle in the alleged negotiations. Duke Franz Albrecht of Saxe-Lauenburg confirmed simply that Wallenstein wished to conclude a treaty of peace – ultimately even against the Emperor's will – but this was within the 'pleins pouvoirs' granted him by the Emperor in 1631. The commission set up to investigate the existence of a plot had found no evidence of the generalissimo's guilt by April 1634. The rhetorical *Relation* concerning the treason was not published until October 1634, but its reliability cannot be confirmed.[52] At the end of the same month Jaroslav Sezima Rašín of Rýzmburk, one of the secret agents of the Bohemian émigrés, wrote a further report, but we now know that its text was improved by Slavata, who was disappointed with Rašín's testimony. Slavata was not the only one to feel thus: why should the last of the imprisoned 'traitors' have been sent to the torture as late as May 1635 if all had been clear as early as the autumn of the preceding year? Thus the one 'proof' remained: the draft of a letter written by Thurn on 14 October 1631 to Gustavus Adolphus in which he assured the King of Wallenstein's good will and his desire to come to terms. But it was only in 1637 that this suspect document was sent to Vienna by a Capuchin friar of Prague; in other words, in 1637 the government at Vienna was still looking for evidence of Wallenstein's treason.

Thus the case against him was never brought to trial. Instead, Vienna defended the thesis of Wallenstein's guilt by legally confirming the rich rewards that were distributed to his assassins: Gallas almost 900,000 florins, Schlick 364,000, Colloredo 351,000, the Irish Colonel Butler, who managed the execution at Eger, 225,000, Piccolomini and Millesimo 215,000 florins each, while Marradas, who made the most strenuous exertions to bring about the fall of his rival, had to be satisfied with a mere 140,000 florins. The pardoned Sezima Rašín was not forgotten, nor was Johann Putz von Adlersthurm. Wallenstein's confidant the astrologer Seni, who played a mysterious rôle in his fall, at least escaped without trouble. The greed of the generals was truly scandalous. After all those vast confiscations, the Imperial treasury remained empty, and down to 1945 a fair proportion of the 'Austrian' nobility continued to live on the blood-money that their military ancestors received for their betrayal of Wallenstein.

It is true that the members of the 'Spanish' party – the Verdugos, Marradas and Huerta – disappeared during the seventeenth century, and the Butlers, Leslies and Gordons did not long survive them. The Taaffes left the country in 1938 at about the same time as Lord Runciman, just before the Munich crisis. Others, according to their own testimony, played important rôles in the preparation of the Munich Agreement: the Buquoys, Clary-Aldringen, Kinský, Khuen-Lützow. These left only after the Second World War, along with the heirs of the Liechtensteins and Dietrichsteins, although their proprietary titles came into question after 1918.[53]

There is really no question but that Wallenstein was a traitor – not, however, so much against the Habsburgs as against that Bohemian society in which his own roots lay. He turned his coat in several ways: as a Protestant who became a Catholic to further his career; as a member of the Estates' community in Moravia who coolly defected to the enemy, taking with him the treasury stained with the blood of his subordinates; as an Imperial commander whose plans for the wasting of the Bohemian countryside were distasteful even to Vienna. This was the Wallenstein who as a military entrepreneur led two regiments of 'evil Walloons' in the Bohemian campaign, who provided the troops covering the public executions of 1621 in the Old Town Square of Prague, who dealt so harshly with the victims of the confiscations as to incur the opprobrium of his own peers, and who cruelly suppressed peasant uprisings as late as 1626.

Even before the Battle of the White Mountain Wallenstein had fastened his hopes upon the Habsburgs (or more accurately, upon the worst of them, Ferdinand of Styria) and in the years between 1621 and 1634 it was thanks to the favour and trust of Vienna and Madrid that he became a great figure in European politics. But he became too powerful and therefore dangerous. He posed dangers to the nonentity who occupied the Imperial throne and to the Jesuit confessor Father Lamormain; he represented a threat to the Imperial princes, of whom he made no secret of his estimation, as well as to his colleagues in the government, in the Estates' assemblies, in the War Council and in the military encampments. Pekař's belief that he was a potential King of Bohemia and Srbik's elevation of him as the preordained saviour of

Germany are equally absurd. But Wallenstein was neither an anachronistic condottiere nor a political and military adventurer, as Steinberg has suggested.[54] Certainly ambition is the simplest motive for his activities. But was it the only motive?

His military talent most likely stood somewhat above average, but in the years 1623 and 1626, surrounded at Hodonín and abandoned near Nové Zámky, he was brought to the edge of disaster. He was lucky that his opponents were no better off than he, and he alone was able to turn the threat of annihilation into triumph. He was capable of learning both from the Spaniards and the Dutch; the Hungarian and the newer Swedish tacticians found in him an attentive pupil. And there is no doubt that this military entrepreneur possessed managerial genius. As the perfect manager he was wholly secular: he subscribed to no faith or dogma, and he harboured no political scruples. He was a great Bohemian magnate while being neither Czech, German nor Austrian. To measure him by nineteenth-century standards or those of our own day would be equally inappropriate. He was a great organizer who was able to appreciate talent; he was a Czech in his realism and in his ability to learn, and, like the Hussites, he believed in flexible defence and devastating counter-attack. In short, there was enough about him to account for his greatness. And this rendered him dangerous to the conservative programme of Catholic universalism.

Wallenstein was a lonely figure among his contemporaries. Toward his Bohemian and Moravian fellow noblemen he maintained an attitude of mild scorn, although they sent their sons to serve with him: two of them died at his side at Eger. His opinion of the 'common people' was not high, but he was intelligent enough to realize that the shortsighted policy of plunder and enserfment of the peasantry was absurd because it was irrational. His greatest weakness was his isolation. Whatever grandiose plans he might conceive, he always lacked a sufficiently broad social basis for their execution. Its potential extent is indicated by the uprising of townsmen and peasants in his favour at Opava in February and March 1634, when he was already dead.[55]

He had little in common with the majority of his colleagues in the Estates when he crossed over to the scanty ranks of the Court party. But neither were the old 'Spaniards' his friends. He hated some of them, particularly Slavata and Martinic, and they fully reciprocated. Slavata, brought up in the same surroundings and like him a renegade and careerist, was Wallenstein's mortal enemy. If Wallenstein was the radical 'reactionary', Slavata was every inch the Bohemian conservative who as early as 1624 composed a memorial against him, *Votum cuiusdam secreti consiliarii.* Lobkowitz's attitude to Wallenstein may have been different, but we have no correspondence between the two which might yield clear indications. Lobkowitz, too, belonged to the conservative politicians, but he disagreed with developments after the Battle of the White Mountain, and he must have seen in Wallenstein a man who helped destroy the old Bohemia. The Supreme Chancellor died in 1627 a broken man, but his son Wenceslas Eusebius remained in Wallenstein's circle almost until the end.

On the other hand, Lobkowitz's successor Vilém Slavata, like Wallenstein or Karl von Liechtenstein, was a Protestant who converted to Rome to further his ambitions. Karl von Liechtenstein was, at least until 1624, Wallenstein's ally, but he died in 1627. His brother Gundaker von Liechtenstein was the real ruler of the Privy Council until 1626. He was relieved of this post by Wallenstein's ally Johann Ulrich von Eggenberg, the chief of the Viennese 'Spanish' party. Gundaker remained Wallenstein's sworn enemy ever afterward, and in his *Memorial* presented to the Emperor on 11 January 1634 he recommended that severe steps be taken against him. Another member of the Privy Council was the president of the Court War Council, Count Heinrich Schlick. Schlick made an agile *volte-face* after the Battle of the White Mountain, where he commanded the Moravian infantry covering the retreat of the rest of the Estates' army, and he rose rapidly in the ranks of the Imperial army. He belonged to Wallenstein's circle, but in the summer of 1633 he became estranged from the generalissimo, and the following winter in Vienna he co-ordinated the generals' plot against Wallenstein.[56]

Wallenstein had never liked the head of the Catholic League, Duke Maximilian of Bavaria. Together with the Archduke Leopold of Passau, Maximilian was the protector of the conservative Catholic group of politicians at Prague known as the 'Roman' (or 'Popish') party. Therefore during their exile between 1618 and 1620 Slavata and Martinic preferred to seek shelter at Passau and Regensburg instead of Vienna. In 1630 Maximilian, the spokesman of the German princes, requested and obtained the generalissimo's recall. Wallenstein therefore saw in him the source of his humiliation. Relations between them deteriorated steadily, particularly after the Swedish occupation of most of Bavaria in 1632–3. Maximilian's conversations with the French were of course scarcely less daring than Wallenstein's negotiations with the Saxons, and the generalissimo, now raised to the dignity of an Imperial prince, was probably convinced that in the realm of policy he could allow himself just as much liberty as a Wittelsbach.

For this reason the Bavarian envoy at Vienna Richel was always among Wallenstein's opponents.[57]

Towards the end of 1633, Wallenstein's relations with the Spanish Ambassador became nearly as strained as those with Richel. Until then Oñate had supported Wallenstein's demands upon Madrid (from 1632 onwards Wallenstein received 50,000 florins monthly from the Spaniards), and he even obtained a further extension of Wallenstein's authority. But Wallenstein came increasingly to oppose the presence of an independent Spanish army in the Empire under the command of a Spanish general. This led to a cooling of relations between the two, and by January 1634 Oñate had joined that small circle at the court which resolved upon Wallenstein's death. The end came so unexpectedly for Madrid that at the end of February Olivares convened a *consulta* of the State Council to consider measures to prevent the overthrow of the Spanish monarchy in light of the news of Wallenstein's fall.[58]

It has never been easy for historians to determine the course of Wallenstein's policies – particularly for those who complicated matters by identifying themselves with one of the power groups which were struggling for hegemony in central Europe in their own day. Therefore it is simpler to focus our attention on those facets of Wallenstein's 'system' about which we are better informed, thanks to the surviving evidence. One of these is Wallenstein's rule in the Duchy of Friedland and in Mecklenburg.[59] The Duchy of Friedland became practically an independent administrative unit in June 1625. Friedland had been a Bohemian fief, and its economic relations with Lusatia and Saxony, which had been established by Wallenstein's predecessors the Redern family, permitted the Duke a certain freedom of action. Besides the Redern estates, the core of the duchy embraced those of the Smiřický family, which represented the most advanced form of economic management. This was reflected in the social organization of these estates, which included large numbers of landless peasants who were not subject to feudal labour and lived from the production of flax and the manufacture of linen. Another characteristic feature was the existence of unfree towns which produced substantial quantities of cloth. Cloth and linen were exported through Lusatia or Leipzig to northwestern Europe.[60]

The administrative centre was the town of Jičín, where the Ducal Chamber superintended a certain amount of planned production and marketing. The system of warehouses that was established at Prague, Pardubice, Pilsen, Tábor and Eger served particularly well to satisfy the demands of a huge and reliable market: the army, particularly when it was quartered in northern Germany. Production therefore reached a peak in the period 1627–30. According to Hallwich, the Duchy of Friedland satisfied the chief needs of an army of nearly 100,000 men in these years. The towns of Friedland were able to deliver 10,000 pairs of boots and 4,000 uniforms within a period of ten weeks. Wallenstein, of course, had not the least interest in philanthropy, and he never lost sight of his own advantage. In the last years of his life his income from various kinds of trade, coining, mining, brewing, as well as the traditional seigneurial revenues, reached an annual figure of 700,000 florins. This was at a time when the Emperor owed Wallenstein at least one million florins in subsidies to the army. The generalissimo's fall meant that the debt was automatically wiped out. It did not, however, mean that the Habsburgs had learned the essentiality of a sound economic policy or that they had improved their financial prospects.

Wallenstein had never been willing to invest in risky enterprises. Ernstberger was mistaken when he concluded that Wallenstein was interested in copper- and iron-mining only because he wished to be self-sufficient in these commodities. From Wallenstein's correspondence with his steward Taxis we know that somehow he had acquired a solid grounding in the natural sciences as they were understood in his day. He was avidly interested in the production of saltpetre, and he personally supervised the iron-works at Raspenava. They reached their first peak of production in 1627–8, when the Italians Tanucci and Zanetti fully exploited the existing possibilities. The end of the First Generalship was a serious blow to Raspenava because in the 1620s it had concentrated on the production of iron for the manufacture of arms. But Wallenstein did not close the works. He merely halted production for the army and shifted to the production of pig iron. Since its marketing within the duchy was assured, by 1632 the output of iron had surpassed that of the 1620s.[61]

We can conclude, therefore, that Wallenstein's fall was a catastrophe first of all for his own lands, the Duchy of Friedland, the 'terra felix' of Bohemia. The year 1634 meant the end of everything which had been preserved there from the heritage of the old Bohemia. With Wallenstein, disappeared those social and economic trends which had been progressive in the earlier course of development. Wallenstein, to be sure, was no capitalist entrepreneur, nor does his banker and adviser Jan de Witte bear comparison with, for example, the De Geers of Sweden and the Netherlands But his economic policies were modern to the extent that their practical measures recall the steps taken in France during the reign of Henry IV at the beginning of the seventeenth century, and Jičín was made to imitate the Parisian quarter Le Marais not only in its urban plan but also in its function. Wallenstein's opponents, the Eger murderers and their instigators at Hluboká, Pilsen and Vienna, succeeded in destroying all this. Raspenava's rapid decline began only in 1634, followed by the decline of all northern Bohemia. But surely the last word belonged to the older Bohemian tradition of estate management. Johann Wenzel Gallas, the heir of Wallenstein's rival Mathias Gallas, after enduring the lessons of the great peasant uprising of 1680 to which the peasants of Friedland had been pressed by primitive and stupid forms of exploitation, returned finally towards the end of the century to Wallenstein's example.[62]

In this sense, and only in this sense, Wallenstein's murder was also a tragedy for Bohemia. The question of his treason lost its relevance in 1918, with the disappearance of the monarchy which he had helped to build with his army. His story is that of a man who consciously abetted the destruction of his country's autonomy, who attempted to turn general catastrophes to his own advantage, and who in the final analysis made himself too dangerous simply because he had made himself too independent. It is just as difficult to speak of the 'Bohemian' aspect of his programme as of its 'German' aspect.

It should not be forgotten, in any case, that there were not only two political programmes or two conceptions of intellectual and social development in Bohemia before the Battle of the White Mountain. Wallenstein's contemporaries could choose among at least three models of political thought, three conceptions of life and society. By his actions before 1621 Wallenstein separated himself from the society to which he had originally belonged: the mainly Protestant nobility, bourgeoisie and intelligentsia who subscribed to Protestant Humanism and took the United Netherlands for their model. Wallenstein was at once attracted and repelled by the Netherlands. He instinctively despised the Dutch merchants, but he listened to the advice of Dutchmen and was willing to learn from them. He maintained his contacts with the Netherlands to the end of his life.[63]

The Prague court in the years of his youth included representatives of practically all trends current in Europe, and its contacts extended overseas. The admirers of the Spanish 'universal' monarchy had unlimited possibilities constantly before their eyes. Wallenstein remained a realist whose head was not turned by the title of Admiral of the Atlantic and Baltic Seas. The Spaniards convinced themselves that they could count on him when differences arose over Spanish policies in Germany, the Netherlands, and perhaps also in Italy.[64]

But Rudolphine Prague contained within its walls still another group of people, who, like the monarch, inclined neither to Spain nor the Netherlands. From the very beginning of his reign – or more precisely, from the unsuccessful Pacification Congress of Cologne in 1579 – Rudolph II attempted to mediate. And thus he was neither a militant Catholic nor a particular friend of the Protestants. The Rudolphine 'mannerists', who were sometimes counted among the followers of Erasmus, belonged to various denominations, but all of them inclined towards religious toleration or religious indifference. They favoured the increase of Imperial power but did not support Spanish hegemony; rather, they advocated a balance of political power in Europe and its defence against the Turks. They admired the Italian and Dutch practitioners of mannerist art and were interested in the emergence of a 'new art', a 'new history', new science and new politics. They defended Giordano Bruno just as they defended Kepler, Tycho Brahe and Jacob Typotius. They believed both in astronomy and astrology, mineralogy and alchemy. The real and the unreal were joined in their ideas and in their aristocratic view of life.

Young Colonel Wallenstein did not belong to the mannerist circle at the court of Rudolph II. In the final analysis he was a soldier and a man of action. But many of his actions and aspirations became more comprehensible if we see in him a late adept of the mannerist programme of the *via media*, the way of compromise, understanding and peace. The revolt of the Bohemian Estates scattered the Prague mannerists. The best of them joined one or the other of the contending parties. Some, like Eggenberg or Nostitz, fought in Vienna against their former colleagues, of whom one, Jesenský-Jessenius, ended his life in the Old Town Square at the execution supervised by Wallenstein's soldiers. Wallenstein was untouched by the crisis of mannerism and returned too late to conceptions that could no longer save him from the tragic end which linked him with the bitter fate of Rudolph II and the Prague mannerists.

The tragedy of the Czech nation began in 1620; the personal tragedy of Albrecht Wallenstein was its epilogue. Pekař was just as wrong as Srbik in saying that Wallenstein died because he had attempted with insufficient forces to hasten that great world-historical process in which Habsburg–Catholic universalism was replaced by the ideal of equal rights for all Christians and self-determination for all nations. It is doubtful whether Srbik rightly understood the process of which he spoke. The contest between the Habsburgs and the Netherlands was in the end a conflict between two forms of civilization. When the Thirty Years' War (and the Eighty Years' War) drew to a close, neither of these conceptions emerged victorious. The Dutch Republic retired in favour of England, and the model of French absolutism replaced that of the Spanish monarchy. Wallenstein was perhaps able to understand this process only indirectly, and it did not begin to be realized until the decades following his death. But he belongs to that process which set Europe on the path of economic expansion and an imperialist foreign policy, religious toleration and scientific progress. He also belongs to a different conflict – that between the forces of change and those of conservatism. Therefore the problem of Wallenstein will never lose any of its relevance, nor will it ever be resolved.

6

The Swedish–French Period, 1635–43

PROBLEMS AND SOURCES

During the last decades the attention of historians dealing with the period 1635–43 has mainly centred on France and Spain.

The best introduction to the complex group of Spanish problems is *Imperial Spain 1469–1716* by J. H. Elliott.[1] He has supplemented it with the large monograph on the revolution in Catalonia which has been mentioned.[2] J. Sanabre has written on the French intervention in Catalonia,[3] and Catalonia itself has been dealt with by P. Vilar.[4] There is no good survey yet of the revolution in Portugal, but F. Mauro has published work on the Portuguese economy.[5] H. Kellenbenz has traced Dutch–Spanish economic relations[6] and also studied the material aspects of the Franco–Swedish alliance.[7]

France in the age of Richelieu has been described by V. L. Tapié and R. Mandrou in works already cited. H. Lonchay has studied French and Spanish activities in the Netherlands[8] – a problem which was also treated in volume IV of the *History of Belgium* by Henri Pirenne.[9] The noteworthy book by A. van der Essen on the Cardinal Infanta and Spanish policy in Europe unfortunately only goes up to 1634.[10]

J. U. Nef has traced the results of the changing military balance in the conflict.[11] A new work on Swedish foreign policy has been published by W. Tham, tracing the rise of Swedish power.[12] A detailed biography of the Chancellor Axel Oxenstierna, the first volume by N. Ahnlund, at present only reaches 1632. Some of the works by the West German historian Walther Hubatsch[13] have introduced novel ideas which have been discussed by J. Peters in the *Zeitschrift für Geschichtswissenschaft*. J. Paul has had partial success in tracing the complex threads of Baltic politics.[14]

S. Daníčková's study of the Swedes in Bohemia and Moravia has continued the earlier work of B. Dudík,[15] B. Bretholz,[16] J. Loserth[17] and P. M. Hebbe.[18] The Bohemian question in the framework of Swedish policy has been treated by S. Göransson,[19] and the campaigns of Banér and Torstenson by L. Tingsten.[20]

The best factual survey for the Bohemian lands in the later years of the War is the once popular work by Antonín Rezek.[21] This remains the basic source of general information about this critical period in Bohemian national history, together with Denis' *Bohemia after the White Mountain*[22] and the unfortunately too general treatment by O. Odložilík in *Československá vlastivěda*, volume IV. My article in the *Survey of Czechoslovak History* I, dealing with the connections between popular movements and European politics, is supplemented by F. Dostál's study of the Wallachian uprising and its suppression in 1644.[23]

With the conclusion of the Peace of Prague, central Europe disappears from sight. France and her ambitions now take centre stage. Her foreign policy and internal conditions have received quite a lot of attention in recent decades. On the other hand, the less dramatic withdrawal of the United Netherlands from the front line of the struggle against the Spanish Habsburgs has so far received far less attention. Historians have generally agreed that the year 1640 was of central, though not yet fully assessed, significance. So far, very little has been done for example, on relations between pre-revolutionary and revolutionary England and European politics, and a dissertation by W. V. Wallace concerning England's attitude to the Bohemian question has remained unpublished.

Whether or not we consider the crisis of the 1640s to be a part of a 'general crisis', it is clear that it will now be necessary to focus attention upon problems that until now have been considered marginal – that is the socio-political crises in England and Spain, the growing tension in the Netherlands, and the structural changes in central Europe that were caused by the military conflict. The polemical views of S. H. Steinberg, F. L. Carsten and their German opponents can be confirmed or overthrown only by micro-analytical studies. Since it was in central Europe that the war resulted in a new orientation of the economic policies of the 'old' and 'new' ruling class, and since it is here – particularly in Czechoslovakia – that the greatest volume of archival material has been preserved, it would be appropriate now to concentrate the efforts of teams of scholars upon this period. The long series of financial accounts, instructions and correspondence invite detailed investigation.

In the furnace of the military conflict a 'new' Austrian nobility was formed. The study of its origins is not an easy task. The reign of

Rudolph II brought with it an inflation of patents of nobility which until the proclamation of the Renewed Constitution could be controlled by the Estates. From 1627–8 the granting of patents of nobility and incolats became a royal prerogative. The chief source remains the confiscation protocols, and it is possible to trace the process of confiscation quite accurately throughout Bohemia in the whole period 1618–34. It can be said in advance that the confiscations did not change the composition of land holdings, and that the great enclaves appeared precisely in those places where the necessary conditions had been established earlier, that is in the border regions, though, of course, the actual membership of the ruling noble oligarchy did change. The bourgeoisie was virtually excluded from the community of the Estates; and a new focus of power arose in the Catholic hierarchy. The war also contributed to a great reduction in the lesser nobility which was pushed to the economic periphery. Thus a completely new socio-political situation was formed in the Bohemian lands, one which differed profoundly from that which had been expected by the former members of the 'Spanish' party.

The deaths of Gustavus Adolphus and of Wallenstein, followed early in the 1640s by Richelieu's, deprived European politics of figures of the first rank. The tragedy of Olivares, the growing difficulties of Oxenstierna, the penetration of large capital into politics in the person of De Geer – none of these things have been convincingly explained in all their aspects. Some answers are now possible on the basis of new materials.

Even after the fall of Wallenstein and the ruin of his 'terra felix', Bohemia and its Crownlands continued to provide the material foundations for Habsburg policy in Europe. Without the productivity of the Bohemian lands – Silesia almost as much as Bohemia itself – the activities of the Habsburg diplomats and generals would not have been possible. Since most of them held estates in Bohemia, the Czech archives now contain much material dealing with their military and diplomatic activities even for the periods when the centre of military activity had shifted elsewhere.

The core of this material is the military correspondence in the 'military chanceries' of Wallenstein's enemies – Gallas, Piccolomini and Schlick. The Piccolomini Collection, which (as we shall see) affords information about the most remote regions of Europe, was deposited at the Piccolomini estate of Náchod. At the end of the last century, however, it suffered serious depletion which has since been only partially rectified by efforts to repurchase the documents which were dispersed. We begin to get a clear picture of the original wealth of these collections when we consider the number of documents from them which have found their way into the later artificial collections of the Waldstein-Wartenbergs or the Desfours-Walderodes. These sources, which chiefly pertain to the study of those parts of Europe which were in the hands of Spain or in which Spain had an overriding interest, are supplemented by the collections of the castle library at Náchod and the castle gallery.

The Schlick archives, on the other hand, are more valuable for their information about the central institutions at Vienna, and on this they are very informative indeed. In this respect they resemble the transcripts in the Colloredo Family Archive.

Another source of material which has still not been evaluated is the archive of Wenceslas Eusebius Lobkowitz, who later became First Minister to Leopold I. These papers are supplemented by manuscripts and books in other Lobkowicz collections which are now gathered together and administered by the University Library at Prague. Important though rarely complete material is provided by the Waldstein collection of autographs from Mnichovo Hradiště, chiefly concerning Spanish and Swedish diplomats and soldiers.

The *State Archive at Zámrsk* is extremely important for the entire second half of the Thirty Years' War because it contains the papers of Piccolomini, Schlick, Colloredo and Kolovrat, together with others of less significance.

The *Piccolomini Family Archive.* Three-quarters of the documents in this archive directly or indirectly concern the affairs of the General, later supreme commander of the Imperial Army, from 1646 commander of the Spanish army in the Netherlands, and thereafter an important diplomatic agent. In the 1880s the entire Piccolomini collection was divided by the archivist Arnold Weyhe-Eimke into forty-eight sections in a scheme that can only be called completely inadequate. One part of the collection was classified by subject matter (for example, the affairs of the Piccolomini estate in Bohemia and Italy, Náchod and Amalfi), and another according to persons (Ottavio I, Ottavio II, etc.). Neither Weyhe-Eimke's catalogue nor Machát's survey provides adequate orientation. Therefore the documents for a particular problem must be searched for in several of the sections.

Section III ('Materials Concerning Various Families') contains valuable documents for the study of European politics in these years.

Section IV ('Affairs of the Duchy of Amalfi') contains the correspondence of Ascanio Piccolomini, Archbishop of Siena, together with news of military actions, chiefly in Italy. Section V ('Materials Concerning the Piccolomini Family') include also correspondence from members of other families such as Strozzi and Montecuccoli. Section VI ('Papers of Ottavio I. Piccolomini'), with 4,000 documents (nos. 10,221–14,199) is the most important of all. Others that are useful are section VIII ('The Thirty Years' War' – nos. 16,430–28,011), which has been mentioned already; sections IX and X, which deal with the end of the conflict; section XII, with Ottavio I's correspondence concerning Italy; section XVI ('Papers concerning England'); XVIII ('The Spanish–Dutch War' – nos. 31,059–45,186), whose contents of course are also important for the years 1635–40 in section VIII. Of the other sections numbers XXX ('History of France') and XXXVIII ('History of Poland') should also be mentioned. All of them are fortunately arranged chronologically.

Of particular importance for this period are the documents in section VI which concern the peace negotiations of 1644 at Nuremberg, the Imperial Diet at Regensburg, the Danish–Swedish conflict (the embassy of Georg von Plettenberg), and embassies to Turkey and Spain. In section VIII are important pieces of correspondence with the Archduke Leopold Wilhelm, together with documents from Piccolomini's mission to Dresden. Piccolomini's English correspondence in section XVI also merits attention.[24]

The *Schlick Family Archive* was organized by Max Dvořák at the end of the nineteenth century into nineteen sections. In 1912 the estate of Kopidlno with the family archive passed to the Weissenwolf family who destroyed the structure of the archive. In 1930 the Schlicks regained the archive, but not all the documents were returned, and the collection was only reassembled when all the material came under the control of the State Archive at Zámrsk and was completely recatalogued. A new inventory completed in 1966 gives easy access to the Schlick papers.

The papers of Heinrich Schlick, who eventually became President of the Court War Council, are composed partly of official copies made for meetings of the Council, and partly of his own correspondence.[25]

The transcript collection contains the rescripts and decrees of Ferdinand II and Ferdinand III, reports to the Emperor, and the correspondence of leading figures among the nobility. Schlick's official correspondence with the Emperor, with the generals, and with the enemy should be mentioned. There are also diplomatic reports by

R. Schmidt from Constantinople (1635–41), reports of the negotiations at Constantinople in 1644, the documentation of offers for peace negotiations, and finally the negotiations with Poland and Sweden.

The *Colloredo-Mansfeld Family Archive* contains material for the Thirty Years' War, as has been mentioned, in the papers of Rudolph and Jerome Colloredo (boxes 1–8). The zenith of Rudolph's career was the defence of Prague in 1648, and there are two important pieces of correspondence with the Archduke Leopold Wilhelm (1640–1). Documents dealing with the supply of the army – particularly grain from Bohemia, supply links with Saxony – are of great significance. Also there are thirteen volumes of copies (the *Archivalische Erhebungen*) from the collection of the Court War Council at Vienna, from the Lower Austrian and Prague War Councils, and from the *Feldakten*.

The *Kolovrat Family Archive* contains the following useful collections: A. 'The Family of the Kolovrat-Libštejnský' (particularly papers of Zdeněk Lev, d. 1647); C. 'The Kolovrat-Krakovský Family'; E. 'The Betengl Confiscation, 1640–48'; K. 'Reports from Silesia' (at the end of the war), revealing attempts at postwar reconstruction and containing papers of Morgenthaler and other mercantilists.

The *Leslie Family Archive* was originally at Nové Město-nad-Metují, where it originated from the purchase of materials from the Dietrichstein-Leslie-Proskowsky Family Archive at Mikulov (1923). The papers of Walter Leslie (boxes 5 and 6) concern the acquisition of Nové Město and contain its registers from 1638; they also contain material for Leslie's diplomatic mission to Turkey. Part of the Eggenberg Family Archive also found its way here through marriage (boxes 16–18), but after 1625 the documents are concerned exclusively with family scandals.

The *Sporck Family Archive* is also richer for the postwar period.

The *State Archive at Litoměřice, branch at Děčín* contains the papers of Gallas, Thun, Clary-Aldringen, Desfours-Walderode, and other families.

The *Military Chancery of Mathias Gallas* is one of the most important parts of the Clam-Gallas Family Archive. Work here is simplified by a catalogue for the years 1638–45. Its most complete section covers the years 1635–43 (28 boxes, about 4,500 documents). The material is supplemented by two further boxes containing private correspondence of Mathias (call-number XXI/1–2), the correspondence of his wife Dorothea (from 1633, call-number XXI/3), and a box of correspondence about the quarrel over the Mantuan plunder, call-number XIX/21). The Gallas papers are not an unknown source: they attracted the attention of H. Hallwich and J. Bergl, but they have never been used systematically.

The *Papers of Rudolph Thun* (d. 1636) in the Thun-Hohenstein Family Archive at Děčín contain sources for the close of Thun's military career – most of it from the year 1635. Most of this collection, of course, covers the preceding period.

The *Desfours-Walderode Family Archive* was originally at Hrubý Rohozec, then at Liberec (Reichenberg), whence it came into the possession of the State Archive at Děčín. The original classification of the papers in this collection, described by K. R. Fischer in *Archivalien*, I, was completely inadequate, so that the entire collection is now being recatalogued. Section II of the Family Archive contains originals and transcriptions from the *Feldakten* and other sources, concerning Nicholas Desfours (1590–1661), a native of Lorraine who served as an officer under Buquoy and made a career for himself in Bohemia, and who was finally made a count and appointed Imperial Chamberlain. He was a member of the Court War Council and Lieutenant Field Marshal. The collection also contains photostats, genealogical material, and so forth. There is similar material among the papers of another branch of the family settled in Moravia at Podštát, which are now deposited at the State Archive at Opava, in its branch at Janovice. An important supplement to this archival material is the Castle Library which concentrates on seventeenth-century Lorraine and the Thirty Years' War.[26]

The *State Archive at Litoměřice, branch at Žitenice* contains in the Family Archive of the Lobkowiczes of Roudnice the papers of Wenceslas Eusebius Lobkowitz (1609–77) who from 1636 was a member of the Court War Council, from 1644 its Vice-President, and from 1650 its President. For the period 1634–9 the collection contains the immensely important correspondence of the Imperial counsellor and Ambassador in Saxony Maximilian Trautmannsdorf, together with 'letters from the Imperial Army', including correspondence of Heinrich Schlick, members of the War Council, military commissars, generals and colonels, including Colloredo, Gallas, Millesimo, Piccolomini, Hatzfeld, Leslie, Enckenfoert (Enkevört), Montecuccoli and Sporck. Reports of military actions to the year 1638 are also to be found, under the call-number Q 16/36; from 1641–5 under R 1/11; news sheets and pamphlets for 1635–43 are under R 1/4.

The *State Archive at Prague, branch at Mnichovo Hradiště* contains in the Waldstein Family Archive (the series 'Autographs I') documents from the military chanceries of Piccolomini and Khevenhüller.

'Autographs II' is composed chiefly of documents originally belonging to the Khevenhüllers. Noteworthy are the letters of Francesco di Caretto (1642–5), F. K. Khevenhüller, H. L. Kufstein (the Imperial Ambassador at Constantinople from 1641–7), K. P. von Liechtenstein, J. L. von Schwarzenberg (formerly steward to Wallenstein), and Ferdinand III. From Piccolomini's military chancery there are letters of Walter Leslie from the years 1641–4, to Marradas. There are also autographs of Piccolomini, Colloredo, and Gallas. Particular attention should be drawn to letters of Lennart Torstenson to the Swedish resident and war counsellor Erskein (1642–6) and letters of Baner.

Important supplementary material is provided by the Castle Library with its rich collection of pamphlets.

The *State Archive at Pilsen, branch at Žlutice*, in the *Family Archive of Nostitz-Rieneck*, has seven letters from the Archduke Leopold Wilhelm to Jan Nostitz, Captain of the Elbogen (Loket) district, from the years 1642–6 (call-number D 4), together with documents of a financial character and fragments of the writings of Jiří Bořita of Martinic (to the year 1643). All this material is located in sections EE 4, FF 1, and NN 7.

The *State Archive at Třeboň, branch at Český Krumlov* contains in the *Schwarzenberg Family Archive* the papers of the Brandenburg diplomat Adam von Schwarzenberg (1634–41, numbers 409–18) and those of the Imperial diplomat Johann Adolf I von Schwarzenberg (1643–6, number 363).

The branch of the same archive at *Jindřichův Hradec*, in the *Family Archive of the Slavatas*, contains fragments of the correspondence and writings of the High Chancellor Slavata to the year 1638. His *Historical Writings* are under number 84–97; drafts of his correspondence under numbers 98–107. For the years after 1637 there is little material. The rest of Slavata's writings are found under number 109 (III A 1, boxes 11–14).

In the collection 'Foreign Families' are the fragmentary papers of Jan Jakartovský of Sudice (1634–95), which include correspondence with Imperial commissars (particularly D. Freissleben) from the period of the conflict with the Swedes in Moravia (chiefly 1634–5), with references to the Moravian Wallachians.

The miscellaneous documents to be found in several of the family archives in the *State Archive at Brno* are of similar character. Most important here are the papers of Johann von Rottal (Rottal Family Archive, formerly at Holešov, 'Old Section I') and those of Franz Magnis (Magnis Family Archive, G 146), which elucidate the connections between members of the Magnis family (including the Capuchin Valerian) and Poland and the Swedes, particularly for the years 1644–6. The collection also contains documents concerning their quarrel with General Enckenfoert.

The *State Archive at Opava, branch at Janovice by Rýmařov* contains fragments of the Žerotín papers (Žerotín Family Archive, Bludov); Dietrichstein's correspondence concerning the property affairs of the Pergar family (under the heading 'Domain of Branice'); fragmentary papers of members of the family Hofmann of Grünpichl (Harrach Family Archive, Janovice); and documents dealing with the history of Lorraine at the end of the Thirty Years' War (the Belrupt-Tissac Family Archive). The papers of Christoph Karel Podstatský of Prusinovice (d. *c.* 1644), Dietrichstein's collaborator, are in the Podstatský-Liechtenstein Family Archive, whose second section is located in the State Archive at Brno.[27]

The massive Dietrichstein Correspondence ceases in 1636 with the death of the Cardinal (State Archive, Brno: Dietrichstein Family Archive). The last correspondents are J. F. Breiner, Ernest Platejs, and Nicholas Esterházy. Several other leading figures also died around this time, including Karel of Žerotín, Podstatský and R. Thun, so that the very broad range of the material now begins to narrow and to assume a different complexion.

THE BOHEMIAN QUESTION AND THE ENGLISH REVOLUTION

The Bohemian Estates' Rebellion of 1618–20 is an historical event occurring during the period which, according to Karl Marx, separates the English Revolution of the seventeenth century from its 'model', the rebellion of the Dutch against Spain. This means that the anti-Habsburg rebellion, ending with the Battle of the White Mountain, could have been influenced only by the pre-revolutionary situation which existed in the orders of English society. In the years 1640–9 independent Bohemia had ceased to exist, and the 'Bohemian question' was the concern only of isolated groups of exiles.[28]

In the conclusion of my book *Anglie a Bílá hora* I asserted that the personal policies of James I toward the Bohemian Rebellion, and particularly the fact that these were at odds with English public opinion, form the first link in the chain of failures in Stuart foreign policy. The diplomatic defeat of James gave Parliament its first opportunity in 1621 to bring thorough criticism to bear upon Stuart attempts at absolutism, and to organize the first anti-Stuart opposition.[29] I reached these conclusions on the basis of an analysis of the opinions of contemporaries and an analysis of the class distribution of public opinion. It was Cromwell's former secretary John Rushworth who most clearly expressed the view that a connection existed between the foreign policy failures of the first two Stuarts and the opposition movement. In the first volume of his *Historical Collections* Rushworth used as the frontispiece an engraving showing a map of England with the battlefields of the Civil War and also, in the heart of Europe, a sketch of Prague and the Battle of the White Mountain.[30] In the text he asserted that the origins of the conflict between Charles I and Parliament cannot be explained without taking into consideration the quarrels between James I and Parliament: 'And finding those proceedings to have their rise in the year 1618 (in which year the blazing-star appeared) I resolved that very instant should be Ne plus ultra of my retrospect.'[31] According to Rushworth it was James I who was primarily responsible for the tragic conclusion to the Bohemian Rebellion. The general revulsion his policies inspired resulted, according to Rushworth, in the first open conflict between the King and Parliament, in 1621. At that time James opposed Parliament's attempt to interfere in his foreign policy, with the result that his own attention was more and more drawn to domestic affairs.

It would be senseless here to review the attempts of the peripatetic agents of the 'Bohemian King' and his English supporters, members of the 'Palatine' or 'Bohemian' party, to enlist English aid for their lost cause.[32] The general picture has been clarified, though not changed in any fundamental way, by the discovery of new evidence in recent years: this includes primarily two volumes of correspondence belonging to the English Ambassador at the Hague, Sir Dudley Carleton; some newly available volumes of the State Papers in the Public Record Office at London; and letters of Achatius and Christoph von Dohna which have been preserved among the *Bohemica* in the papers of Christian of Anhalt the Elder.[33] It would be enough, then, to compare the information offered by this new material with the results of the most recent work on the foreign policy of the Stuarts. Besides the work of Christopher Hill and Edward McCabe, this also includes articles by the Soviet historians V. F. Semenov, S. I. Archangelsky, and B. F. Porshnev. In his article 'English absolutism in the first half of the seventeenth century and the coming of the Revolution', Semenov simply notes the opposition between the views of James I and those of Parliament on the attitude to be taken toward Frederick of the Palatinate and focuses upon the critical importance of this policy in

Parliament at the end of 1621. S. I. Archangelsky deals more informatively with the Bohemian question.[34] His article on the 'Foreign policy of English absolutism in the first half of the seventeenth century' indirectly characterizes the struggle of the Bohemian Estates as a struggle for national liberation with a progressive programme of religious reformation. But unfortunately Archangelsky makes no mention of the negotiations of the Bohemian Directors with the English before the election of Frederick of the Palatinate as King of Bohemia, and he deals with the negotiations for aid to the Bohemians as an aspect of Anglo-Spanish relations. Nevertheless he points out very clearly the ambiguity of James' policy and Parliament's judgement of it in November 1621.

A valuable contribution to problems of Jacobean England is a book by the American historian D. Harris Willson about King James VI (of Scotland) and I (of England).[35] In the chapter pointedly entitled 'The crisis of government, 1618–1622' the author, on the basis chiefly of printed sources, offers a detailed analysis of James' position on the Bohemian question from the time of the defenestration of Prague. He gives appropriate attention to the anti-Spanish group in the Council of State, to the complicated relations between England and the Netherlands, and to the popular opposition to James' double-dealing. According to Willson 'the Puritans won over Buckingham to the new Spanish party' at court. Willson deals very carefully with the meetings of Parliament in 1621 – both the spring session and that of November and December – and analyses the parliamentary petitions, from which 'the gulf separating James from the nation was entirely obvious'.[36] Against those historians who have celebrated James the Peacemaker, Willson concludes that James' foreign policy ended in scandalous failure, a catastrophe for England's allies which did much to discredit England herself. It simply was not possible for James to pose at once as the defender of Protestantism and the friend of the Spaniards. While the conflict was breaking out on the continent, James could not remain friendly with both sides at once. His policies were entirely personal; the people could not understand them, and they opposed them. The King's obvious mistakes 'roused the Parliament to its first attempt to gain a share in the formulation of foreign policy'.[37]

What is important here is that the core of the opposition which appeared in Parliament in 1621, during its struggle with James' opinions on foreign policy, included men who later became leaders of the Revolution – for example, John Pym, who later became the 'ruler of Parliament' and the protector of Comenius. Of course the sharp criticism of the Stuart government did not cease with the dissolution of Parliament in 1621. The anonymous author of the pamphlet of 1622 'Tom-Tell-Troath' asserted that Frederick of the Palatinate was ten times better loved than his father-in-law James, whose name was only an object of ridicule. And the Bohemian War, he continues, is proof of how James' incompetence added 'dishonour abroad' to the 'dissension' that already existed at home. A 'general wave of discontent' is rising in the land 'which will lead to conflict'. Among the least contented are the merchants, whose trade is ruined, the lawyers and the common people.[38] The author concludes that only a firm and faithful alliance with the Netherlands can 'lead the children of His Majesty back into Germany'.

However, neither James nor his successor Charles I was prepared to follow such a course. In the parliamentary proceedings of 1624 there is no mention at all of the Bohemian question. In the long run the King was brought to declare war against the Spaniards. There was no more discussion about Bohemia, only about the restitution of the Palatinate. But since Spanish power on land presented no threat to English commerce, the spokesmen of the City pressed for naval actions – raids upon colonies and upon the Spanish fleets carrying American silver. Therefore the Palatine campaign collapsed just as grievously as had the defence of the Palatinate by English troops under Vere in 1621–2. The Bohemian question was sacrificed to the Palatine question. It is true that a handful of Englishmen and Scots found their way into the ranks of the Anglo-Dutch regiment of Ruthven which joined the troops of Mansfeld and Denmark, then followed a circuitous path across the Elbe into Silesia in the autumn of 1626, thence in the winter into Moravia and Upper Hungary. But this enterprise, too, for lack of supplies, ended catastrophically.[39] The parliamentary opposition served only as a warning, which was reinforced, it seems, by Parliament's financial control over the war preparations for which it voted the revenue. In any case Charles I learned nothing from his father's mistakes. He answered Parliament's criticism by dissolving it, and after a time he returned to his father's unfortunate hispanophile policies.

While the fighting continued on the continent and domestic critics repeatedly asked what Charles I was going to do for the 'Protestant Cause', the English navy limited itself to minor conflicts with the Dutch over fishing rights – the Dutch who were fighting the Spaniards on land and at sea and who at the same time offered their hospitality at The Hague to Frederick of the Palatinate and his wife, the King's sister. At the end of the 1620s the English court favoured the Catholics;

the Anglican Church persecuted the Calvinists; and the English fleet attacked only Dutch fishing boats. This, at any rate, was the simplified view of Charles' subjects. In 1630 Charles even concluded an agreement with the Spaniards by which Spanish silver would be coined in English mints and carried in English ships to Flanders, where it was to be used to pay the troops fighting against the Dutch. Charles in fact became the ally of the Spaniards and let himself be subsidized by them.[40]

The Protestant critics of the King's policy did not forget about Frederick of the Palatinate, nor especially about his wife, the crowned Protestant Queen of Bohemia, 'our blessed and courageous Lady', the Queen of Hearts and mother of a growing brood of handsome children. Pictures of her, most of them cheap woodcuts, circulated in great numbers throughout England whose own King waited in vain for an heir. Great hopes were raised at the beginning of the 1630s when, in connection with Anstruther's mission, England again sought an alliance with Protestant northern Europe. But the hopes which Frederick of the Palatinate – and also Comenius – placed on Gustavus Adolphus of Sweden were brutally disappointed on the battlefield of Lützen in 1632. Frederick himself did not long survive Gustavus Adolphus, and there remained only the tragic widow to defend the lost claims of her children. Elizabeth received some help from her brother, but she tried in vain to secure a binding promise that he would help her eldest living son, Charles Louis, back to the Palatinate, or that he would help to free from his Austrian prison her favourite son, Prince Rupert, born at Prague in December 1619 and in his cradle proclaimed Prince of Lusatia. At last, in the mid-1630s, both of them appeared at their uncle's court, probably not very much to his delight. Even the most zealous defenders of the 'Bohemian Queen' no longer thought of a reconquest of Bohemia. Neither, apparently, did Charles Louis nor the adventurous Rupert, who amused himself with plans for conquering a colonial domain somewhere in Madagascar.

His prudent brother maintained close contact with the Dutch and Venetian ambassadors and cultivated the acquaintance of a group of opposition noblemen, particularly those who disagreed with Charles' hispanophile naval and colonial policies. The Soviet historians Semenov and Archangelsky have emphasized, as has been mentioned, the significance of colonial questions for the conflict between the King and his opposition in the 1630s. An expansionist, anti-Spanish policy was favoured by those who opposed the King's attempts to monopolize domestic production, and they protested against the royal acts limiting the privileges of the colonial companies and of individual proprietors.[41] This group included Warwick, Essex and Hertford, Lord Saye, Lord Brooke, John Hampden and John Pym – many of whom undoubtedly had commercial talents. The opposition to the King was further strengthened by the case of the Providence Island Company, which had founded three small settlements in the West Indies that James I had ceded to the Spaniards. Most of the new friends of the Count Palatine Charles Louis were members of this Company. The Puritan lawyer Oliver St John became their legal representative, and their secretary was John Pym. In 1632 the Spaniards destroyed one of the Company's settlements. The interests of the opposition group were well-founded, because in 1637 they invested another 100,000 pounds in a venture which only was able to subsist by piracy against Spanish shipping.

The King's foreign and religious policies were conducted so maladroitly that they fanned the flames of discontent. The popularity of the 'Bohemian Queen' also played a part. When the 1636 edition of the Prayer Book left out the prayer for Elizabeth, Queen of Bohemia, and her children, the omission was pilloried by William Prynne in his pamphlet *News from Ipswich.* In June 1637 Prynne stood trial with two other critics of the King's religious policies before the Star Chamber, and their trial became the demonstration of serious dissatisfaction with the royal policies.[42]

We still do not know enough about the fate of individual Bohemian exile groups. Therefore we are unable to say what connections existed between Elizabeth and her sons and members of the émigré groups in the Netherlands, not to mention those in Saxony, Hungary or Poland. We do know that from the beginning of the 1630s the Leszno group tried to obtain material help from England. Archbishop Laud was an opponent of any substantial aid. On the other hand, significant contributions arrived from certain religious communities supported by the mercantile patriciate, particularly the Dutch Church in London, whose parishioners generally included Calvinists from the Continent.[43] Bohemian émigré students were to be found particularly at Emmanuel College, Cambridge, the 'hotbed of Puritanism', some of whose members, for instance Hugh Peters, left at least for a time during the 1630s for New England. The opposition to the court and to the court nobility also manifested itself in the field of education. From the 1630s voices were raised in criticism of the humanist educational background of most courtiers. The first of these critics was apparently Lord Herbert of Cherbury who was later joined by a group including Samuel

Hartlib, John Dury and John Pym, advocates of the new educational ideas of Comenius.

As early as 26 November 1636 John Pym promised Hartlib his help in bringing Comenius to England, 'as soon as it shall please God to restore the freedom of trade and travel'.[44] The project did not materialize at the time, but Comenius sent Hartlib an interesting essay describing how in human society ('in morals and politics') there exist 'according to principles which are generally valid, mathematical laws which are the same as in Nature'.[45] In another letter Comenius acknowledged Bacon's philosophical work.

The Parliament which was summoned in 1640 by Charles I when he was forced into a corner by domestic opposition and rebellion in Scotland gave Pym and his associates the necessary authority to negotiate Comenius' journey to England. A group which included members of the Long Parliament such as Pym (who was now apparently in close contact with Comenius' future son-in-law Figulus), the political writer John Selden, and Laud's opponent, Bishop John Williams, stood behind Comenius' journey to England. The long-planned journey had a twofold aim: Comenius was to solicit support for the Bohemian Brethren and for the émigré colony at Leszno, and at the same time interest 'some leading man, or else the King, or both' in plans for the foundation of a college of scholars for the advancement of the schools and of education. It seemed that the situation was propitious. Archbishop Laud, who had blocked aid for Leszno eight years earlier, was now out of power. In 1641 the Parliaments at both London and Edinburgh discussed the chances of restoring to the Palatine family 'that which they lost through the fault of evil counsellors'.[46] On 1 March 1641 the Count Palatine Charles Louis returned to England.

It is of course true that the discussions in Parliament had no concrete result and that the Count did nothing to oppose the marriage of his cousin the Princess Mary, to the son of the Dutch Stadholder Frederick Hendrik, who later became William II. Mary had in fact earlier been promised to Charles Louis himself. Nevertheless on the autumn day in 1641 when Comenius arrived in England, the general situation seemed to favour the aspirations of the Bohemian émigrés. In this year Comenius' collaborator and friend Samuel Hartlib dedicated to the English Parliament his utopian treatise *A Description of the Glorious Kingdom of Makaria* with its picture of planned production and suggestions for social experimentation.[47] Comenius was given the opportunity to explain his own views to a group of his followers.

Important in this respect is Comenius' *Brevissima delineatio*, concerning the measures necessary for a thorough and general reform of religion. The fourth section dealt with the question of 'whether it is correct and lawful to employ secular powers to carry out a Reformation'. Comenius answered in the affirmative. It is lawful and proper to use the secular authority to this end, but it would be better attained through education.[48] His own set aims were the reformation of the schools, peace among the Protestant Churches, and Pansophy. These were also the tasks which take first place in a list of things which, in October 1641, Comenius noted as necessary 'to the encouragement of general truth and peace'. It is not out of place to note in conclusion that Comenius' residence in England was of great significance for his later work, not so much in the outline programme of action for the betterment of the world which is found in his *Via lucis* (in any case only published in 1668 in Amsterdam) but rather in the kinds of activity with which he was soon to occupy himself. His relationship with his host Hartlib, and his close friendship with the irenist John Dury on the one hand, and on the other the unsatisfactory development of the political situation – all this must have confirmed Comenius' conviction that a general improvement in human affairs would only be realizable through education.

John Williams, Bishop of Lincoln and later Archbishop of York, who according to Comenius was a most acute observer of the political scene ('politicissimus'), at first played an important rôle in the Long Parliament and contributed significantly to the fall of Strafford.[49] Later he became more and more disillusioned with his rôle as intermediary between the King and the opposition peers. In December 1641, Bishop Williams was insulted by a crowd of journeymen and prevented from entering the House of Lords. In the name of all the bishops Williams protested against their being prevented from taking part in the debates. Contemporaries believed that the bishops' protest was approved by the King who hoped thereby to strengthen the shaky position of his court. The House of Lords refused to receive Williams and his associates, and at Pym's suggestion the lower house decided to bring charges of treason against him. On the last day of December 1641 (11 January 1642 new style) the 'political bishop' Williams was imprisoned in the Tower, where he joined his opponent Laud.

Parliament did not consider the discussions about a Pansophical College to be very important. This was largely because Sir John Culpeper, who was carrying on discussions with Comenius, on hearing of the Grand Remonstrance joined the ranks of Pym's opponents at the end of November 1641, along with Hyde (Clarendon) and Falkland.[50] And the Count Palatine Charles Louis even accompanied Charles I on his attempted coup, when it was intended to arrest five members of Parliament, among them Pym and Hampden (4 January 1642).[51]

Thus by the beginning of 1642 the original group of Comenius' supporters had dissolved. Comenius, who in November and December of 1641 still hoped for the success of his pansophical plans in England, was, from February, 1642, resigned to leaving England, and in the middle of April he accepted the offer of the Dutch–Swedish munitions manufacturer De Geer to come to Sweden. In his later memoirs Comenius emphasized that he did so with the agreement of his English followers, among whom he named Lord Brooke (Robert Greville), Bishop Williams, and John Pym. It is of course difficult to determine what could have connected Pym and Brooke, the author of the uncompromisingly Puritan *Discourse on Bishops*, with Bishop Williams by the spring of 1642. In England, where, after the failure of Charles' attempted coup, both sides were preparing for war, the plans of Comenius, Dury and Hartlib were all doomed to failure. Comenius may have still witnessed the attempts of Charles and Parliament to gain control of the armed forces, or he may have heard in April of the refusal of the governor of the city of Hull to submit to the King, but at the outbreak of hostilities he was no longer in England. He left with Figulus and Dury for the Netherlands, charging his friends to remain faithful to their efforts on behalf of Pansophy. This was in June, and on 22 August at Nottingham Charles launched open warfare against Parliament.[52]

After 1642, Comenius became estranged from the mainstream of the Revolution in England. This can be explained by the divided class loyalties of his supporters, which became apparent during the time of Comenius' stay in England. After 1646, following the death of Pym and the end of the first Civil War, none of Comenius' original supporters was any longer in a position of power or influence. Hartlib and Dury, of course, remained loyal to Parliament, and Dury, according to Perez Zagorin, was to be found among the official theoreticians of the Commonwealth during the 1650s. But by this time Comenius' relations with both parties had grown more distant. The conflict between Parliament and the King was foreign to Comenius, but not because he was by nature a monarchist. His essay of 1648 concerning his attitude towards the leaders of the English Revolution, the Independents – even in its title, *Independence, the Eternal Source of All*

Confusion – recommended to the English a compromise union of feudal and non-feudal elements of government which was perhaps best exemplified in the constitution of the United Netherlands.[53]

Thus Comenius never identified himself with the ideology of the English Revolution, nor, it seems, did he trust Cromwell completely even though he tried to persuade him to join the anti–Habsburg camp. England interested him as a necessary element in the anti-Habsburg coalition which in 1654–6 he tried to gather together from Leszno. Comenius and his friends regretted that England, which had not even participated in the peace negotiations at Münster and Osnabrück, had taken no part in the struggle against the Habsburgs.[54]

We may conclude, then, that a sober assessment of Comenius' activities as the spokesman of the Leszno group in revolutionary England in 1641–2 does not confirm the accepted judgement that he played a significant political rôle at this time – that perhaps he even acted as mediator between the King and Parliament. It is obvious that even his call to England was not the work of Parliament as a whole, but rather of a group of influential members – a group which fell apart just before the outbreak of hostilities.[55] Comenius' attitude towards England was basically passive, although he regarded the Revolution as an unfortunate conflict which sapped the strength of the coalition that he hoped would be victorious in the interest of his defeated homeland.

If the predominantly bourgeois Bohemian émigrés saw in England their natural saviour and defender, the nobility in Bohemia after the Battle of the White Mountain took a decidedly negative view of revolutionary England. At any rate the pamphlets, relations and passages from the correspondence that can be found in the manorial libraries and archives in Bohemia reveal a uniform horror and alarm in their comment upon the Revolution, the execution of Charles I, and the proclamation of the Republic.[56]

This raises a second question which deserves an answer: what was the attitude of the Austrian and Spanish Habsburgs towards revolutionary England? The most important recent conclusions are those of the Soviet historian B. F. Porshnev. He emphasizes the great influence of the English Revolution on French policy in the 1640s, under Mazarin, and believes that is was not only the internal difficulties of France, but also the fears aroused by the English Revolution, which led Mazarin to support the conclusion of the Peace of Westphalia.[57] Porshnev's argument, which relies chiefly on Chéruel's edition of Mazarin's correspondence, can also be supported by sources for the history of Mazarin's policy and of the Fronde in Bohemian archives and libraries, even though the real significance of the fighting on the barricades of Paris on 26 and 27 August 1648 for the conclusion of the Westphalian agreement still remains obscure. The situation was doubtless more complicated: the United Netherlands concluded a separate peace with Spain as early as January 1648, and in Sweden Salvius' party, with Queen Christina's support, triumphed over Oxenstierna's group, which advocated a struggle *à outrance*.[58]

It is difficult to infer that the conclusion of the Peace of Westphalia, which increased the danger of intervention by France and Spain, encouraged the English to proceed with the execution of Charles I, which took place on 30 January 1649. On the other hand, Porshnev's observation that in France there was sympathy for the English Revolution, and that the rebels at Bordeaux in the beginning of the 1650s were in contact with the Leveller Sexby, is of considerable interest. Although some of his assumptions based on pamphlet and newspaper literature will have to be checked against other sources,[59] it will certainly be necessary to base the further study of the Fronde and its relation to England upon scrutiny of Porshnev's conclusions.

Here we shall only review some of these: those concerning the relationship of the Austrian and Spanish Habsburgs to revolutionary England, which can be done on the basis of the correspondence of Ottavio Piccolomini.[60] Piccolomini's contacts with English, Scottish and Irish Catholics certainly went back to the period of Wallenstein's army. Most of all Piccolomini needed men for his army, and from the middle of the 1630s he employed recruiting agents. Thus in 1635 Captain George Shawe wrote to him from Brussels that through the influence of friends at court he was going to attempt to ease restrictions upon the activities of his agent in England, and that after his return home he would recruit a whole regiment of English Catholics himself.[61] The letter also contained information about conditions in England – the situation at court, the arrival of the Count Palatine Charles Louis – and Piccolomini continued to seek this kind of news. Along with transcriptions and reports he also received copies of proclamations and diplomatic documents.[62] But Piccolomini's papers become more important after the winter of 1641–2 – that is, in the period when Comenius was offered shelter in Hartlib's London house in Duke's Place. On 8 February 1642 Shawe sent Piccolomini a report in which he gave prominence to the progress of the Irish rebellion which had erupted the previous November. In January and February there was already discussion of Queen Henrietta Maria's agreement with the Catholic rebels in Ireland. Shawe did not think the King's setback of January

1642 important and mentioned that a group of bishops had been sent to the Tower following a quarrel with Parliament.[63] Piccolomini answered on 11 April in a letter now lost, but apparently he asked for further news, which Shawe provided in the middle of May. Tension was increasing: the Irish rebellion was successful, but Parliament had prevented the King from travelling to Ireland and stood by the city of Hull's refusal to give the King access to the great arsenal that was located there.[64] Shawe also wrote that he had received news of the defeat of the Irish, of the sufferings of the Catholics, and of the continued resistance of Colonel Hotham at Hull. Shawe's well-informed friends had heard some rumour ('algun ruydo') about an outbreak of hostilities between the King and Parliament.[65]

In June 1642 Shawe was in London, probably to recruit soldiers for Piccolomini and for Mello's army in the Spanish Netherlands. According to him there was no agreement in Parliament, but the small group of parliamentary leaders had not lost courage, so that there was small hope of mediation.[66] The situation had not changed by the end of the month: the Irish were defeated, while in England both sides prepared for war.[67] Once the war began, the hope of recruitment for the Spaniards vanished, and the correspondence ceased.

There are no Bohemian sources for the first years of the Civil War. So we do not know how Brussels and Vienna reacted to news that their former prisoner Prince Rupert was leading the King's cavalry with great courage but little tactical adroitness. In March 1643 those surrounding the King at his temporary seat in Oxford welcomed the news that Piccolomini was on his way to England. Letters from Edward Herbert, Charles' chief adviser, and from Charles' confidant Endymion Porter are filled with jubilation. An important guest was expected from Flanders whose arrival must be a good omen.[68] Porter added that 'Emperors and Kings must help each other against treacherous vassals.' The correspondence contains no information about Piccolomini's journey. According to letters from another English Catholic, Henry Gage, Piccolomini's *maestro del campo* who was recruiting troops in England at this time, Piccolomini left England from the southern port of Weymouth. This places the visit sometime in May or June 1644, but its aims will have to be clarified on the basis of other material.[69]

Piccolomini remained in contact with Herbert, Porter and Henry Gage after the royalist defeat at Marston Moor in July. In the autumn Herbert informed him of his appointment as commander of the Royal Navy,[70] and at the end of the year Gage reported that he wished to leave Oxford to return to Flanders. Since the parliamentary forces had failed to follow up their victory and there was no prospect for a quick victory on either side, it was obvious that nothing would come of the plans to recruit one *tercio* (*i.e.* two infantry regiments) in England.[71]

During the winter Piccolomini, perhaps on the basis of Gage's information, shifted his interest to Ireland, where F. Foissotte was recruiting soldiers for the Spanish Netherlands.[72] The prospects appeared favourable, and Foissotte was trying to bring Piccolomini into contact with the Catholic confederates. There were many Irish soldiers of the type represented by Butler, Taaffe or Geraldine (Fitzgerald) in the Imperial service, so that it is not surprising that the Catholic Irish regarded the Habsburgs as their natural spokesmen.[73] The deteriorating position of the royalists doubtless rendered continued recruitment for the Spanish Netherlands fruitless, and the correspondence is interrupted in the spring of 1645. For the entire year there is only one letter of significance. It came in the middle of April from Lord Newcastle, who asked Piccolomini's advice about accepting a commission in the royalist army. Piccolomini's response was apparently negative because Newcastle later replied thanking him for his help.[74]

After their defeat at Naseby, more and more royalists fled to France. Among them was Endymion Porter, Spanish on his mother's side, who first arrived in England in the entourage of Buckingham and Charles. He was a diplomat and courtier who belonged to the inner circle of Charles' trusted advisers. In the 1620s these men were commonly reviled as opportunists and monopolists; on the other hand, Porter became famous as the patron of the poets Herrick and Davenport and the painter Mytens. He belonged to Strafford's faction and took part in all the 'popish plots'. Therefore in 1645 he thought it wise to leave for France.[75] On 24 February 1646 he wrote to Piccolomini from Paris that he was ill.[76] On 14 April he informed him that he had 'lost King and Country'. and that he wished now to serve Piccolomini. At the same time he recommended his son to him.[77]

With the influx of royalists onto the Continent, Endymion Porter assumed greater importance for Piccolomini, and from Paris he sent his 'Lord and Patron' news of Queen Henrietta Maria and her son.[78] On 20 May he recommended to Piccolomini the Earl of Norwich, George Goring, who had been in France since the end of 1644. At present he was in Brussels, and Porter pointed him out as a significant figure who might prove useful as a mediator between the King of Spain and the Dutch 'rebels'. Goring is a cavalier, is well-disposed toward Spain and holds the respect of the Stadholder Frederick

Hendrik.[79] In July Porter also sent Piccolomini his own son – probably his younger son Philip, who had served for two years as a 'sargeant major' (*i.e.* lieutenant-colonel) in the Prince of Wales' cavalry regiment.[80] Shortly afterwards Philip Porter was commissioned as a captain in the Spanish army.[81]

At the beginning of 1647 Endymion Porter's elder son George Porter also began to write to Piccolomini. He had served in the First Civil War under Prince Rupert and Newcastle and had fought as a major-general at Marston Moor, where he was captured and imprisoned for a time in the Tower, then exchanged. From June 1645 he served in the Spanish forces under Ormond. George Porter had great influence with his father-in-law, the Earl of Norwich. In January he was in London to recruit soldiers for the Spanish Netherlands, and he promised Piccolomini that he would send news of the situation in England.[82] There appear to have been several other recruiting officers in London at this time because George Porter complained of French and Irish competition and requested a commission. On 5 February he reported that the Scottish army had turned over Charles I, with whom it failed to reach an understanding, to Parliament. Porter complained that the Scots had sold the King for a Judas' ransom of one million pounds, though in fact they only received a promise of 400,000 to cover expenses. According to Porter, the 'arrogant rabble' who composed Parliament planned to hold the King prisoner at Holmby near Northampton.[83]

This was very up to date and accurate information. It was confirmed somewhat later by another royalist, perhaps also a recruiting officer but otherwise completely unknown, Alexander Keynes. On 15 March 1647 Keynes wrote from London that in spite of the Irish invasion of Scotland, the situation in England was practically hopeless and could be saved only by an agreement between Parliament and the Spaniards.[84] Meanwhile Keynes' rival George Porter urged Piccolomini to grant him a recruiting patent, since in London there were 'many gentlemen who would like to enter the service of Piccolomini'. He warned of the dangers of waiting for the resumption of hostilities and added that two regiments were also being recruited for Prince Rupert.[85] But Piccolomini apparently favoured Keynes, who at the end of March wrote that he had recruited 600 men, for each of whom he requested fifty shillings. At the beginning of May, George Porter still had not received his commission, while Keynes had already begun to send shiploads of soldiers. He reported that the Independents appeared to have gained the ascendancy over the Presbyterians,[86] and on 9 June he crossed with the last of his recruits to Brussels. He stated that during his residence in England he had spoken with the King for a whole hour at Holmby. Charles had concurred that his followers should enter the service of Spain in Flanders, and he conveyed his greetings to Piccolomini and the Archduke.[87] At the beginning of June Keynes did not know whether he would be returning to England with the same mission, but the 'new war' that George Porter mentioned in his letter of 14 June from London ruined the chances for further recruitment.

Keynes and the son of the Earl of Norwich, who was also named George Goring, wished to serve directly under Piccolomini. The younger Goring had served in the Dutch army in the 1630s, was wounded, returned to England as a colonel, and in 1639 served in the war against the Scots. Then he fought without much success in the royalist army under Newcastle before leaving for France in 1646, and the following year he was a colonel-general in the Spanish army.

From July 1647 Goring complained regularly to Piccolomini of the inadequacies in the supply and equipment of his 'Ingleses'. His infantry was poorly paid and required reinforcements, and he and Keynes both requested that their men not be sent against the French. The English regiments arrived at the encampment near Dixmuiden only in October, their ranks weakened, their commanders ill and plainly eager to return to their winter quarters.[88] Thus by the end of 1647 Piccolomini had no source of information about English affairs. In January 1648 the Dutch concluded a separate peace with Spain, so that the situation on the French front was eased. At the end of April Keynes complained of the Spanish commanders who had decided upon Piccolomini's transfer from the Netherlands. Therefore there was a growing desire among the English royalists to transfer to the service of the Prince of Wales, who was marching from France through Holland on his way to Scotland.[89]

Keynes judged the situation there to be quite hopeful. According to his information the journeymen of London had risen in favour of Charles, and the King's restoration was practically a certainty. He feared only that Queen Henrietta Maria, under the influence of Cardinal Mazarin, might squander precious time. Keynes believed that excessive caution at this point could only enhance the influence of the Scots and the Presbyterians, and 'we should be thrown from the frying-pan into the fire'.[90]

On 11 June 1648 George Goring requested that he be released from Spanish service for the reason that the Queen had asked him to depart for England. At the same time he assured Piccolomini that he would continue to do his utmost for the Habsburg cause.[91] Keynes, too, was waiting for Goring and the Prince of Wales, and he also expressed his devotion to Piccolomini.[92] The reports from England were optimistic. Keynes wrote on 13 June that everyone in the land was against Parliament, that a part of the navy had gone over to the royalist side and that they controlled Rochester and Dover. It was expected that 100,000 men would gather on Blackheath Field by Greenwich. Marmaduke Longdale, who had once served under Goring, had more than 14,000 men in the southeast. Parliament had sent Cromwell against the royalist forces, but according to the news he had been beaten and killed.[93]

One month later Keynes was already in the entourage of the Duke of York at The Hague. The Prince of Wales was waiting for a ship at Calais; the Dutch provided nine large ships. What was not known was whether the royalists from the Netherlands and France were going to be transported to Scotland, whose army under the Duke of Hamilton had invaded the north of England, or to southeastern England, where the royalist forces were concentrated near Colchester. There, too, were Charles Lucas and the elder Goring. Keynes complained that the Duke of York had surrounded himself with inexperienced counsellors who included not only non-Catholics but also anti-Catholics. Parliament protested to the Dutch against their provision of ships to the royalists, a point on which the views of the States General and the Stadholder diverged widely. The younger Goring had so far remained at Brussels, where he succeeded in gathering only sixty men for the English campaign. Keynes himself was prepared to go to Scotland or England in order to make some money or acquire some landed property. Afterwards he hoped to be able to leave his family there and return to the service of Spain.[94]

Thus among the royalist commanders, whose numbers were apparently quite small, there was very little unselfish zeal for the King's cause. Their failure was not far off. Charles I's execution on 30 January 1649 provoked horror on the Continent and indignation among rulers. Its echo is also to be found in Piccolomini's correspondence.[95] Alexander Keynes, who somehow survived the defeat of the Scottish expedition, once again offered his services to the 'Duke of Amalfi, at Vienna or at Prague', even in the modest capacity of captain. He described the atrocities that followed the 'cruel tragedy of our King' and mentioned that a number of his and Piccolomini's acquaintances, among them the elder Goring, had been brought to trial. The single remaining hope was Scotland and Ireland, where Prince Rupert continued to hold out. In England the royalists were being systematically ruined by taxation. 'A new party has appeared in the army and in Parliament, called the English Levellers, which is to say those who believe that all people in the land should be equal, and they wish to allow no differences in property or power.' Keynes thought that their strength was great enough to begin to cause Cromwell and Fairfax some concern.[96]

The younger Goring, 'shaken by the news of the King and of my father', wrote to Piccolomini from Brussels. The 'young King' Charles II had fled in May 1648 to Ireland, where he was awaited by 20,000 foot and 4,000 horse, virtually all of them Catholics. But he was bitterly disappointed by the Archduke Leopold Wilhelm's unwillingness to help him. The Scots, it is true, were negotiating with Charles II, but they could not be relied upon. The elder Goring had been sentenced to death by Parliament after the capitulation of 27 August 1648, but he was still being held in prison. In these circumstances the younger Goring wished to continue to serve Spain and Charles II.[97]

With this the reports concerning revolutionary England end. Piccolomini, of course, continued to receive news of England, chiefly from Keynes, who was once again in Scotland with Charles II until he returned to Brussels after the defeat at Worcester in September 1651.[98] In 1653 Piccolomini was interested in the Anglo-Dutch war and in Charles II's attitude toward it. Alexander Keynes returned to England in the 1650s, and he wrote to Piccolomini from London and Canterbury, but his last letter, an urgent plea for financial assistance, arrived from Vienna in 1656.[99]

Endymion Porter died on 20 August the same year in England, having returned in 1648 to reconcile himself with Parliament. The younger Goring died one year later in Madrid in the same poverty of which Keynes had complained in Vienna. His father the Earl of Norwich lived in France at the émigré court of Charles II. After the Battle of Worcester there was no longer any hope that the royalists would be able to bring about another rising in England. Cromwellian England was too strong, and it had become one of the chief actors in European politics. But it was no longer revolutionary, and its leaders began to seek accommodation with those elements which in the beginning they had fought against.

7

War, revolution, peace negotiations 1643–50

PROBLEMS AND SOURCES

The central problems of the period 1643–50 are the final contraction of Spanish power, which was dealt a fatal blow by the revolutionary wave of 1640; the exclusion of England from European politics during the revolutionary years 1640–2; the dominance of conflict-ridden France over her Swedish and German allies; and Sweden's halfhearted attempts to decide the war on the battlefield, or at least to gain an advantageous position for diplomatic negotiations which would lead automatically to peace by compromise.

Besides the works about Spain that have already been mentioned (particularly those by Elliott) others calling for notice are the balanced survey by Juan Reglá, *Introducción a la historia de España*, and his article in the *New Cambridge Modern History*.[1] Spain has also been the subject of work by V. Palacio,[2] José Maria Jover,[3] and M. Fraga Iribarne.[4]

The basic recent work on England and her seventeenth-century revolution is by Christopher Hill.[5] J. R. Jones has studied the position of England in Europe in the seventeenth century, particularly with reference to her relations with the United Netherlands.[6] The same theme also attracted C. R. Boxer in his monograph of 1965.[7]

In his studies B. F. Porshnev has argued that France under Mazarin was prompted by its struggle against revolutionary England and by its own internal crisis to a readier acceptance of the Peace of Westphalia which was not to the advantage of France's allies.[8] I have analysed this point on the basis of Piccolomini's papers.[9] It seems that action against revolutionary England in the years 1647–8 was supported not so much by Spain or France as by the Dutch Stadholder Frederick Hendrik, and still more by his son William II of Orange. This question has also been dealt with by Peter Geyl in his book *A History of the Low*

Countries.[10] C. Smit[11] and J. J. Poelhekke[12] have studied the Dutch withdrawal from the war.

J. A. van Houtte has analysed the economic and social development of the Netherlands before the conclusion of the separate Peace of Münster.[13] H. A. Enno van Gelder has written about the 'Golden Age' of Dutch culture.[14] Tibor Wittman has produced a popular survey of this period.[15] J. Presser has dealt with another side of the 'Golden Age' in his articles about the poor in this era.[16] Together with the archivist S. Hart I have discussed the social composition of Amsterdam in an article entitled 'Prague and Amsterdam in the seventeenth and eighteenth centuries'.[17]

Porshnev's book on the popular uprisings before the Fronde[18] is complemented by Roland Mousnier's edition of *Lettres et mémoires adressés au chancelier Séguier (1633–1649).*[19] There is also an important article by Robert Mandrou on this subject; and a valuable work on the Fronde is by the Dutch historian Ernst H. Kossmann.[20]

The Porte was still active in European politics in 1645, and its aims are elucidated by the work of Ernst Werner on Turkish feudalism.[21] This conflicts with the views of Turkish historians, in particular Professor O. Barkan.

The classic work of modern historiography on the Peace of Westphalia is the book by Fritz Dickmann.[22] M. Braubach published an anniversary study in 1948,[23] and important sources are contained in the *Acta Pacis Westphalicae.*[24] The articles by Bedřich Šindelář have attracted attention, and his monograph *The Peace of Westphalia and the Bohemian Question* has been published.[25]

There have been a number of studies dealing with the general effects of the war. S. H. Steinberg, writing about the work of R. Ergang, has warned against accepting premature results.[26] Ergang's book is not widely available,[27] and the works by K. F. Olechnowitz[28] and J. A. van Houtte,[29] which Steinberg cites, deal only with restricted localities and thus do not permit any general conclusions. None will probably be forthcoming in the near future. The summary of these problems has been published by Theodore K. Rabb in his *The Struggle for Stability,* mentioned above.

The situation in any one town, district or country shows how risky it is to generalize. But it is possible to assess the situation after the war in Bohemia, and without exaggeration it can be called tragic. The economic condition of the country was indicated by V. Pešák's work on the towns' indebtedness, of which they were never able to free themselves.[30] The position of the peasant population is indicated by the extensive though incomplete edition of the *Tax Roll* (*Berní rula*) of 1654–6. Of the thirty-three volumes that have been planned, only sixteen have appeared, but the information is summarized in the second volume, edited by Karel Doskočil, *Popis Čech roku 1654* (*A Description of Bohemia, 1654*).[31]

The large volume of written sources which are available for the last years of the Thirty Years' War concerns the diplomatic activities which were finally concluded at Münster, Osnabrück and Nuremberg. They also include sources for military history, because it became increasingly clear that neither side would be able to achieve a decisive victory. Therefore the aim was to win victories of prestige and to occupy the best possible bargaining position.

The most important collection is undoubtedly the chancery of Ottavio Piccolomini, with valuable information about Dutch–Spanish relations, conditions in Italy, and the socio-political crises in France and England. Piccolomini's papers follow the peace negotiations until the agreement with the Swedish representatives at Nuremberg in 1650. Supplementary material for this basic collection is available in the papers of Schlick and Colloredo, and also, of course, in the Autograph Collection at Mnichovo Hradiště.

The second place belongs to the Military Chancery of the not very successful Mathias Gallas of Friedland, the contents of which end in April 1647. Together with the Schlick collection it elucidates the actual military actions – a theme which is further illuminated by the transcript collections of the Colloredo–Mansfeld archives. But there is also a third collection, so far little used – the papers of the Imperial diplomat Johann Adolf I von Schwarzenberg, which from 1645 cover the group surrounding the Archduke Leopold Wilhelm, both in the army and at Brussels. This collection offers a valuable supplement to the Piccolomini material and enables us to trace the last phases of the negotiations for the Peace of Westphalia. The Schwarzenberg correspondence, with the Spanish Ambassador Brun and the Imperial Ambassador at Madrid Caretto, throws new light on the activities of the triangle Brussels–Madrid–Vienna. The negotiations at Münster from 1644 are also covered by papers in the Dietrichstein Family Archive and by some of the contents of the Trautmannsdorf collections.

The papers of the families of Belrupt, Martinic, Magnis, and those of Wencelas Eusebius Lobkowitz further elucidate the situation at the end of the war. The material at Opava helps to explain the question of Silesia which was so important at the close of the military conflict.

There is significant Bohemian material from the period of the Swedish campaign against Brno and Vienna, the Battles at Jankov and Třebel, and the occupation of the Lesser Town of Prague. Since the appearance of P. M. Hebbe's study, the question of the Swedish occupation of northern Bohemia and Moravia has taken on a new significance, so that it will be necessary to evaluate the contents of the municipal archives (for example Olomouc, Brno, Kroměříž, etc.).

Finally, on the question of the actual effects of the war, there is so much material in the archives that it is scarcely possible to estimate its extent. From the 1640s we have the 'patrimonial registers', which in many instances continue in the records of the noble domains down to the twentieth century. There is, however, hardly any material with which to compare the results available for the last decade of the war, and in many cases there is no material for the pre-war period, though the work by Josef Petráň represents a significant step forward.

The *Papers of Ottavio Piccolomini in the State Archive at Zámrsk* represent the most important collection because Piccolomini was the key figure in the Habsburg Austro-Spanish coalition in the last period of the Thirty Years' War. Sections IX and X ('The Conclusion of the Peace, The Nuremberg Tracts', 'Militaria 1646–48', nos. 28,012 to 29,729) are the most important for this period. Here are copies of the correspondence of Ferdinand III with his ambassadors (particularly Francesco di Caretto at Madrid and the envoys at Münster), drafts of Piccolomini's letters to the Emperor, reports of the progress of the negotiations at Nuremberg (1649–50). In subsection B are reports of the negotiations at Münster and of the ratification of the Peace Treaty (1649), correspondence with Leopold Wilhelm and with several others, some of them leading figures, others less prominent. Section X contains Ottavio's correspondence with Ferdinand III from 1649 concerning the organization of the Imperial army, particularly that part which became the permanent standing army. There is also correspondence with the Court War Council.

Also important are section VI (the background of the Westphalian negotiations, reports of the Hispano-Dutch separate peace of January 1648, reports on the Fronde and on English affairs, etc.); section VII (negotiations for a Spanish commission, reports of the great battles at the end of the war, correspondence with the Emperor and with several others in 1648); sections XVI–XIX (correspondence with English royalists, with Philip IV of Spain from Brussels), and finally sections XLII (Spanish affairs to 1650) and XLVIII ('Handwritten and Printed

Reports: Footnotes to the Thirty Years' War'). One example of how this material can be used will be found below.[32]

The correspondence of Heinrich Schlick in the *Schlick Family Archive* (State Archive at Zámrsk) also contains material relevant to the study of the peace negotiations. Most of the sections in this collection, which have been described earlier, extend to the year 1648 and some of them to 1650.[33]

The so-called *Military Chancery of Mathias Gallas* (State Archive at Litoměřice, branch at Děčín) extends to April 1647. For the period 1644–7 there are fifteen boxes with about 2,500 documents. Particularly important is section XIX (17–20) containing Gallas' papers collected at his death; they include information about his plundering expeditions to Italy in search of works of art.

The series 'Letters from the Imperial Army' in the papers of Wenceslas Eusebius Lobkowitz (*Lobkowicz Family Archive*, State Archive at Litoměřice, branch at Žitenice) extends to the year 1650.

For the last years of the war the collection 'Autographs II', of the *Waldstein Family Archive* (State Archive at Prague, branch at Mnichovo Hradiště) contains letters of H. L. Kufstein from Turkey, as well as letters of K. P. von Liechtenstein, Ferdinand III, Ottavio Piccolomini, and L. Torstenson, which, however, are important primarily as supplements to other collections. The chief importance of these collections lies in the earlier period – at least this must be the provisional conclusion until the collections are reorganized.

The *Nostitz-Rieneck Family Archive* (State Archive at Pilsen, branch at Žlutice) contains imperial papers (EE 2), propaganda pamphlets (HH 2), cameral affairs (LL 2) and military affairs (SS 1), which extend to the end of the 1640s.

The 'Smečno Transcripts' in the *Martinic Manuscript Collection* (State Archive at Prague, branch at Křivoklát) contain, under numbers 110, 113 and 119, some interesting documents from the last phase of the conflict, particularly from the year 1643. Number 110 includes papers concerning the renewal of the high offices of the Kingdom of Bohemia, accomplished on the initiative of Vilém Slavata and Jaroslav Bořita of Martinic. Number 113 (*Copiale rerum notatu dignarum*) contains reports from Prague from 1643 written by Freissleben, copies of the Italian correspondence of Bohemian noblemen from 1644, and copies of diplomatic correspondence – for example the letter of the Dutch States General to Queen Christina of Sweden in January 1644. Number 119 (*Quodlibet in lingua germanica et latina*) contains copies of pamphlets (for instance on the death of Richelieu), peace plans from

1643, and important papers from the Münster negotiations in April 1644. These volumes of transcripts are apparently fragments of the Martinic Archive which was for the most part destroyed during the Swedish attack on the Lesser Town of Prague in 1648. The rest of the archive was destroyed when the Martinic palace in Hradčany burned down in 1676. The papers of the defenestrated Jaroslav Bořita of Martinic have thus only survived in the correspondence of others.[34]

The *Schwarzenberg Family Archive* (State Archive at Třeboň, branch at Český Krumlov) contains diplomatic and military correspondence of several members of the family. Georg Ludwig von Schwarzenberg was the organizer of the military frontier against the Turks (nos. 285–7), and he recruited the Croatian light cavalry for the Imperial Army (no. 286). In his correspondence with his secretary J. Walther there is important information about the negotiations at Münster and Osnabrück in 1645–6 (no. 287).

But of greater significance are the papers of Johann Adolf I von Schwarzenberg, from 1645–1661 the High Chamberlain to the Archduke Leopold Wilhelm, who from 1647 to 1652 was governor in the Spanish Netherlands. Johann Adolf mediated in the quarrels between Leopold Wilhelm and his brother Ferdinand III (no. 355), and he also managed the court at Brussels (no. 356). He gathered information about the persons associated with the court, about officials and pages ('Beschreibung der span. Niederlände, 1647'). His diplomatic correspondence is very important, particularly that with Maximilian of Bavaria concerning the negotiations at Münster and Osnabrück (no. 363), and with Ferdinand IV, King of Hungary (1648, no. 366).

Here is also Johann Adolf's correspondence with Imperial generals and diplomats, which is arranged alphabetically. From the period around 1648 there are letters of W. Leslie, Khevenhüller, Count Caprara, Franz Fürstenberg, J. M. Lamberg, Johann Werth (nos. 367 and 368). Other important correspondence is from de Brun, the Spanish Ambassador at Münster and later at The Hague (1647–50, no. 369); from Francesco di Caretto, the Imperial Ambassador at Madrid (1647–50, nos. 369–70), with reports from Spain, the Netherlands and France. Other letters are from the Spanish correspondent Count Fuensaldaña, the Marquis de Lede, and Andrés de Andrade (containing information about Catalonia) (1647ff, no. 370). The correspondence in the section 'Histories' (no. 374) contains reports of the peace negotiations in the Westphalian cities in 1647.

The papers of Maximilian von Trautmannsdorf, on the other hand, have only been partially preserved in the *Trautmannsdorf Family*

Archive (State Archive at Pilsen, branch at Klatovy); and the collection is more valuable for the second half of the seventeenth century. Other Trautmannsdorf papers are in the Family Archive at Zámrsk, and in several collections of correspondence in other archives.

Among the Moravian collections two deserve particular notice: the *Magnis Family Archive* (State Archive at Brno), which continues to 1649; and the *Belrupt Family Archive* (State Archive at Opava, branch at Janovice). Sources for the history of Olomouc in the period of the Swedish occupation are scattered in the artificial 'Dudík Collection' of the District and Municipal Archives of Olomouc.

Slovak collections for the period are partly in family archives and partly in district and municipal archives. The State Central Archive at Bratislava contains some fragmentary material in the *Erdödy Family Archive*, and pro-Habsburg documents in the *Esterházy Family Archive* (with reports of noble resistance and uprisings, particularly that of George Rákóczy; reports of Daniel Esterházy on the defence of the Turkish frontier in 1642–5; and personal papers of Colonel Johann Esterházy from 1637). The *Pálffy Family Archive* contains the papers of the Palatine Paul Pálffy (d. 1653), and the *Révay* and the *Zay Family Archives* contain miscellaneous information about political affairs (both families belonged to the Estates' opposition).

The State Archive at Bratislava contains the correspondence of the Illésházy family. The State Archive at Banská Bystrica, branch at Bytča contains the Koháry and Thurzo family papers. The State Archive at Košice, branches at Levoča and Prešov, contain the family archives of Andrássy, Csáky, Horváth-Stansith, Drugeth of Humenné and others.[35]

These collections form quite a good basis for the study of the links between the Estates' opposition to the Habsburgs – particularly that of George Rákóczy – and the Turkish Wars. This material is complemented by documents from the various district archives in Slovakia and from such rich municipal archives as those at Bratislava, Kremnica, Banská Bystrica and Levoča.[36]

BOHEMIAN SOURCES FOR THE HISTORY OF THE NEAPOLITAN UPRISING, 1647–8

The arms of Amalfi, which are placed over the gate of the castle at Náchod remind us not only that Ottavio Piccolomini was Duke of Amalfi from 1639, but also that throughout the seventeenth century and into the eighteenth there existed quite close relations between

Bohemia and the Kingdom of the Two Sicilies. These were manifested in many ways. Among them is the fact that after 1635 Mathias Gallas was not only lord of Friedland in Bohemia but also of the Duchy of Lucera, and that his nephew Johann Wenzel Gallas served as Viceroy of Naples, as did Cardinal Schrattenbach Bishop of Olomouc and Count T. A. R. Harrach of Prague. Finally, many traces of Neapolitan influence have survived in the Bishops' Palace at Kroměříž and in the Clam-Gallas Palace in Prague.[37] The connections between Bohemia and Naples are also evident in extant written records: a small part of this material enables us to trace a picture of the social and political crisis that Naples experienced in 1647–8 – the crisis which is usually called Masaniello's Rebellion. The Bohemian sources enable us to correct some details of the traditional interpretation of this event.[38]

The manifestoes issued by the 'most faithful Neapolitan people' in 1647 and 1648 usually portray the poverty brought upon the people by the war. Their standard of living declined in proportion to the warlike spirit of the Viceroy Osuna, whose policies led to an increase in direct as well as indirect taxes, which bore most heavily on the poorest. Fiscalism was and is pointed out as the cause of inflation, poverty, unemployment, prostitution, and banditry. The resulting unease found a target in the Spanish government, but also in the Neapolitan barons – and the result was the uprising in 1622 which was brutally crushed by the Viceroy Zapata, Osuna's successor.[39]

Osuna's fall at the end of 1620 meant an extension of the power of the barons, who until 1642 at least in theory shared power with the Viceroy. It led to the persecution and arrest of several of Osuna's domestic advisers from the ranks of the anti-baronial opposition which included the future adviser of Masaniello, Genoino. The entry of Spain into the Mantuan War meant not only the beginning of the brief 'Italian' period of the Thirty Years' War, but also a further worsening of the situation in Naples. For it was Naples which in 1619–20 during the Bohemian campaign, and now together with Milan, bore the financial burden of the conflict and, what was equally important, provided the human material for the Spanish armies.[40]

Of all the Neapolitan mercenaries who served in Bohemia or elsewhere in Europe, only a few were able to make brilliant careers for themselves. The coincidence between the policies of the Austrian and Spanish branches of the Habsburg family only enabled the magnates, such as Piccolomini or Gallas, to acquire property and profit in central and southern Europe.[41] To central Europeans Mediterranean Europe had so far been no more than an enchanted land of high culture, containing a compelling pattern of Catholic–Humanist conceptions of life. This attraction is evinced in the decoration of one of the salons of the Waldstein castle at Mnichovo Hradiště, and also in the collection of the Waldstein Library. The pamphlets and reports at Mnichovo Hradiště, together with the papers of Wallenstein's protégé Piccolomini, form the documentary basis for the study of the Neapolitan uprising of 1647, whose leader is traditionally said to be one Tommaso Aniello Amalfitano, or Masaniello, the son of the fisherman Cino of Amalfi.[42]

In his stimulating book about the Italian south G. Pepe has traced the changing picture of Masaniello's uprising in Italian historiography.[43] In the period of the risorgimento it was generally assessed positively, and Masaniello's character was portrayed sympathetically. Later the sympathy began to evaporate; shadows were discovered in the portrait; the importance of the popular movement receded before evidence of anti-Spanish intrigues by France and Savoy. The popular survey by L. Salvatorelli presents the events of 1647–8 as the actions of 'the people', led, however, by Genoino and others. Elsewhere there is talk of a Neapolitan 'sotto-proletariato', or of 'rabble, thieves, mobs' (*popolo*, *popolaccio*, *popolino*, etc.).[44]

The history of the Neapolitan uprising of 1647–8 takes on new meaning when it is considered in connection with a general view of the history of the seventeenth century. It was not simply by chance that Marx interested himself in this episode – one of the six 'contemporaneous revolutions' which shook nearly the entire European continent in the middle of the seventeenth century.[45] Therefore it is important to explain the relationship between the popular uprising and the politics of the great powers. The Neapolitan uprising recedes of course before the uprising in Catalonia and Portugal in 1640. Olivares' successor, his nephew Don Luis de Haro, faced catastrophe. One road led to peace negotiations. Intervention in central Europe was phased out after 1644, finally coming to an end with the separate peace concluded with the Netherlands in January of 1648. In October 1647, twenty years after the state bankruptcy of 1627, that phenomenon was repeated which was usually termed euphemistically 'consolidation of the liquid public debt'; crises still occurred in 1652 and 1662. Step by step Spain was pressed to the realization that the United Netherlands were now independent, as was Portugal, and finally that there would have to be a separate administration for Catalonia. The trouble in Naples and Sicily, coming so closely on the heels of all this, meant the peak of the crisis for the Spanish monarchy. It is no wonder, therefore, that French policy was to use this critical situation to attain a final triumph.[46]

Beside this chief problem there stands another which is far more complex. This is the problem of the social psychology of the Neapolitan masses, and, in the final analysis, of individual psychology, necessary for an understanding of Masaniello's behaviour during the last days of his life. Too few source materials however have survived to answer these questions.

As far as can be ascertained, the uprising of 1647 had nothing in common with preceding revolts, for example that of 1636 which was provoked by French and Savoyard intrigue. On the contrary, all the testimony indicates that the cause of the uprising was unutterable poverty, intensified by the fiscal policies of the Spanish Viceroy d'Arcos. In December 1646, d'Arcos decreed some new taxes (*gabella, balzelli*), of which that on the sale of fruit weighed particularly upon the poorest part of the population, mainly dependent upon fruit and fish. Later Spanish allegations that the uprising was the work of conspirators cannot be proved; they were manufactured for the usual reasons – to exaggerate the extent of the danger and inflate the significance of the saviours of order. The events began spontaneously. One night, at the beginning of June 1647, the offices of the tax collectors in the Neapolitan *Mercato* were destroyed by fire, and Tommaso Aniello Masaniello, then about twenty-seven-years old, a fishmonger's assistant, gathered together some young people who were not content to express their outrage only by shouting *senza gabella.*[47] It was the Naples administration that had to answer for the outbreak of violence, and it is therefore no wonder that at first the Spanish officials tended to minimize the seriousness of the situation. On Sunday 7 July 1647 fighting broke out between the shopkeepers and merchants on the one hand and the tax collectors on the other. The incident began with the throwing of ripe and over-ripe figs, but when Masaniello appeared on horseback in the midst of the crowd it became a demonstration. He had had previous trouble with the authorities and had spent some time in prison. To the sound of the bells of the nearby Carmine monastery, which soon became the headquarters of the rebellion, the conflict spread, and the officials of the Viceroy's government soon found it prudent to seal off the whole quarter.

In any case, it appeared that the uprising was not at all directed against the Spaniards, for the crowd kept shouting 'No taxes, long live the King of Spain, down with bad government!' ('Non vogliamo la gabella, viva il rè di Spagna, mora il malgoverno'). On 8 July the

Archbishop of Naples Cardinal Filomarino wrote to the Pope, who had previously served as Nuncio in Naples and who continued to interest himself in the affairs of the city, that 'the whole city has taken up arms', and that it was still too early to tell what would develop from the revolt. The policy of the Curia towards Spain at this time was one of neutrality; but of course it could have no objection to any affair which would tie the Spaniards' hands even tighter.[48]

In a letter written on 12 July Filomarino, who was of bourgeois background and disliked the Spaniards as much as the Neapolitan barons, gave a valuable analysis of further developments. The unrest which began on Sunday had spread and intensified to the point that the Viceroy sent two representatives who were 'buon affetti al popolo' to meet the crowds, who were 'in all ways highly excited'. However both of them, the Duke of Madelino and the prior of a monastery, were received so poorly that they 'nearly fled'. On the night of 8 July several fires broke out in the city, testifying to the people's revenge upon the property of the tax collectors and more generally upon the pillars of the established régime.

Filomarino emphasized that there had not been widespread destruction or looting, and for this he gave credit to Masaniello who he said had

> such authority and power to command and at the same time commands such respect and obedience that the whole city is under his spell. His orders are carried out by his followers with all precision and thoroughness. In a word, he has become king in this city, and moreover the most glorious one that ever ruled in the world. He wore nothing more than a shirt and trousers of white linen; in the manner of fishermen he went barefoot and bareheaded.[49]

Here Filomarino made no attempt to conceal his sympathy, but there is other testimony in favour of Masaniello. The historian Schipa, who regards Masaniello with equal sympathy, points to the part played by those who surrounded him, particularly Genoino. G. Pepe cites the pro-Spanish chronicler who emphasized that Masaniello's entourage included more than one patrician ('di condizione onorata') who had taken the part of the people out of hatred of the Spaniards, the counsellors of the Viceroy, or the native barons. The Neapolitan physician Donzelli, also cited by Pepe, came from the same educated bourgeois background as Genoino. In his dramatic portrayal of the uprising he, too, described how Masaniello prevented the people from burning the 'traitors who have shed our blood', so that only their dwellings were put to the torch.

At some time on Monday Cardinal Filomarino himself intervened. He rejected the idea of sending a nobleman as his representative to Masaniello, 'for the people were highly suspicious of the nobility'. Instead he sent the popular preacher Frà Francesco. Frà Francesco and the Cardinal presented the people's petitions to the Viceroy, who received them in silence. Substantially they amounted to the request that the freedoms – real and imagined – that had been granted by the Emperor Charles V be exercised in public life. 'On Tuesday morning [9 July] the elders of the city [*eletti*] brought to the people the *privilegia* and placed them in the Carmine monastery for safe-keeping.' The Cardinal, too, was willing to support the 'defence of liberty' and appeared personally at the 'Office of the People' (*Castro del Popolo*).[50] During the day the Viceroy issued several decrees designed to appease the populace, and on the night of 9 July there were only isolated instances of violence.

In the meantime, of course, Masaniello and his followers became aware that in fact the Viceroy had promised them nothing concrete, and they drew up a new list of demands. Again Filomarino acted as mediator between the two sides, 'and on Wednesday morning [10 July] he achieved an agreement between the Viceroy and his Council [*Collaterale*] and the people', which was solemnly confirmed by a religious service.

But the Viceroy's entourage was not satisfied. The Duke of Madelino, whom the people had refused to accept as an intermediary, and also a number of other noblemen (among them Don Giuseppe Caraffa, one of the family so prominent in post-Rebellion Bohemia) urged that the uprising be crushed by force, and they suggested that this could be achieved most easily by the assassination of its leader Masaniello. According to Filomarino the nobleman invited 200 bandits into the city and entrusted to them the job of murdering the 'head of the people'. But the plan failed: on 10 July the bandits, along with Don Giuseppe Caraffa, were wiped out: 'The number of corpses was so great that it inspired terror. But it is necessary to remember that in spite of the great numbers killed, there was none among them who died guiltless.'[51]

The night of Thursday 11 July was again very uneasy. The wrath of the people turned against the nobles. Filomarino estimated that hundreds of thousands of people were armed. Since the entire population of the city was scarcely 100,000 this is an obvious exaggeration. But the threat of violence was sufficient to ensure that the last of the Spanish soldiers were removed from the city and that banditry was suppressed. Meanwhile, with the help of Filomarino and on the advice of Genoino, Masaniello continued to apply pressure on the Viceroy. When rumours that the bandits had poisoned the water supply were disproved, and when Genoese war galleys that had appeared in the harbour were neutralized, a list of twenty-three articles was agreed upon in which the Viceroy guaranteed certain 'liberties' of the Neapolitan people. In essence the specific demands of the urban population were recognized, though there was no mention of demands from the people of the Neapolitan countryside and towns.[52]

On Friday 12 July, with the election of a 'new *eletto*, called by the will of the people', Masaniello reached the pinnacle of his success. But at the same time his fall was being prepared. He became the 'Captain-General of the most faithful Neapolitan people' (*Capitano generale del fedelissimo popolo*) and was driven in solemn procession in the Viceroy's carriage, accompanied by the armed popular militia and amid the cheers of the people, to the Viceroy's palace.[53] Almost immediately he returned to his lodging in the popular quarter, but the peace, whose renewal was praised by Filomarino in a letter to Rome written that day, was not to last long.

Masaniello's relations with the great lords aroused mistrust among many of his followers. Those who concluded that he had served his function and could now be disposed of knew how to use this mistrust. The solemn parade through the city was enough to spread the rumour that Masaniello, 'who earlier had hated honours, treasure and grandeur, had become proud and ambitious'. In his second letter to Innocent X written on 16 July Filomarino, who had stood behind the tribune of the people until now, wrote that Masaniello had 'lost his former quality of deliberation, his judgement and his temperance, and has acquired such a self-willed daring and tyranny that nobody could be sure of him, neither the people nor his followers; therefore this morning he was killed and his head cut off'.[54] Donzelli, who had been closer to Masaniello, wrote that 'the people, led by their suspicion, saw signs of betrayal in everything' – they feared that Masaniello, too, would betray them. Filomarino himself unwittingly contributed to the rift between Masaniello and the people. It seems that stories of the near insanity displayed by the leader of the people prompted Masaniello's followers among the bourgeoisie (such as Genoino) to action. If we look for reports of the symptoms of this madness we can find little reliable testimony, certainly not enough for even a perfunctory diagnosis of mental imbalance. If Masaniello feared for his safety after he had so narrowly escaped one assassination attempt, his behaviour appears perfectly normal. True, he did give one order which was ill-considered. This was when he decreed that the weight of loaves of bread should be increased without making certain that there were sufficient stores of grain. But if this were sufficient indication of insanity, all the psychiatric clinics in the world would be unable to accommodate the politicians.

The symptoms of Masaniello's 'insanity', then, are so vague that at most we can speak of some mental stress, or perhaps neurosis, which of course remained constant and therefore could have become worse. But the period from 12 to 16 July is too brief and too poorly documented for us to come to any conclusion at all.

Masaniello's 'friends' at first, apparently, tried to get rid of the 'mad' Masaniello without bloodshed. However, when he escaped from prison he was killed – it seems by conspirators in the service of Spain. But the blame for his death must be borne by those who allowed it to happen. The people, who had permitted their tribune to fall because they suspected that he had gone over to the side of their oppressors, now demonstrated such loyalty to him that the conspirators, who at first had thrown his body in a dust-heap, now found it expedient to placate the rising storm. Masaniello's body was carried to the Carmine monastery and buried 'with flags tilted towards the earth, and to the sound of muffled drums; the body was accompanied by 30,000 armed men and 10,000 women'.

With Masaniello's death the Neapolitan uprising entered a new phase. Genoino and his followers came to power, and they reached an agreement with the Viceroy. But in August 1647 there were new outbreaks of violence, and Genoino, whose fall the Viceroy did nothing to prevent, died as a prisoner on the way to Spain where he was to be tried as a rebel.[55] The new 'Generalissimo of the people', the Prince di Massa, tried to follow a pro-Spanish line, but by October this course had lost all its attractiveness. Di Massa tried in vain to turn the popular resentment against the barons. The Spanish offer of collaboration addressed to the patriciate was refused, and the 'Generalissimo of the people' was killed in a new wave of violence.[56] Under a red and black flag the people of Naples rose against the Spaniards, and on 22 October 1647 a new leader, a gunsmith named Gennaro Annese, proclaimed a republic. Of course, it was a republic in which the barons gradually rose to power alongside the bourgeoisie; they emphasized the anti-Spanish character of a régime which was to ensure their privileges and their feudal pre-eminence.

The pamphlet literature of the period now began to emphasize that the people could be led (today we might say 'manipulated') and that the leadership of the republic belonged rightfully to the nobility. It was only the bourgeois republicans who wished to turn to the Netherlands and Venice, Catalonia and Portugal, for aid against the Spaniards.[57] But the influence of France became ever more prominent. Mazarin, in spite of his domestic troubles, was willing to follow Richelieu's example and make full use of the difficulties facing the Spanish enemy. At first the French considered supporting the attempts by Prince Thomas of Savoy to seize control of Naples. But the situation was complicated by the appearance in Naples of another pretender, Henry of Lorraine, Duke of Guise, who also was successfully elected 'Duke of the Republic' (24 December 1647).

In the beginning of 1648 the Neapolitan Republic was a painful thorn in the side of the Spanish monarchy. But by now only a few individuals, among them Gennaro Annese, connected it with Masaniello's popular movement. The Spaniards, who continued to hold their citadels on Neapolitan soil naturally had no intention of giving up Naples. As d'Arcos' successor the Spaniards took care not to send an unknown and untried figure (though they were running short of capable men): they sent the Count d'Oñate, formerly Spanish Ambassador in Prague and Vienna, the man who had brought about Wallenstein's fall. Oñate arrived with a fleet whose commander was the illegitimate son of Philip IV, Don Juan José d'Austria. He was able to make good use of the popular opposition to the barons who had become supporters of the Guise régime. Guise himself lasted until February 1648; in the meantime he tried unsuccessfully to make use of an uprising in Palermo and to obtain help for his government from the papal Curia.[58]

After concluding a secret agreement with the Spaniards, Gennaro Annese overthrew Henry of Guise in February 1648. Before long, however, he realized that Oñate had no intention of respecting the 'liberties' of the Neapolitan people. His attempt to drive out the Spaniards, this time with French help, ended in failure, and he was killed in the struggle.[59]

Thus the Spaniards once more controlled Naples – actually without even having to make a very great show of strength. This was not only because Mazarin, whose own government was threatened by the disaffection of a wide segment of the populace, hesitated to involve himself too deeply in Italian affairs just as the war in Germany was coming to an end. He had several other irons in the fire to use against Spain: there were Catalonia and Portugal, and he had recently heard of preparations for a revolution in Aragon. But the anti-Spanish uprising in Naples was doomed so long as its social basis was limited to the nobility. After Masaniello's death it became the affair of a small group of Neapolitan bourgeoisie and bourgeois intelligentsia who followed their own aims and used the support of the people only when they needed it.

Among the people there arose opposition not only to the barons and the Spaniards, but also against the self-styled 'saviours' from France and against their own unsuccessful leaders. In a bitter satire entitled 'Pluto's antechamber: on the Revolution in Naples' ('Anticamera di Plutone sopra le Rivoluzioni di Napoli') there appear representatives of all the various interests which we have seen at work. There are the Duke of Osuna and Don 'Pepe' Caraffa, as well as Tommaso Aniello Masaniello.[60] And it is he who concludes the meeting at which each is made to reveal his real plans and aims. Masaniello ironically thanks them for their 'love' for the Neapolitan people and promises to explain to the people how brutally they were duped and what lessons they might learn from the whole affair.

PART TWO

THE EFFECTS OF THE THIRTY YEARS' WAR

8

The aftermath of conflict

The general exhaustion of all the participants in the conflict made the compromises and partial peace treaties of 1648 a necessity. But two parts of the European conflict – those between France and Spain and between Sweden and Poland – were not resolved at this time: they prolonged the general political crisis until 1660. With the Turkish danger still looming on the horizon, the Habsburgs had to reconcile themselves to the impracticability of their far-reaching plans.

The programme of feudal and Catholic restoration could therefore be forced through only in certain regions – those very regions in which the conflict had started, the Bohemian lands and (partially, at least) Upper Hungary. For these regions, and for most of Germany as well, the Thirty Years' War meant retrogression. In the west and north of Europe – although even there the suffering caused by the war was immense – the social changes which were speeded up by the conflict left the way open for unprecedented progress.[1]

It is not easy to state just what the Thirty Years' War did mean to Europe as a whole, or even to its different parts.

Generalizations about this 'pre-statistical' age are always risky.[2] The case of Bohemia and Moravia shows that any methods of investigation that are adequate must also be complicated; even so they provide us with information that is of uneven value at best. With appropriate caution we can say that the loss in population was not made good in central Europe until the beginning of the eighteenth century. The economic optimism of the sixteenth century still lingered on in the middle of the seventeenth century, but economic life revived fully only after 1700.[3]

If the havoc wrought by the war was serious, the changes which were prepared by its termination were even worse. If we can hardly speak of the introduction of a 'second serfdom' in central Europe (the situation was different in Hungary and Poland even before the war began), the regression is nevertheless clearly documented for the Bohemian lands and for Lower and Upper Austria. The Bohemian Peasant War in 1680 marks a watershed: at least some of the 'servile' methods of exploitation had to be abandoned soon afterwards, since they clearly involved too many risks and in the long run were economically unprofitable.[4]

It is more difficult to come to a conclusion for the whole of central Europe. A uniform 'Germany' did not exist; and even in the Austrian provinces the differences were enormous. Nevertheless, a few characteristic features do emerge for Europe as a whole. The war did not fundamentally alter the supremacy of Dutch and English commerce in some branches and in some areas; it even helped to strengthen it by stages. Italy and her economy, by contrast, remained depressed for a long period.

The impact of the conflict in the realm of thought and the arts remains a fascinating subject. The conflict of ideas was clearly evident long before the war. The prewar type of humanist culture, imbued with the ideas of the Reformation, gave way to the beginnings of the Enlightenment in western Europe. Even when 'Baroque' thought prevailed formally in central Europe, its frontiers were by no means rigid, as can be seen in the work of Jan Amos Comenius.[5]

In the arts, the Mannerism which had flourished in Prague around the beginning of the seventeenth century vanished. The Baroque, although its origins were Italian and Spanish, was not originally bound to either religious denomination. In Bohemia, it achieved its typical expression only during the 1630s and 1640s, when the local brand of realism, present in the Mannerist tradition, became one with the influence of northern Italy. The contradictions between Baroque and Classicism only showed up later, making their appearance especially in the lands that had belonged to the anti-Habsburg camp.[6]

We can certainly agree with the view that the Thirty Years' War has remained one of the burning problems of European civilization for the last three centuries. The historians of the seventeenth century provide us anew with a starting point for a modern kind of research. The liberal historiography of the nineteenth and early twentieth centuries was much more distant from the conflicts than we can now afford to be. The role of religion – the 'nationalism' of the sixteenth century, as Lewis Namier put it – was underestimated and its close relations with politics and economics were forgotten.[7]

Where contemporaries saw only events governed by providence or by fortune, we can try to assess 'what really happened' and especially why it happened. We still do not know enough about how the war and its far-reaching results affected the lives of the common people. We can follow the traces of hunger, plague, the great 'dying-off' all over Europe. The transformations that European society underwent during these thirty years of open conflict between two conceptions of civilization were enormous. By the 1650s it was clear that neither the Spanish nor the Dutch model was victorious. Meanwhile England, separated from the Continent but never completely severed from it, was trying to solve in her own way the inherent inner contradictions which existed in her political and social situation. Imperial Spain was moribund and France in ascendancy. New conceptions of life and society were emerging; and one painful, even 'traumatic', period of transition was over.

9

Changes in the composition of the Bohemian nobility

In recent years a good deal of attention has been given the problems of the nobility in early modern Europe: what changes did this dominant element in the 'Estates' community' undergo in various parts of Europe in this period of transition from feudalism to capitalism? The larger themes of the period, including the questions of the origin of absolutism, the class structure of society, and the nature of class tensions within society, have recently formed the subjects of two conferences. One, held at Moscow in 1966, was devoted to 'theoretical and historiographical problems in the rise of capitalism'. The other, at Paris in 1968, considered problems of social stratification.[1] At the Moscow conference A. N. Chistozvonov pointed to the need for further study of social changes in Austria, Prussia and Spain, while at Paris Roland Mousnier found among his colleagues only one who was concerned with these phenomena in central Europe: F. L. Carsten, whose contribution dealt with Brandenburg and Prussia in the sixteenth and seventeenth centuries.

A general treatment of developments in the Habsburg lands has been provided by Victor L. Tapié in his chapter in the fourth volume of the *New Cambridge Modern History*.[2] Here his authority for Bohemia was Otto Placht, whose conclusions he accepted quite uncritically, in spite of the serious difficulties that are described in the introduction to Placht's volume. The same source appears again in Tapié's book on the peoples of the Danube basin.[3] Tapié has used Placht's information about the decrease in numbers of the Czech 'nobility' (900 knightly families in the year 1557 had declined to 460 in 1615, and of them only 238 remained by the reign of Leopold; the number of baronial families dropped in the same period from sixty-nine to twenty) to explain the significance of the influx of foreign noblemen into Bohemia and to emphasize the importance of the 'new nationalism' among the Bohemian nobility in the seventeenth century.[4]

Finally the example of Bohemia and the decline suffered by her population (including the nobility) as a result of the Thirty Years' War is reviewed by Henry Kamen in his book *The Iron Century*.[5] Here the source is the book by Eduard Winter.

In all these studies, of course, the structural changes in Bohemian society and its nobility have been given only cursory attention. But the work done by Lawrence Stone and Pierre Goubert has shown that this kind of problem can be dealt with in more detail, by using complex methods and analysing large quantities of data.[6] This kind of approach, unfortunately, is lacking in the most recent contribution to the study of the central European nobility: Jean Meyer's paper read at the International Congress at Moscow in 1970.[7] His basic mistake here was to equate 'Central Europe' with 'Germany', with the result that in his own study he accepted uncritically the work of German historians, in particular Hellmuth Rössler's two volumes on the German nobility. The only other source of information about Bohemian conditions appears to be the books by Tapié mentioned above, together with his *Baroque and Classicism*, which in its time was sharply criticized by P. Francastel.[8]

Meyer argues that the nobility in central Europe suffered from internal contradictions which exploded on the eve of the Thirty Years' War. The immediate trigger for the war was a threat to the material interests of the Bohemian Protestant nobility. The Protestant noblemen had outstripped their Catholic counterparts in the field of economic activity, and with their defeat and expulsion the land was deprived of its economically most dynamic elements. But like Tapié, Meyer does not conclude that the Habsburgs were entirely successful in liquidating the old Bohemian nobility, although according to him only a fifth of the old Protestant Bohemian families survived in the decade 1630–40. He points out, however, that it is impossible to discover the size of the emigration, and therefore its concrete results cannot be estimated.[9]

Meyer believes that this question is an important one not only for the history of Bohemia; the Battle of the White Mountain was a setback for the whole of the Protestant camp, and therefore for the economically 'dynamic' sections of society in all of central Europe. The Thirty Years' War meant a 'renewal' for the nobility, chiefly German, which was of significance for all of eastern Europe in the seventeenth and eighteenth centuries. But to what extent did the 'old nobility' survive the Thirty Years' War, and how large was the rôle of the 'new nobility' in this period which was certainly one of 'refeudalization'?[10]

We believe that these questions can now begin to be answered, provided that the historian does not allow himself to be blinded by certain individual phenomena nor to forget that the nobility formed only a part of the structure of society in the sixteenth and seventeenth centuries. At the same time it is important, when dealing with a 'pre-statistical' age, to proceed far more cautiously and critically than did for example Otto Placht. It is also necessary to re-examine some of the older theses that have persisted about Bohemian society – for instance the idea, incorporated also in Placht's work, of the 'dying out' of the Bohemian nobility at the end of the sixteenth century, which was explored more than a century ago by A. V. Šembera and as recently as fifteen years ago by Karel Stloukal. It is true that several families became extinct at this time – the Boskovices, the barons of Hradec, and the Rožmberks were the most prominent; they were joined by the Šelnberks, Hasištejnský-Lobkowitzes, Krajířes and several others. But it is important to consider also that all of them continued to exist on the distaff side, so that for example the Švamberk family became the heirs of the Rožmberks, the Lobkowitz of the Pernštejns, Liechtenstein of the Boskovices, Slavata of the barons of Hradec, and so forth. The most recent contribution to the study of this phenomenon among the Bohemian nobility is a demographic survey by Jaroslav Honc of the 125 baronial families which were in existence in the year 1502.[11] One limitation of this kind of study, of course, is that in focusing entirely on the baronial Estate as it existed at a given point in time, the evolution of the social class itself is lost sight of. In this way Honc's work has served to perpetuate a number of earlier misconceptions. But there are three important questions that are only touched upon in Honc's study: 1. What can be done to establish the composition of the 'ruling class' of the old Bohemian state, that is the nobility in both its Estates, the baronial and the knightly? 2. Was the confiscation of landed property from the nobility and their subsequent emigration a direct result of their 'crimes' and 'punishment' – in other words, of their political activities between 1618 and 1620? 3. What changes took place in the composition of the Bohemian nobility between 1620 (the defeat of the Rebellion) and 1656 (the compilation of the first comprehensive land survey after the Battle of the White Mountain)?

Most of the work on social and economic problems by Czech historians appearing in the last twenty-five years has made at least some mention of the character of the Bohemian nobility. It is clear, however, that the tax records, upon which most of this work has relied, are neither complete nor entirely reliable.[12] At the same time, most historians have shown a tendency to try to generalize from the reports or impressions of contemporary writers – particularly Václav Březan, Pavel Skála ze Zhoře, and Pavel Stránský.

Until now the consensus has been that the sixteenth century saw but little change in the composition of the Bohemian nobility, with the exception of the ennoblement policies of Rudolph II, which were necessitated by that ruler's financial difficulties, and the 'dying out' of the old noble families, mentioned above, at the end of the century. Jaroslav Honc's analysis of the genealogies of the 125 families that he studied reveals that the male line survived intact for an average of five generations. Some of the families, of course, disappeared sooner, others survived much longer, but the result coincides quite well with that obtained by Perroy's analysis of the French nobility of Forez in an earlier age.[13]

The question of Rudolph II's influence on the numbers of the Bohemian noble class may be studied quite conveniently, thanks to the interest of the Moravian magnate Karel of Žerotín in the Habsburgs' ennoblement policies. Žerotín commissioned an index or *Extrakt* of all incolats registered in the *Tabulae regni* (*Desky zemské*, *Landtafel*) between 1544 and 1615.[14] The *Extrakt* is quite a reliable compilation, made probably at the end of 1615, and a valuable aid to the study of the nobility. Certainly it is more convenient than the individual volumes of the *Tabulae regni* themselves, all of whose entries, whatever their nature, are arranged chronologically. A nineteenth-century index of incolats (the *Incolatio*), however, affords a survey of the later period. Žerotín's register contains the text of the regulations governing the granting of the incolat, the formula for the 'oath to the Land' (*přísaha k zemi*), and a chronological list, arranged according to individual years and sessions of the Diet, of the new members of the Estates' community. These are divided into three categories: 'inhabitants' (*obyvatel země*), who were usually foreign, non-Bohemian noblemen, or else non-noble Bohemians who wished to acquire feudal landed property; the knights (*rytíři*, *Ritter*, *Milites*); and the barons (*páni*, *Herren*, *barones regni*). The entries are distributed as follows:

	Inhabitants	*Knights*	*Barons*	*Total*
1542–50	8	42	5	55
1551–60	15	71	4	90
1561–70	27	41	7	75
1571–80	46	27	4	77
1581–90	48	28	3	79

	Inhabitants	*Knights*	*Barons*	*Total*
1591–1600	57	29	4	90
1601–10	56	14	18	88
1611–15	16	–	8	24

Together there are 529 entries, including 53 new baronial and 228 new knightly families. For the 'inhabitants', it was usually merely a question of time before they were accepted into one of the legal noble Estates. The numbers of 'new' noble families are relatively high, as can be appreciated from a comparison with the figures for the total noble population obtained from the tax records for 1557, 1603, and 1615:[15]

	1557	*1603*	*1615*
Families in the baronial Estate	184	216	197
Families in the knightly Estate	1,438	1,131	977

If, between 1542 and 1615, fifty-three baronial and 228 knightly families were given new status, then in the year 1615 a quarter of the baronial families and about a fifth of the knightly families were 'new' in the sense that they had not existed in their present Estate before 1542. In both Estates about three-quarters of the new creations were of domestic origin – non-noble Bohemian families – while the rest were foreign noblemen, most of them Germans from the Austrian provinces or from southern Germany, with a few from Poland and Hungary.

The thesis that Rudolph was obliged by financial difficulty to create a new nobility is not confirmed by these figures. His grandfather Ferdinand I, in fact, surpassed him in the creation of new noblemen. Under Ferdinand a total of 191 persons were received into the land, which for the twenty-two years of his reign works out to a yearly average of 8.68, though the heaviest influx occurred in the decade 1551–60. Rudolph II comes only in second place, with 283 creations over thirty-four years. Then comes Maximilian II with 69 creations over twelve years. Under Ferdinand I acceptances into the knightly Estate predominated, and most of the individuals in question were officials in the administration of the realm (secretaries in the office of the *Tabulae regni*, chancery officials, comptrollers), with also some officials of royal estates and estates belonging to magnate families, as well as a few doctors and lawyers. The official positions of the new barons were of course somewhat higher. Among them were vice-chancellors of the realm, imperial chamberlains, counsellors, counsellors of the court chamber. In Maximilian's reign the ranks of the nobility did not increase very substantially (the yearly average of new acceptances was 5.75). Under Rudolph the yearly average increased to 8.32, but the new knights were no longer the most numerous, having been overtaken by the category of inhabitants; after 1600 the number of new barons rose astonishingly: twenty-two to 1610 thereafter a further eight. It seems, therefore, that the pre-Rebellion nobility of Bohemia must be considered a living, evolving organism which responded to the fluctuating political and economic fortunes of the individual noble families. This is certainly the case, for example, of the Trčkas, Rederns and Smiřickýs, whose economic rise was followed by appropriate adjustment in socio-legal status.

It seems reasonable to accept Alois Míka's view that the differences between the baronial and knightly Estates, as far as economic and therefore political power are concerned, were not very great, and that in the century before the Rebellion they underwent no striking changes. Míka's tables taken from the tax records may be supplemented with the results for the incomplete registers for the year 1620. Then the feudal landholders may be divided according to the extent of their holdings: category A, those with under 100 unfree holdings on their lands; B, medium landholders with between 100 and 500 holdings; C, large proprietors with from 500 to 900 holdings; and D, the wealthiest noblemen, with over 900 holdings. The distribution of total landed wealth among the various categories may be tabulated as follows:[16]

Category	*1557*	*1603*	*1605*	*1620*
		(percentage)		
A	28.0	24.1	22.1	18.1
B	32.4	34.9	32.0	28.8
C	13.5	14.0	12.7	11.3
D	25.8	27.0	33.2	41.8

Briefly this means that in a period of generally peaceful development the less wealthy portions of the nobility became poorer, while the wealthier became richer at their expense. In the case of the Protestant families the way to wealth was, in fact, often through economic enterprise and innovation – witness the examples of the Smiřický, Trčka, Redern, Vchynský (Kinský), Hrzán, Hodějovský of Hodějov, or Vrchotecký of Loutkov families. But of these only the Smiřickýs and Kinskýs demonstrated any serious interest in political activity during the years before the Rebellion. In fact most of the political activity in this period was carried on by members of families whose landed holdings rank them only among the moderately wealthy (category B in the table above). This was the situation, for example, of Václav Budovec z Budova, of Thurn and also of the Šternberks. Among Catholic families and families attached to the court there were doubtless also possibilities for economic gain, or for the acquisition of property through marriage to wealthy heiresses. The latter included the case of the Catholic Lobkowitzes, but the practice was even more prevalent among the 'new Catholics', converts from the Czech Brethren or from the Utraquist groups, such as the Slavata, Liechtenstein and Waldstein (Wallenstein) families.

Because most of the nobility were members of the anti-Habsburg opposition and in one way or another participated in the Rebellion of 1618–20, after the Battle of the White Mountain they became prime targets for the vengeance or the rapacity of the victors. Even those individuals who maintained a neutral or moderate stance during the Rebellion (Adam Waldstein or Cardinal Dietrichstein) changed their tone after 1621 and tried to gain what they could from the situation.[17]

The wealthiest noble families were to be found on both sides during the Rebellion; most of them (the Smiřickýs, Švamberks, Hodějovskýs, Hrzáns, Rederns or Kinskýs) contributed at least moderately prominent rebels. But the majority of the 'opposition party' was formed of noblemen whose wealth places them in categories A or B, that is, among the small and medium property-holders, who in any case, of course, were the most numerous. Some of the great noblemen remained loyal to the Habsburgs: this was true of the Lobkowitz, Slavata and Berka families, but also of the impoverished Pernštejns and the not very wealthy Kolovrats and Vratislavs of Mitrovice. However, as noted above, there was also a third group: those who tried consciously to preserve a neutral course (they were the exception), or who simply waited to see who would win. These 'moderates' included, besides Adam Waldstein (who at least stated his position clearly early in the Rebellion), the Trčka family, Vencelík of Vrchoviště and several others. A few of them, for example Liechtenstein and Dietrichstein in Moravia, eventually joined the Imperial side after protracted calculation.

Some conclusions about the period immediately after the Battle of the White Mountain can be made on the basis of older studies: Tomáš Bílek's massive compilation from the records of the Confiscation Commission, carried out in the 1880s, and Břetislav Jelínek's later supplementary index of participants in the Rebellion. But there is also a source which has not yet been used: a collection of drafts found among the papers of the Imperial prosecutor Přibík Jeníšek z Újezda.[18] Jeníšek's material is particularly valuable because it permits a closer glimpse of the activities of individual noblemen during the Rebellion: it specifies the accusations made against them in full. Though it does not by any means contain a complete list of the participants, it does reveal the rôles played by 134 of the noble families during the Rebellion. Of these, thirty-three families participated in some capacity from the beginning of the Rebellion; sixty-six first became active in 1619; twenty-five in 1620; and nine were accused of subversive activities in 1621. Most of them were accused because one or more of their members held office in the administration of the realm or of one of the regions (*kraje*) (twenty-two), or served in some capacity in the Estates' army (twenty-five cases, notably during the siege of Pilsen, the two campaigns against Vienna, the siege of Budweis, or the defence of Třeboň, Tábor, Zvíkov, etc.). A few of them performed diplomatic tasks for the government of the Estates or later for that of Frederick of the Palatinate.

If the cases recorded in Jeníšek's drafts are plotted on a map, it appears that the most active rebel noblemen came from the Čáslav region (five families), from Chrudimsko, Hradecko, Litoměřicko (four families each), then from Žatecko and Prácheňsko (three families). The western region of Pilsen and the central regions of Kouřimsko, Slánsko and the northern Boleslavsko are less well represented, and there is hardly a trace of activity on the part of the small nobility of southern Bohemia.

Since the material is only partial, covering at best only about a sixth of the total number of cases that came before the Confiscation Commissions during the 1620s, the results of this microanalysis must be used with caution. Yet they do suggest some modification of Josef Pekař's thesis – that the Estates' Rebellion of 1618–20 was the work of northern Bohemia, just as the southern part of the country had been responsible for the Hussite Revolution. It appears, partly from Jeníšek's papers but also from the proceedings of the sessions of the Diet between 1618 and 1620, that most of the active participants in the Rebellion generally came from central and northeastern Bohemia. This is a territory which on the one hand possessed convenient communications with Prague and, on the other, whose economy had throughout the sixteenth century supported a high level of political and cultural activity. This region extended from Louny and Roudnice, the valley of the River Moldau north of Prague, to Jaroměř, Litomyšl and Chrudim in the east.

At the same time, what we now know of the numbers of the rebel nobility warns us against accepting the figures of tens of thousands which regularly appear in the literature about the emigrations after the Battle of the White Mountain.

If we compare Jeníšek's information with that of Bílek and Jelínek and with the *Tabulae regni* after the Rebellion, we must conclude that the specific accusations lodged against the participants were not decisive in determining their guilt or punishment. This conclusion is also suggested by the correspondence of Dietrichstein with such adventurers as Marradas or Verdugo. More important seems to have been whether this or that landed estate was attractive to one or another of the military or civil officials of the Habsburg régime. Finally, the suffering to which the nobility was subjected should be viewed in proper perspective. A survey of the death sentences or the relative value of the confiscated property, not to mention the effects of inflation and economic ruin (for all this was regarded as part of the 'punishment' of the rebels), makes it clear that it was the bourgeoisie, not the nobility, who suffered the greater losses.

For the influx of 'new' noblemen after the Battle of the White Mountain we have no source as convenient as Žerotín's register for the sixteenth century. Some help is given by a dissertation by L. Mikeštíková-Kubátová, which traces how the granting of the incolat, which before the Rebellion was in the hands of the Diet, became with the Renewed Constitution of 1627 the almost exclusive prerogative of the ruler.[19]

The chief source, therefore, is the *Tabulae regni*, which may be compared with the *Berní rula* (*Tax Roll*) of 1654–6. For the years 1621–56 there are together 417 entries in the *Tabulae regni* dealing with incolats – in other words 417 new members of the landholding classes: the barons, knights and 'inhabitants', in this period usually referred to as the 'vladycký stav' but legally indistinguishable from the knightly Estate. The figure of 417 incolats for a period of roughly thirty years (if we begin with the date of the Renewed Constitution, 1627–56) may be compared with the data above for the roughly seventy-year period from 1546 to 1615. The annual average of new acceptances was 7.56 for the earlier period and 11.91 for the later. Therefore the first surprise is simply that the increase, though substantial, is not nearly so large as we should expect on the basis of the existing literature.

But of these 417 new members of the Estates' community, or of the ruling class, only 253 can be found listed in the *Berní rula*. Among the missing names are Eggenberg, Harrach, and Herberstein, and this shows that neither the *Berní rula* nor the *Tabulae regni* can be accepted as entirely reliable or complete. These magnates appear to have been in no hurry to complete the official registration of their ownership of landed property or their membership in the Estates of the realm.

Of the 417 entries nearly half were Germans – 200 precisely. But no longer were they chiefly from the Habsburgs' Alpine lands: they now included also a larger proportion of officials of bourgeois origin. The second most numerous group – 107 or about a quarter of the total – were people from Bohemia (89), Moravia (7), Silesia and Lusatia (11). But many of these, particularly those from Moravia, remained merely 'paper incolats', apparently never acquired estates at all, and received the incolat as Catholic supporters of the Habsburg régime. Then there were forty-three Italians, twenty Frenchmen (chiefly from Lorraine), eleven Spaniards, and seven from the Spanish Netherlands. Most of the increase is accounted for by 324 'new noblemen' who were registered in the *Tabulae regni* in three periods: the first from 1627 to 1631, in which there were 119 incolats; the second between 1635 and 1638 (in which there were eighty-six, most of whom acquired property from the Wallenstein confiscation), and finally, the postwar years 1650 to 1656 (119 incolats).

In the first period there were on the average twelve new noble 'settlers' each year. Of the 119 who were registered, only fifty-six appear in the *Berní rula.* Most of the new noblemen of this period were army officers: Buquoy, Marradas, Aldringen, Clary, Paradis, Huerta, Magnis, Verdugo, St Julien. Some members of families already established in other Habsburg lands also appear: Liechtenstein, Metternich, Nostitz, Eggenberg, Trautmannsdorf. But there were also some Bohemians, even a few who had taken part in the Rebellion: Jan Jezberovský z Kolivé Hory and even Benjamin Früwein, one of the former directors of the rebel government.

From 1632 to 1634 there were only nine new entries, most of them members of bourgeois administrative or professional families. More significant is the 'second wave', the arrivals between 1635 and 1638, who were chiefly the new proprietors of lands confiscated from Albrecht Wallenstein, the Trčkas and Vilém Vchynský. Nine of these had received the incolat earlier (among them Nostitz, Thun, Aldringen, Paradis). There were also eleven officials, some of whom had married noble heiresses. But most of the new incolats were generals and subordinate officers who had abandoned Wallenstein in time: Piccolomini, Tiefenbach, Desfours, Morzin, Butler, Taaffe, Gallas. The Colloredo, Schlick, Dietrichstein and Aldringen families were also among those who gained from the confiscations, while those who had betrayed Wallenstein and those who had carried out the assassination also applied for their reward: Leslie, Geraldine, Johann Putz von Adlersthurm, and Captain Carlo Villani. Finally, the Duke of Saxe-Lauenburg also became a 'new nobleman' by marriage to a widow of one of the Kolovrats.

Altogether seventy-six new noble families arrived between 1635 and 1638.

Immigration in the 1640s was a good deal less remarkable. From 1639 to 1649 an average of six incolats were granted each year. Together there were sixty-eight incolats to members of fifty-one families, and twenty of these are not to be found in the *Berní rula.* Of those who remained by 1656 (twenty-three) the largest group is composed of soldiers (sixteen) who were paid for their service with lands in Bohemia. Some of the successful soldiers of the 1630s were now being followed into Bohemia by their relatives from other parts of the continent.

The 'third wave' of immigration took place from 1650 to 1656, when 110 incolats were granted to members of ninety-six families, of which only sixty-seven are listed in the *Berní rula.* Some of the twenty-eight 'missing' families received the incolat before they took over their estates, or else these were in the process of transfer when the surveys for the *Berní rula* were being carried out. This explains why a few of the large landholders, such as the Schwarzenbergs, are absent. Some of the new families were Moravian magnates (Kounic and Rottal), but again the military represents a sizeable proportion (twenty-five families, among them Wallis, Kaiserstein, Iselin de Laman), though their share is smaller than in the two earlier periods of heavy immigration. Eighteen of the new noblemen were office-holders of varying rank. Firmer conclusions about this group are impossible because many of them only acquired property after the compilation of the *Berní rula.*

Together, then, about 400 individuals representing 334 new noble families received the incolat between 1627 and 1656 from the Habsburg ruler.[20] But only 192 of the families appear in the *Berní rula*, so that 40 per cent 'disappeared'. It would be useful, therefore, to carry the analysis further, at least to the middle of the eighteenth century, or to 1741–2, the last rebellion of the Bohemian nobles against the Habsburgs, during the Franco-Bavarian invasion.[21]

Bohuslav Balbín in his *Disputatio* pointed to the 'dying out' of the new nobles as a hopeful sign and expected that they would disappear altogether in the not too distant future. Although his speculations were not fulfilled, the fact remains that eighty-one of the new families did not remain permanently as landholding noblemen. If we look at the figures in terms of the time of arrival, the results are these: of the 102 families who received the incolat before 1631, forty-five disappeared, or 45 per cent. Of the forty-eight families from the second wave of 1635–8, fifteen disappeared, or 31 per cent. Of the forty-four families who came during the 1640s, twenty-one disappeared, or 48 per cent. Often this disappearance was caused by the early death of a new nobleman, whose widow generally remarried into one of the other families, old or new.

Some difficulty is caused by the fact that between 1627 and 1656 the Habsburgs ceased granting the lowest title of nobility (*vladycký stav*). There are only twelve of these patents, most of them issued before 1630. On the other hand, they now granted imperial titles to Bohemian noblemen (*Grafenstand*, *Reichsherrenstand*). In practice a distinction began to be drawn between the 'old' and 'new' members of the old Bohemian noble Estates. From the 1630s patents often specified 'new' or 'old' knightly Estate, 'new' or 'old' baronial Estate. Such knightly families as Černín, Vratislav of Mitrovice, Kolovrat, Hyzrle z Chodů, Koc z Dobrše and Lažanský were accepted into the baronial Estate. But because the 'old' Bohemian baronial Estate was now becoming confused with the Imperial baronial title, these families did their utmost to acquire a countly or even a princely title, designations hitherto unknown or at least officially unrecognized in Bohemia. Altogether sixty-five of these imperial titles were given, about four per year.

One basic question remains: what was the balance of strength, numerical and economic, between the 'old' and 'new' groups of the nobility in Bohemia? Using the *Berní rula* we can trace the outcome of the earlier evolution:

	1557	*1615*	*1656*
Baronial families	169	194	297
Knightly families	1,019	938	573
Total	1,188	1,132	870

The ratio of new families to old was 128 to 169 in the baronial Estate in 1656, and 116 to 457 in the knightly Estate. The total number of noble families fell, and the 'new' nobility penetrated most strikingly into the baronial Estate. However, in 1656 the new nobility formed only about 28 per cent of the total number of noble families in the realm, so that Bohemian families were far more numerous than foreign ones. But in terms of power and wealth the relation was quite different. The old nobility, according to the *Berní rula*, controlled 27,180 unfree holdings, the new nobility 26,749, so that the possessions of the two groups were nearly equal.[22]

It is useful to look at the geographical distribution of the landed holdings of the old and the new nobility. Throughout the country, of course, the new noble families were to be found in control of the most extensive estates. But their position was strongest in the border regions, where the latifundia were located, and where, moreover, most of Wallenstein's holdings had been concentrated. The situation in some of the *kraje* was as follows:

Kraj	*Old noble families*	*Villein holdings*	*New noble families*	*Villein holdings*
Litoměřicko	40	2,165	40	2,840
Žatecko	33	2,256	27	1,250
Boleslavsko	32	1,857	32	3,352
Bechyňsko	68	3,393	20	5,267
Prácheňsko	106	2,339	14	2,187
Loketsko	13	411	11	561

The predominance of the new nobility in Litoměřicko, Boleslavsko, Loketsko, but also in the southern region of Bechyňsko, is quite clear. In the western Pilsen region there were 128 old families but only thirty-one new ones, while the distribution of villein holdings was 3,795 to 2,187. The other *kraje* – Slánsko, Kouřimsko, Podbrdsko, and Rakovnicko, all of them in the central part of the kingdom – continued to be heavily dominated by old noble families. Yet on the whole the Eggenbergs, Schwarzenbergs, Thuns, Buquoys and Trautmannsdorfs were, in terms of the lands they held, more than a match for the old magnate families such as Slavata, Lobkowitz, Berka z Dubé, Černín and Šternberk.

This is clearly revealed by a table showing the changes that took place in landholding patterns between 1615 and 1656 (using the categories established above p. 207):

Category		*1615* (percentage)	*1656*
A	proprietors:	81.6	80
	holdings:	22.1	14
B	proprietors:	15.1	15
	holdings:	32.1	31
C	proprietors:	1.8	3
	holdings:	12.7	20
D	proprietors:	1.4	2
	holdings:	33.2	35

It appears that in this respect as well the war and the changes resulting from it strengthened the effect of older trends of development. The dominance of the latifundia and the large landholders was increased, while the position of the small holdings was further eroded.

The relative position of the old and new nobility in 1656 was as follows:

Category		*No. of families*	*No. of holdings*
A	new nobility:	137	3,620
	old nobility:	262	4,125
B	new nobility:	41	8,776
	old nobility:	37	7,428
C	new nobility:	5	3,447
	old nobility:	10	7,483
D	new nobility:	5	10,346
	old nobility:	6	8,823

Among the small noble property-holders the old families still predominated numerically, but their average possessions were smaller than those of the new noble families. Among the medium landowners, the new nobles held a slight majority. Most of the large landholders (category C) were old Bohemian Catholic, pro-Habsburg families. But the holdings of the new magnate families (category D) were larger than those of the old.

It emerges, therefore, that the most important changes were not quantitative, but qualitative. These resulted in a clear position of dominance for the recently arrived families. Because these were families and individuals who had no connection with the established traditions of feudal economic exploitation in Bohemia, the changes in control of landed property meant in most cases a worsening, often a very marked worsening, of the situation of the peasants. The forms of exploitation that were introduced on noblemen's estates after the Rebellion led directly to the Bohemian peasant war of 1680.[23]

The provisional results of this analysis of the composition of the Bohemian nobility and its evolution in the sixteenth and seventeenth centuries enable us to answer at least some of the questions left unanswered by Jean Meyer, whose conclusions, like those of Tapié, were limited by their dependence on the questionable data contained in the work of Otto Placht and older German historians.

If we return to the three problems that were stated at the beginning of this study, which has combined a micro- and macroanalysis of a limited body of source material, the conclusions may be summarized as follows:

1. In contrast to the older view that the 'dynamic' period of the

evolution of the Bohemian ruling class came only after the Rebellion, while the earlier period was 'static', we may conclude from the analysis of the entries in the *Tabulae regni* that the situation did not change very much from a quantitative point of view, while qualitative changes were clearly more important.

2. The confiscation of landed property after the Battle of the White Mountain was only one form of the punishment which affected the whole of the Bohemian state and *de facto* its entire population. Nor did it have much to do with the real or imagined crimes committed by the rebel noblemen. The aim was simply to get rid of the rebels and destroy those social elements which from the point of view of the Habsburg régime posed actual or potential dangers. The figures for the value of confiscated property do not give a complete picture of the effects of the process. The value of confiscated noble property is usually estimated at between five and eight million Bohemian schocken (*kop*), and that confiscated from the bourgeoisie at two and a half million. But since by the time of the Rebellion the towns and the bourgeoisie controlled only about a tenth of the land they were relatively much more heavily affected by the confiscations than was the nobility. At the same time the other forms of punishment, including exile, also contributed to the destruction of the bourgeoisie, which was regarded as the most dangerous element in the country.

3. The changes that took place within the Bohemian nobility after the Battle of the White Mountain were most important in qualitative terms because the 'new families', though numerically in the minority, became more than the equal partners of the old nobility in material terms. The disappearance of families who received the incolat but never acquired estates points to the creation of a nobility not so much 'new' or 'old' as 'Austrian', which owed its status primarily to its connections with the civil and military apparatus of the monarchy, had little connection with the land, and owed its position to the Habsburgs, whose chief support it remained until the end of the dynasty.

Conclusion

As a conclusion to this report on the present state of research into the Thirty Years' War and the new sources at our disposal, we can see that in general terms the problem to be dealt with is one which for three centuries has been to a greater or lesser degree a burning issue for European society. One might take the view that the social changes during the war cannot be understood even in these rich records, and that the task is impossible. But such a severe judgement would rule out any attempt to come to grips with a period which more and more historians are coming to see as the foundation of the modern world we still live in. Thirty-five years ago Otakar Odložilík, face to face with the disintegration of the European political system, posed the question: 'Are we living in the seventeenth century?' We are of course living in the twentieth century and have survived the first three decades of the Atomic Age; but the seventeenth century, so little known, seems to have more in common with our own than we generally care to admit.

New research must be directed towards problems which are not parochial but affect European society as a whole and even extend beyond the confines of the continent. We should not forget that it was no accident that from the middle of the sixteenth century the Spanish silver-fleets carried with their cargo the hopes and fears even of far-off Bohemia. American silver for the Spaniards, East-Indian spices for the Dutch and the English, the struggles to close off or keep open the Baltic and the Mediterranean, Turkish domination of the Balkans: all these are reflected in one way or another in the documents of this conflict, as it were, of world-wide proportions. This means that attention must be paid to the history of the 'international confrontation' between two types of social and political organization, the Spanish on the one hand and the Dutch on the other. From these were forged, in the clash of armies and states, a new pair of models represented by France and England which were to set the tone of European life until the nineteenth century. But to appreciate the full implications of this change we should have to step past the limit of 1650 and seek in the destinies of the next generation the direct consequences of the Thirty Years' War. It is, however, not unreasonable to hope that on the basis of the research already accomplished we may proceed to a better understanding of the rise in Europe, during the first half of the seventeenth century, of new conceptions of life and society.

Notes

INTRODUCTION

1. P. Daix, 'Le XVIIe siècle, cet inconnu' *Les lettres françaises*, no. 1152.
2. P. Vilar, 'Le temps des hidalgos', in *L'Espagne au temps de Philippe II*, ed. F. Braudel (Paris 1965), 81–111. P. Chaunu, *La civilisation de l'Europe classique* (Paris 1966). P. Goubert, *Louis XIV et vingt millions de Français* (Paris 1966). F. Braudel, *Civilisation matérielle et capitalisme. XVe–XVIIIe siècle* (Paris 1968).
3. T. Aston, ed., *Crisis in Europe 1560–1660* (London 1965). *Historians of Early Modern Europe, Newsletter*, nos. 1 (1966), 2 (1967).
4. O. Odložilík, 'We live in the seventeenth century' (separatum, n.p. n.d.).
5. R. Mandrou, *La France aux XVIIe et XVIIIe siècles* (Paris 1967).
6. R. Mandrou, *Magistrats et sorciers en France au XVIIe siècle. Une analyse de psychologie historique* (Paris 1968). C. Hill, *The World Turned Upside Down.* (London 1970). Cf. also A. L. Morton, *The World of the Ranters.* (London 1970).
7. C. Brinton, J. B. Christopher, R. L. Wolff, *Modern Civilization. A History of the Last Five Centuries* (Englewood Cliffs 1957). *Civilization in the West* (Englewood Cliffs 1964).
8. A. G. Dickens, *Reformation and Society in Sixteenth Century Europe* (London 1966). J. H. Elliott, *Europe Divided 1559–1598* (London–Glasgow 1968). H. Lutz, *Christianitas Afflicta* (Göttingen 1964).
9. A. Meusel, 'Revolution and Counterrevolution', in *Encyclopaedia of the Social Sciences, XIII* (London 1934), 367–76. K. Griewank, *Der neuzeitliche Revolutionsbegriff. Entstehung und Entwicklung* (Weimar 1955).
10. T. K. Rabb, ed., *The Thirty Years' War: Problems of Motive, Extent and Effect* (Boston 1964), x.
11. J. V. Polišenský, *Anglie a Bílá hora* (Prague 1949), 194.
12. *Ibid.*
13. G. Ritter, *Die Neugestaltung Europas im 16. Jahrhundert. Die kirchlichen und staatlichen Wandlungen im Zeitalter der Reformation und der Glaubenskämpfe* (Berlin 1950). F. Braudel, *La Méditerranée et le monde méditerranéen à l'epoque de Philippe II* (Paris 1949).
14. Ritter, *Die Neugestaltung Europas im 16. Jahrhundert*, 338.
15. D. Gerhard, 'Regionalismus und ständisches Wesen als ein Grundthema europäischer Geschichte', *Historische Zeitschrift* (hereafter *HZ*), 174/2 (1952), 307–37.

16. F. H. Schubert, 'Die Niederlande zur Zeit des Dreissigjährigen Krieges im Urteil des diplomatischen Korps im Haag', *Historisches Jahrbuch*, LXXIV (1954), 252–64.
17. R. Mousnier, ed., *Problèmes de la stratification sociale. Actes du Colloque International (1966)* (Paris 1968).
18. I. Schöffer, 'La stratification sociale de la République des Provinces Unies au XVIIe siècle', in *Problèmes de la stratification sociale*, 121–32. Cf. also *idem*, De Nederlandse revolutië', in *Zeven revoluties* (Amsterdam n.d.), viz. 27–8 for the modern bibliography. H. R. Trevor-Roper, *Religion, the Reformation and Social Change* (London 1967), 1–45.
19. J. A. Maravall, 'La comédie espagnole et la stratification sociale à l'âge baroque', in *Problèmes de la stratification sociale*, 249–65. N. Salomon, *La campagne de Nouvelle Castille à la fin du XVIe siècle d'après les Relaciones topográficas* (Paris 1964).
20. The most recent report of the state of the problems is in A. Ubieto, J. Reglá, J. M. Jover, C. Seco, *Introducción a la historia de España* (Barcelona 1967) 381ff.
21. J. G. da Silva, *Desarrollo económico, subsistencia y decadencia en España* (Madrid 1967), 218ff.
22. J. Tazbir, 'The commonwealth of the gentry, 1492–1696', in *History of Poland* (Warsaw 1968), 169–271.
23. For the holdings of the Czechoslovak archives see J. V. Polišenský, *Otázky studia obecných dějin*, I, II (Prague 1957, 1963); *The Thirty Years' War* (London 1972), 266–95.
24. For problems of periodization see J. V. Polišenský, 'The Thirty Years' War and the crises and revolutions of seventeenth century Europe', *Past and Present*, XXXIX (1958), 34–43; *The Thirty Years' War* (London 1971), 1–11.
25. F. L. Carsten, *Princes and Parliaments in Germany* (Oxford 1959). S. H. Steinberg, *Der Dreissigjährige Krieg und der Kampf um die Vorherrschaft in Europa 1600–1660* (Göttingen 1967).

1. ATTEMPTS AT A REINTERPRETATION OF THE CONFLICT

1. See J. V. Polišenský, *Třicetiletá válka a český národ* (Prague 1960) 9–29.
2. V. M. Alekseyev, *Tridsatiletnaya voyna* (Leningrad 1961).
3. S. H. Steinberg, *Der Dreissigjährige Krieg und der Kampf um die Vorherrschaft in Europa 1600–1660* (Göttingen 1967).
4. T. K. Rabb, 'The effects of the Thirty Years' War on the German economy', *The Journal of Modern History*, XXXV (1962), 40–51. See also Rabb's *The Struggle for Stability in Early Modern Europe* (New York 1975), with extensive bibliography.
5. *Idem, The Thirty Years' War. Problems of Motive, Extent and Effect* (Boston 1964).
6. T. Aston, ed., *Crisis in Europe 1560–1660*, preface by Christopher Hill (London 1965).
7. H. Kamen, 'The economic and social consequences of the Thirty Years' War', *Past and Present*, XXXIX (1968), 44–61.
8. J. V. Polišenský, 'The Thirty Years' War and the crises and revolutions of seventeenth century Europe', *ibid.* 34–43.

9. R. Mousnier, *Les XVIe et XVIIe siècles. Les progrès de la civilisation européenne...*, *Histoire générale des civilisations*, IV (Paris 1954).
10. R. Mandrou, *Classes et luttes de classes en France au début du XVIIe siècle* (Florence 1965).
11. P. Vilar, 'Le temps des hidalgos', in *L'Espagne au temps de Philippe II*, ed. F. Braudel (Paris 1965).
12. P. Chaunu, *La civilisation de l'Europe classique* (Paris 1966).
13. J. V. Polišenský, 'Současný stav bádání o "španělské odchylce" či "úpadku Španělska" v 16. až 17. století', *Československý časopis historický* (hereafter *ČSČH*), XI (1963), 341–52.
14. T. Wittman, 'España en la "Monarquía Española" de Campanella', *Acta Historica*, XV (Szeged 1964), 3–17; "A spanyol abszolutizmus néhány vonása a XVI. században', *ibid.* 19–29; "Apuntes sobre los métodos de investigación de la decadencia castellana (Siglos XVI–XVII),' *Nouvelles études historiques* (Budapest 1965), 243–59; 'Sobre el presunto caracter "turco" del absolutismo español del "siglo de oro"', *Rosario* (1964), 309–20; 'Vitoriától suárezig. A XVI századi spanyol államelmélet mérlege', *Filológiai Közlöny* (Budapest 1966), 53–66; *II Fülöp* (Budapest 1967).
15. A. N. Chistozvonov, 'Nekotoriye aspekty genesisa absolutisma', *Voprosy istorii* (1968–1), 46–62.
16. N. Salomon, *La campagne de Nouvelle Castille à la fin du XVIe siècle d'après les Relaciones topográficas* (Paris 1964).
17. A. Ubieto, J. Reglá, J. M. Jover, C. Seco, *Introducción a la historia de España* (Barcelona 1967).
18. B. Chudoba, *Španělé na Bílé hoře* (Prague 1945); *Spain and the Empire 1519–1643* (Chicago 1952).
19. E. Beladiez, *España y el Sacro Imperio Romano Germanico. Wallenstein 1583–1634* (Madrid 1967).
20. J. M. Castroviejo, F. de P. Fernández de Córdoba, *El Conde de Gondomar. Un azor entre ocasos* (Madrid 1967).
21. J. Presser, *De Tachtigjarige Oorlog* (2nd edn, Amsterdam 1964).
22. *Algemene Geschiedenis der Nederlanden*, IV and V (Utrecht 1952).
23. *Bijdragen voor de Geschiedenis der Nederlanden*, IX (1954), 324–8; X (1955–1956), 58–67, 239–48; XI (1956), 103–6.
24. E. Kuttner, *Het Hongerjaar 1566* (Amsterdam 1949).
25. J. V. Polišenský, *Nizozemská politika a Bílá hora* (Prague 1958), 32–4, 37, 57–8.
26. G. Griffiths, 'The revolutionary character of the revolt in the Netherlands', *Comparative Studies in Society and History*, II (1959–60), 452–72.
27. I. Schöffer, *ibid.* III (1961–2), 470–7.
28. *Idem*, 'De Nederlandse revolutië' in *Zeven revoluties* (Amsterdam n.d.), 9–28.
29. *Idem*, 'Did Holland's Golden Age coincide with a period of crisis?', *Acta Historiae Neerlandica*, I (Leiden 1966), 82–107.
30. *Idem*, 'De Engelse revolutië', in *Zeven revoluties*, 29–50.
31. C. Hill, 'The century of revolution 1603–1714', in *History of England*, V (Edinburgh 1961); *Reformation to Industrial Revolution* (London 1967); *Change and Continuity in Seventeenth Century England* (London 1974).
32. H. R. Trevor-Roper, *Religion, the Reformation and Social Change* (London 1967).
33. B. F. Porshnev, *Feodalizm i narodnye massy* (Moscow 1964).

34. *Idem, Les soulèvements populaires en France de 1623 à 1648* (Paris 1963).
35. R. Mandrou, *Introduction à la France moderne (1500–1640)* (Paris 1961); *La France aux XVIIe et XVIIIe siècles* (Paris 1967).
36. Apart from the bibliographical section of J. V. Polišenský, *The Thirty Years' War* (London 1971), see now volumes I, II, III, IV of the *Documenta Bohemica Bellum Tricennale Illustrantia* (Prague and Vienna 1971, 1972, 1976, 1974), especially I (1971).
37. B. Chudoba, 'Roudnická politica (zastoupení renesanční politické vědy v knihovně českého státníka na rozhraní XVI. a XVII. století)' (separatum, 1934). See *Sborník Historického kroužku* XXXII (1932) and XXXIII (1934). See also *idem, Španělé na Bílé hoře* (Prague 1945) 178ff.
38. I thank Dr E. Urbánková for making available to me the catalogue of the Roudnice Library, now under the administration of the University Library at Prague but inadequately housed at Postoloprty. Besides this catalogue (*Standrepertorium, Schlossbibliothek zu Raudnitz, 1900*) I have also used the *Verzeichnis der Lobkovic-Handschriften* and the *Katalog der Prager Lobkovic-Bücherei.*
39. O. Odložilík, 'Political thought of Bohemia in the early 17th century', *VIIe Congrès International des Sciences Historiques, Zürich 1938, Communications...*, II (Paris 1938), 635–7.
40. J. V. Polišenský, 'Viléma Slavaty relace o jednáni v příčině knížetství Opavského 1614–1615. (Příspěvek k poznání politického myšlení předbělohorských Čech)', *Slezský sborník*, XXXI (1953), 488ff.
41. O. Odložilík, 'Poslední Smiřičtí', in *Pekařův sborník II* (Prague 1930), 70–87, which may be supplemented by the study by V. Pešák of the economic régime on the Smiřický estates, 'Panství rodu Smiřických v letech 1609–1618', *Sborník archivu ministerstva vnitra* (hereafter *SAMV*), XIII (Prague 1940), 7–203.
42. See most recently H. Kunstmann, *Die Nürnberger Universität Altdorf und Böhmen* (Cologne-Graz 1963). See also Polišenský, *Nizozemská politika a Bílá hora*, 128ff.
43. N. Mout, J. V. Polišenský, *Komenský v Amsterodamu* (Prague 1970).
44. J. V. Polišenský, *České dějepisectví předbělohorského období a pražská Akademie* (*AUC, Historia Univ. Carolinae Pragensis*, IV, 1963), 115–17.
45. For this party of the 'centre' see J. V. Polišenský, *Jan Jesenský-Jessenius* (Prague 1965), 35ff.
46. See the documentation in the study by Polišenský, *K politické činnosti Jana Jesenského-Jessenia* (*AUC, Historia Univ. Carolinae Pragensis*, II, 1961), 87–128.
47. R. Zuber, *Mladá léta kardinála Dietrichštejna* (dissertation, Prague 1946). Dietrichstein's correspondence is partly in the Family Archive and the 'Historica' of the Dietrichstein Collection in the State Archive at Brno, and partly in the 'Unbound Correspondence' of the former archepiscopal archive from Kroměříž, now at Olomouc.
48. Chudoba, *Španělé na Bílé hoře*, 180.
49. See above, n. 44.
50. Polišenský, 'Viléma Slavaty relace...,' 492.
51. V. L. Tapié, *Bílá hora a francouzská politika* (Prague 1936); *La politique étrangère de la France et le début de la guerre de Trente ans (1616–1621)* (Paris 1934).

52. On the Castle Library at Český Krumlov see *Knihovna Národního musea* (Prague 1959), 131–2, which lists further literature.
53. The following catalogues have been used: *Catalogus der. . .Büchern so anno 1721 verrichtet*, State Archive at Český Krumlov, Schwarzenberg Family Archive, I 7 є 23 h, MS 202; *Alterthümer, Historische und Biographische Werke E* (*1779–1780*), *ibid.*
54. See *Knihovna Národního musea*, 54–5.
55. Pavel Ješín of Bezděz, *Posmrtná paměť českým hrdinům. . .*, published by K. Hrdina (Prague 1938).

2. THE BOHEMIAN WAR, 1618–1620

1. H. Hantsch, *Die Geschichte Österreichs*, 2 vols. (Graz 1953, 1959).
2. E. Zöllner, *Geschichte Österreichs* (Vienna 1961; 4th edn, 1970).
3. H. Sturmberger, *Georg Erasmus Tschernembl. Religion, Libertät und Widerstand* (Linz 1953); 'Die Anfänge des Bruderzwistes in Habsburg', *Mitteilungen des Oberösterreichischen Landesarchivs*, v (1957); *Kaiser Ferdinand II. und das Problem des Absolutismus* (Vienna 1957).
4. G. Mecenseffy, *Geschichte des Protestantismus in Österreich* (Graz-Cologne 1956); K. Richter, 'Die böhmischen Länder von 1471–1740', in *Handbuch der Geschichte der böhmischen Länder* (Stuttgart, 1974), 99–313.
5. V. L. Tapié, 'Méthodes et problèmes de l'histoire de l'Europe centrale', in *Mélanges Pierre Renouvin. Études d'histoire des rélations internationale* (Paris 1966), 33–49.
6. A. Wandruszka, *Das Haus Habsburg. Die Geschichte einer europäischen Dynastie* (Vienna 1956).
7. R. Belvederi, *Dell' elezione di un rè dei Romani nel carteggio inedito del Cardinale Guido Bentivoglio* (*1609–1614*) (Rome 1951); 'Un nunzio pontifico di fronte alle tensioni delle potenze europee nei primi decenni del secolo XVII', *Humanitas*, x (1955), 561ff.
8. R. F. Schmiedt, 'Vorgeschichte, Verlauf und Wirkungen des Dreissigjährigen Krieges', in Max Steinmetz, ed., *Deutschland 1476–1648* (Berlin 1965), 271–383; 'Deutschland von 1608 bis 1648', in *Deutsche Geschichte*, I (Berlin 1965), 593–628.
9. J. B. Novák, *Rudolf II a jeho pád* (Praha 1935).
10. Gertrude von Schwarzenfeld, *Rudolf II. Der Saturnische Kaiser* (Munich 1961).
11. G. R. Hocke, *Die Welt als Labyrinth. Manier und Manie in der europäischen Kunst* (Hamburg 1957); R. J. W. Evans, *Rudolf II and his World. A Study in Intellectual History 1576–1612* (Oxford 1973); E. H. N. Mout, *Bohemen en de Nederlanden in de 16. eeuw* (Leiden 1975).
12. T. Wittman, *Az osztrák Habsburg-hatalom válságos éveinek történetéhez* (*1606–1618*) (*Acta Universitatis Szegedinensis, Sectio Historica*, 1959).
13. *25 ans d'historiographie tchécoslovaque 1936–1960* (Prague 1960).
14. V. Pešák, *Začátky organizace české komory za Ferdinanda I.* (Prague 1930). K. Stloukal, *Česká kancelář dvorská*, (Prague 1931).
15. M. Volf, *Nástin správy českých berní v době předbělohorské* (Prague 1941).
16. V. Pešák, *Berní rejstříky z roku 1544 a 1620* (Prague 1953).
17. J. Kolman, *Berní rejstříky a berně z roku 1567* (Prague 1963).
18. J. Janáček, *Rudolfinské drahotní řády* (Prague 1957).
19. S. Hoszowski, 'L'Europe centrale devant la révolution des prix XVIe et XVIIe siècles', *Annales E. S. C.*, XIX (1961–3), 441–56.

20. T. Wittman, '"Revolutsia tsen" i yeye vlyanye na Vengriu vo vtoroy polovine XVI v.', *Sredniye veka* xx (1961), 166–88.
21. J. Petráň, 'K problémům tzv. "cenové revoluce" ve střední Evropě'. *Numismatický sborník*, VIII (1964), 47–74.
22. *Kolokvium o dějinách cen a mezd v 16. a 17. století*, (*Zápisky katedry čsl. dějin a arch. studia UK*, Prague 1962).
23. M. Hroch, J. Petráň, 'K charakteristice krize feudalismu v XVI.–XVII. století', *ČSČH*, XII (1964), 347–64; 'Europejska gospodarka i politika XVI i XVII vieku: kryzys czy regres?', *Przeglad Historyczny*, LV (1964), 1–21; *17. Století krize feudální společnosti?* (Prague 1976).
24. J. Válka, *Hospodářská politika feudálního velkostatku na předbělohorské Moravě* (Prague 1962).
25. J. Petráň, *Zemědělská výroba v Čechác h v druhé polovině 16. a počátkem 17. století* (Prague 1964).
26. F. Matějek, 'Gospodarka szłachecka i chłopska na środkowym Śląsku w XVI wieku', *Studia i materiały z dziejów Śląska*, IV (n.d.), 423–52.
27. J. Petráň, 'Pozdněfeudální lidová hnutí', *Úvahy o problémech a metodách* (1967), 107–50. (Separatum.)
28. *Dějiny Prahy* (Prague 1964).
29. F. Kavka, *Majetková, sociální a třídní struktura českých měst v první polovině 16. století* (Prague 1959).
30. J. Marek, *Společenská struktura moravských měst v 15. a 16. století* (Prague 1965).
31. See the article by J. V. Polišenský, 'Nové poznatky o Komenského rodišti a rodě', *Listy filologické*, XC (1967), 404–10.
32. E. Schieche, 'Die Rosenbergsche Bibliothek vor und nach Juli 1648', *Stifter-Jahrbuch*, V (1957), 102–40.
33. J. V. Polišenský, B. Badura, 'Falešný obraz Bilé hory', *ČSČH*, III (1955), 674–9.
34. K. Stloukal, *Papežská politika a císařský dvůr pražský na předělu XVI. a XVII. století* (Prague 1925); *Počátky nunciatury v Praze* (Prague 1928).
35. J. Matoušek, *Turecká válka v evropské politice v letech 1592–1594* (Prague 1935).
36. W. Konopczyński, *Dzieje Polski nowożytnej, T. I, 1506–1648* (Warsaw 1936).
37. G. Mecenseffy, *Habsburger im 17. Jahrhundert. Die Beziehungen der Höfe von Wien und Madrid während des Dreissigjährigen Krieges* (*Archiv für österreichische Geschichte*, CXXI, Vienna 1955).
38. C. H. Carter, *The Secret Diplomacy of the Habsburgs 1598–1625* (New York 1964).
39. J. H. Elliott, *Imperial Spain 1469–1716* (London 1963).
40. *Idem, The Revolt of the Catalans. A Study in the Decline of Spain* (*1598–1640*) (Cambridge 1963).
41. K. Krofta, *Nesmrtelný národ* (Prague 1940).
42. J. V. Polišenský, ed., *Historie o válce české 1618–1620* (Prague 1964).
43. J. V. Polišenský, J. Kolman, 'Edice pramenů k dějinám předbělohorských a bělohorských Čech', *ČSČH*, I (1953), 494–7.
44. J. V. Polišenský, 'Viléma Slavaty relace o jednání v příčině knížectví Opavského 1614–1615', *Slezský sborník*, XXXI (1953), 488–98; 'Slezsko a válka třicetiletá', *Českopolský sborník vědeckých prací* (Prague 1955), 311–28

45. J. V. Polišenský, J. Hrubeš, 'Turecké války, uherská povstání a veřejné mínění předbělohorských Čech', *Historický časopis*, VII (1959), 74–103.
46. F. Kameníček, *Vpády Bočkajovců, Časopis Českého Musea* (*1894*) (monograph).
47. J. V. Polišenský, ed., *Kniha o bolesti a smutku. Výbor z moravských kronik XVII. století* (Prague 1948).
48. K. Benda, *A Bocskai szabadságharc* (Budapest 1955).
49. V. Březan, *Poslední Rožmberkové*, ed. J. Dostál (Prague 1941).
50. O. Hulec, 'Konspirační charakter předbělohorské protihabsburské opozice', *Jihočeský sborník historický* (hereafter *JSH*), XXX (1961).
51. K. Stloukal, 'Konec rodu pánů z Hradce', *JSH*, XXXIII (1964).
52. F. Hrubý, *Ladislav Velen ze Žerotína* (Prague 1930).
53. O. Odložilík, *Karel st. ze Žerotína 1564–1636* (Prague 1936).
54. V. Kybal, *Jindřich IV. a Evropa v letech 1609–1610* (Prague 1911).
55. A. Gindely, *Dějiny českého povstání léta 1618*, 4 vols. (Prague 1879–1880).
56. J. Pekař, *Bílá hora* (Prague 1921).
57. K. Krofta, *Bílá hora* (Prague 1913).
58. *Doba bělohorská a Albrecht z Valdštejna* (Prague 1934).
59. J. Prokeš, ed., *Protokol vyšlé korespondence kanceláře českých direktorů z let 1618 a 1619* (Prague 1934).
60. V. L. Tapié, *La politique étrangère de la France et le début de la guerre de Trente ans* (*1616–1621*) (Paris 1934).
61. *Idem*, *Bílá hora a francouzská politika* (Prague 1936).
62. J. Macůrek, *České povstání r. 1618 až 1620 a Polsko* (Brno 1937).
63. W. Czapliński, 'Ślask i Polska w pierwszych latach wojny trzydziestoletniej', *Sobótka*, III (1948), 141–81.
64. J. Macůrek, M. Rejnuš, *České země a Slovensko ve století před Bílou horou* (Prague 1958), especially 130–47. R. Neck, in *Mitteilungen des österreichischen Staatsarchive*, X (1957), 434–68. R. Heinisch, 'Habsburg, die Pforte und der böhmische Aufstand', *Südost-Forschungen*, XXXIII (1974), 125–65. C. Rotman 'Zur Frage osmanischer Teilnahme am Dreissigjährigen Krieg' (offprint, n.d.).
65. J. V. Polišenský, *Anglie a Bílá hora* (Prague 1949); *Nizozemská politika a Bílá hora* (Prague 1958).
66. M. Hroch, J. V. Polišenský, 'Švédská politika a české stavovské povstání 1618–1620', *Sborník historický* (hereafter *SbH*), VII (1960), 157–90.
67. B. Badura, 'Zápas o Valtellinu a český odboj protihabsburský 1618–1620', *SbH*, VII (1960), 123–56.
68. *Prameny k dějinám třicetileté války. Regesta fondu Militare archivu* ministerstva vnitra *ČSR v Praze* III, *1618–1625*, ed. V. Líva (Prague 1951).
69. J. Dobiáš, *Dějiny Pelhřimova*, II (Pelhřimov 1936), V (Prague 1970); *Zrádné proudy v českém povstání r. 1618* (Prague 1939).
70. Z. Kalista, ed., *Buquoyův itinerář z konce českého tažení*, in *Vojensko-historický sborník* (n.d.), 100–58, 5–106.
71. F. Hrubý, 'Švýcarský svědek Bílé hory', *Český časopis historický* (hereafter *ČČH*), XXXVII (1931), 42–78.
72. *JSH*, XXIX–XXXIII (1960–4).
73. M. Volf, 'Pokus budějovického patriciátu připojit se k českému povstání r. 1618', *Časopis společnosti přátel starožitností českých* (hereafter *ČSPSČ*), LXIX (1961).

74. F. Macháček, 'Defenestrace pražská 1618', *ČČH*, XIV (1908). J. Petráň, *Staroměstská exekuce* (Prague 1971).
75. H. Sturmberger, *Aufstand in Böhmen. Der Beginn des Dreissigjährigen Krieges* (Munich–Vienna 1959).
76. D. Albrecht, *Die auswärtige Politik Maximilians von Bayern, 1618–1635* (Göttingen 1962).
77. R. Stanka, *Die böhmischen Confœderationsakte von 1619* (Berlin 1932).
78. H. Weigel, *Franken, Kurpfalz und der böhmische Aufstand*, I (Erlangen 1932).
79. I. G. Weiss, 'Beiträge zur Beurteilung des Kurfürsten Friedrich V. von der Pfalz', *Zeitschrift für Geschichte des Oberrheins*, LXXXV (1932), 385–422.
80. Basic information is available in the survey *Otázky studia obecných dějin*, I: *Prameny k obecným dějinám v českých archivech a knihovnách* (Prague 1957), and II: *Prameny k obecným dějinám ve slovenských archivech a knihovnách* (Prague 1963). Then the individual volumes of the guides to the archives (*Průvodce po archivních fondech*) should be consulted. Also the descriptions of sources in the *Archivalien zur neueren Geschichte Österreichs* (Vienna 1913) are still useful for their thoroughness.
81. The significance of these holdings is beginning to be recognized by non-Czech scholars. See for example L. Forster, 'German Baroque literature in Czechoslovak libraries', *German Life and Letters*, XV (1962), 210–17; W. Urban, 'Niektóre polonica z XVI i XVII wieku w zbiorach czechoslowackich', *Zeszyty naukowe uniwerzytetu Jagiellońskiego Kraków*, LVI (1962), 171–91; G. Gille, 'Les archives privées', *Revue historique*, fasc. 475 (1965), 29–46.
82. *Otázky*, I, 55–6; L. Hofmann, 'Bericht über das gräflich Buquoysche Archiv in Gratzen', *Archivalien*, I, 35–51.
83. *Průvodce po Státním archivu v Brně* (Brno 1954).
84. F. Hrubý, ed., *Moravské korespondence a akta z let 1620–1636* (Brno 1934).
85. B. Bretholz, 'Das Schlossarchiv der Fürsten von Collalto, ehemals in Pirnitz (Mähren), heute im Landesarchiv in Brünn,' *Archivalien*, I, 290–321.
86. See *Průvodce po fondech státního archivu Brno*, II, 110ff., where further literature is listed.
87. *Státní archiv v Litoměřicích. Průvodce po archivních fondech*, II (Prague 1963), 93ff.
88. K. Tříska, 'Černínský archiv v Jindřichově Hradci', *Časopis Archivní školy* (hereafter *ČAŠ*) (1936), 63–89.
89. See *Státní ústřední archiv Praha. Průvodce po archivních fondech*, II (Prague 1955), for further literature.
90. *Prameny k dějinám třicetileté války*, III, *1618–1625*, ed. Líva.
91. See *Průvodce po ústředním archivu ministerstva vnitra* (Prague 1952), for examples of the handwriting.
92. M. Pařízková, *Jan Jeník z Bratřic jako historik bělohorských a předbělohorských Čech* (M.A. dissertation Charles University, Prague 1952).
93. *Státní archiv v Litoměřicích*, II, note 8, 34ff.
94. J. Šusta, 'Gräflich Kolowratsches Archiv in Reichenau', *Archivalien*, I, 196–205.
95. L. Hofmann, 'Das fürstlich Colloredo-Mannsfeldsche Archiv in Opočno', *Archivalien*, I, 180–96.
96. J. Šusta, 'Das gräflich Waldstein-Wartenbergsche Archiv in Dux', *Archivalien*, I, 173–6.

97. A. Mörath, 'Archivalien des fürstlich Schwarzenbergschen Zentralarchives in Krumau (1907)', *Archivalien*, I, 28–34.
98. M. Kušík, 'Archive in der Slowakei und ihre Bestände', *Studia Historica Slovaca* III (1965) 255ff. J. Kočiš, Oravský komposesorát – thurzovská korešpondencia 1541–1626', *Inventar* (State Central Archive at Bratislava, 1962).
99. Kušík, 'Archive in der Slowakei', 232ff.
100. *Europa recens descripta à Guilielmo Blaeuw* (Amsterdam, various edns).
101. J. V. Polišenský, 'Bohemia, the Turk and the Christian Commonwealth (1462–1620)', *Byzantinoslavica*, XIV (1953), particularly 81–5. See also Stanley Pargellis, ed., *The Quest for Political Unity in World History* (Washington 1944), and for the conception of general history, E. Joukov (Zhukov), 'Des principes d'une histoire universelle', *Cahiers d'histoire mondiale*, III (1956), 527–35.
102. Significant for these conceptions is for example the pamphlet 'Pesso polytico de todo el mundo por el Conde Don Antonio Xerley al Conde de Olivares' (1622) (Egerton MS 1824, British Museum). About the author of the pamphlet see E. Denison Ross, *Sir Anthony Sherley and his Persian Adventure* (London 1933), and Polišenský, *Anglie a Bílá hora*, 43–4. For the negotiations to bring Persia into the anti-Turkish coalition see G. Le Strange, ed., *Don Juan of Persia, a Shi'ah Catholic 1560–1604* (London 1926). See also J. Matoušek, *Turecká válka v evropské politice v letech 1592–1594* (Prague 1935), and J. Macůrek, *Zápas Polska a Habsburků o přístup k Černému moři na sklonku 16. století* (Prague 1931).
103. B. F. Porshnev, *Les rapports politiques de l'Europe occidentale et de l'Europe orientale à l'époque de la guerre de Trente ans. Rapport pour le XIe Congrès International des Sciences Historiques* (Stockholm 1960) (24 pp). The results of Swedish research have been summarized in Hroch, Polišenský, 'Švédská politika', 157–90.
104. A. E. Christensen, *Dutch Trade to the Baltic about 1600* (Copenhagen, 1941). T. S. Jansma, 'De economische en sociale ontwikkeling van het Noorden', *Algemene Geschiedenis der Nederlanden*, VI, 89–146. Polišenský, *Nizozemská politika a Bílá hora*, 133ff.
105. A critique of older views of the Thirty Years' War may be found in S. H. Steinberg, 'The Thirty Years' War: a new interpretation', *History*, XXXII (1947), 89–102.
106. R. Quazza, 'Il periodo italiano della guerra dei Trent' Anni', in *Miscell. Carlo Emanuele I*, (Turin 1930). B. F. Porshnev, 'Russkiye subsidii Shvetsii vo vremya Tridsatiletnoy voyny', *Izvestia AN SSSR*, II, no. 5 (1945). O. L. Vainstein, *Rossiya i Tridsatiletnaya voyna* (Moscow, Leningrad 1947). J. Presser, ed., *De Tachtigjarige Oorlog* (3rd edn., Amsterdam 1948). For interpretations of Dutch and Belgian historians H. A. Enno van Gelder, L. van der Essen, J. C. H. Pater and J. A. van Houtte, see the fifth volume of the *Algemene Geschiedenis der Nederlanden*. Compare A. N. Chistozvonov, *Niderlandskaya bourgeoisnaya revolutsiya XVI veka* (Moscow 1958).
107. An attempt at a Marxist explanation may be found in J. V. Polišenský's article 'The Thirty Years' War', *Past and Present*, VI (1954), 31–43. See also *idem*, *Přehled československých dějin*, I (Prague 1958), 335ff.
108. This is the thesis defended in the study of Dutch policy and the Battle of the White Mountain cited above, n. 104. See also A. N. Chistozvonov's

assessment of the general significance of the Dutch struggle for independence, in *Vsemirnaya istoria*, IV (Moscow 1958), and G. Griffiths, *William of Hornes, Lord of Hèze and the Netherlands (1576–1580)* (Berkeley 1954).

109. See Polišenský, *Přehled československých dějin*, I, 335ff, and 'Zur Problematik des Dreissigjährigen Krieges und der Wallensteinfrage', in *Aus 500 Jahren deutsch-tschechoslowakischer Geschichte* (Berlin 1958), 99–136. H. Sturmberger follows the traditional interpretation of the conflict as a religious war in his otherwise remarkable sketch *Aufstand in Böhmen*.

110. On the ideology of the leaders of the Estates opposition see H. Sturmberger, *Georg Erasmus Tschernembl. Religion, Libertät und Widerstand* (Linz 1953); F. H. Schubert, *Ludwig Camerarius 1573–1651. Eine Biographie* (Kallmünz 1955).

111. The most recent work on Ferdinand II is by H. Sturmberger: *Kaiser Ferdinand II. und das Problem des Absolutismus* (Vienna 1957).

112. The propaganda from the time of the Bohemian Estates' Rebellion has not yet been systematically investigated. See J. Gebauer, *Die Publicistik über den böhmischen Aufstand von 1618* (Halle 1892), and A. Markus, *Stavovské apologie z roku 1618* (Prague 1911).

113. B. Jenšovský, 'O stavovských konfederacích v českém povstání. Poznámky diplomatické', in *Novákův sborník*, 495–505; Stanka, *Die böhmischen Conföderationsakte;* Sturmberger, *Aufstand*, 47ff.

114. Polišenský, *Nizozemská politika a Bílá hora*, 191 *et passim*. See also R. Belvederi, *Oldenbarnevelt e Maurizio d'Orange* (Bari 1956).

115. For the negotiations of Palatine diplomats with Charles Emmanuel of Savoy, see R. Quazza, *Storia politica d'Italia. Preponderanza spagnuola, 1559–1700* (2nd edn, Milan 1950), 431ff. The negotiations have been clarified in new ways by Zdeněk Šolle in his dissertation *Savojsko a Bílá hora* (Charles University, Prague 1950) which unfortunately has remained unpublished.

116. S. R. Gardiner's *History of England from the Accession of James I to the Outbreak of the Civil War 1603–1642* (London 1883–4) is still indispensable for English policy under James and Charles I. See also Polišenský, *Anglie a Bílá hora*, 7ff. The most recent work on James I is D. Harris Willson's *King James VI and I* (London 1956).

117. For the policy of the Palatinate and the Union, see Weigel, *Franken, Kurpfalz und böhmischer Aufstand*, I; Weiss, 'Beiträge zur Beurteilung des Kurfürsten Friedrich V', 385–422. For the situation in Saxony see J. V. Polišenský, 'Die Universität Jena und der Aufstand der böhmischen Stände in den Jahren 1618–1620', *Wissenschaftliche Zeitschrift der Universität Jena*, VII, (1957), 441–7.

118. The resolute policy of Albert has been discussed by H. Pirenne, *Histoire de Belgique*, IV (Brussels 1927), 247–8. Further evidence may be found in the edition by H. Lonchay and J. Cuvelier, *Correspondance de la cour d'Espagne sur les affaires des Pays-Bas au XVIIe siècle*, I, *1598–1621*, (Brussels 1923); and in the correspondence of Zeelandre from Vienna, (Archives Nationales, Bruxelles, Secrétairerie d'État allemande, fos. 173ff.).

119. A survey of the modern literature on Spanish policy in this period may be found in C. Pérez-Bustamante, *Compendio de historia de España* (6th edn., Madrid 1957), 280ff. For the policy of the Papal Curia see Belvederi, 'Un nunzio pontifico', 561ff. For the dynastic Habsburg–Vasa pact of 1613 see

F. Hejl, 'Od českopolské státní smlouvy k habsbursko–vasovskému dynastickému paktu (1589–1613)', *Sbornik prací filosofické fakulty brnčnské university* (hereafter *SbFFBU*), VIII (1959), 39–54.

120. Carleton to the Secretary of State Naunton, 13 September 1619, The Hague, PRO, London, S.P. 84/92, fos. 3–4. See also Polišenský, *Nizozemská politika a Bílá hora*, 190.

121. *Ibid.*

122. For Bethlen's policy see G. Szekfü, *Bethlen Gábor* (Budapest 1929); T. Wittman, *Bethlen Gábor* (Budapest 1952); *idem*, *A nemzeti monarchia megteremtéséért vivott harc a cseh magyar szövetseg keretebén a reterjeszkedö Habsburghatalom ellen 1619–1620* (dissertation, Budapest 1954).

123. For Bavarian policy see S. Riezler, *Geschichte Bayerns*, v (Gotha 1903).

124. Mecenseffy, *Habsburger im 17. Jahrhundert.*

125. J. Macůrek, *České povstání r. 1618–1620 a Polsko* (Brno 1937).

126. V. L. Tapié has pointed to the significance of the Ulm agreement in his book *La politique étrangère de la France et le début de la guerre de Trente ans (1616–1621)* (Paris 1934).

127. Polišenský, *Nizozemská politika a Bílá hora*, 252ff.

128. *Ibid.* 236–7; 280–1.

129. F. Nethersole to Secretary Naunton, 5 November 1620, Prague, English, PRO London, S. P. 81/19, fos. 129–58.

130. Count Palatine Johann Casimir to Gustavus Adolphus, 5 April 1620, Stockholm, German, Riksarkivet Stockholm, Germ. A III, Förhandlingar.

131. Polišenský, *Nizozemská politika a Bílá hora*, 291ff.

3. THE DUTCH PERIOD OF THE CONFLICT, 1621–5

1. A. Gindely, *Geschichte des Dreissigjährigen Krieges*, IV, *Die Strafdekrete Ferdinands II. und der Pfälzische Krieg* (Prague 1880); *Geschichte der Gegenreformation in Böhmen* (Prague 1894).
2. J. Goll, *Die französische Heirath* (Prague 1876).
3. O. Odložilík, *Ze zápasů pobělohorské emigrace* (offprint from the *Časopis Matice moravské*, LVI (1932); LVII (1933)) (Brno 1933); *Z korespondence pobělohorské emigrace z let 1621–1624* (Prague 1933); *Povstalec a emigrant. Kapitoly z dějin třicetileté války* (biography of Heinrich von Thurn) (London 1944).
4. F. Hrubý, 'Pád českého povstání na Moravě', *ČČH*, XXIX (1923).
5. F. Hrubý, ed., *Moravské korespondence a akta z let 1620–1636*, I, *1620–1624* (Brno 1934).
6. E. Nohejlová-Prátová, *Dlouhá mince v Čechách v r. 1621–1623* (Prague 1946).
7. V. Pešák, *Vojenské vlivy na správu kontribuce v Čechách 1621–1623* (Prague 1936).
8. *Prameny k dějinám třicetileté války*, III, 1618–1625, ed. V. Líva (Prague 1951).
9. T. V. Bílek, *Dějiny konfiskací v Čechách po r. 1618* (Prague 1882–3); *Jmění jesuitských kolejí* (Prague 1888).
10. J. V. Polišenský, 'Die Universität Jena und der Aufstand der böhmischen Stände in den Jahren 1618–1620,' *Wissenschaftliche Zeitschrift der Universität Jena*, VII, (1957), 441–7.
11. *Idem*, 'Od Bílé hory k Masaniellovu povstání r. 1647', *SbH*, III (1955), 146ff.

12. *Idem*, 'Anglická a jiná svědectví o bitvě na Bílé hoře', *ČSPSČ*. LXVIII (1906). 203–8. 'Denmark–Norway and the Bohemian cause in the early part of the Thirty Years' War', in *Festgabe für L. Hammerich* (Copenhagen 1962), 215–28.
13. M. Hroch, J. V. Polišenský, 'Die böhmische Frage und die politischen Beziehungen zwischen dem europäischen Westen und Osten zur Zeit des Dreissigjährigen Krieges,' in *Probleme der Ökonomie und Politik*. . ., (Berlin 1960), 23–55. In Czech: *Acta Comeniana*, XIX (1960), 125–40. In Russian: *Srednye veka*, XXIV (1963), 240–58.
14. V. Fialová, *Jan Adam z Víckova, moravský emigrant a vůdce Valachů 1620–1628* (Brno 1935).
15. V. Fialová, ed., *Kronika holešovská 1615–1645* (Holešov 1967).
16. F. Dostál, *Valašská povstání za třicetileté války (1621–1644)* (Prague 1956).
17. F. H. Schubert, 'Die pfälzische Exilregierung im Dreissigjährigen Krieg. Ein Beitrag zur Geschichte des politischen Protestantismus', *Zeitschrift für Geschichte des Oberrheins*, CII (1954), 575–680.
18. *Idem*, *Ludwig Camerarius (1573–1651). Eine Biographie* (Kallmünz 1955).
19. R. Quazza, *Storia politica d'Italia. Preponderanza spagnuola, 1559–1700* (2nd edn., Milan 1950); *Politica Europea nella Questione Valtellinica: la lega franco–veneto–savoiarda e la pace di Moncon* (Venice 1921). A. Pfister, *Georg Jenatsch, sein Leben und seine Zeit* (Basle 1939).
20. T. Christiansen, *Die Stellung König Christians IV. von Dänemark zu den Kriegsereignissen im Reich und zu den Plänen einer evangelischen Allianz 1618–1625* (Kiel 1937).
21. A. Ernstberger, *Hans de Witte, Finanzmann Wallensteins* (Wiesbaden 1954). The dissertation by K. Vít is unfortunately not available.
22. B. Bretholz, 'Das fürstlich Dietrichsteinsche Schlossarchiv in Nikolsburg', *Archivalien zur neueren Geschichte Österreichs* (Vienna 1913), 98–113. H. Weisner, 'Das Graf Dietrichsteinsche Fideikommissarchiv', *Festschrift zur Feier des 200j. Bestandes des Haus-, Hof- und Staatsarchivs*, I (1949), 180–91.
23. W. Novotný. 'Das gräflich Nostizsche Archiv zu Prag', *Archivalien*, I, 126–32.
24. A. Mörath, 'Archivalien des fürstlich Schwarzenbergschen Zentralarchives in Krumau (1907)', *Archivalien*, I, 12–27.
25. V. Budil has described the present condition of the Wallenstein collection in the series *Průvodce po archivních fondech*, III, *Státní archiv Praha* (in press).
26. J. Loserth, 'Über einige Handschriften und Bücher im gräfl. Schlickschen Archiv zu Kopidlno', *Mitteilungen des Vereins für die Geschichte der Deutschen in Böhmen* (hereafter *MVGDB*) (1918), 114–20. The modern catalogue of 1966 permits a rapid orientation.
27. M. Kušík, 'Archive in der Slowakei und ihre Bestände', *Studia Historica Slovaca*, III (1965), 253ff. Jozef Watzka *et al.*, *Sprievodca po archívnych fondoch a zbierkach*, *Štátny archív Bratislava* (Bratislava 1959), 161ff.
28. *Archiv města Bratislavy. Sprievodca po fondoch a zbierkach* (Prague 1955). T. Lamoš, ed., *Archív mesta Kremnice, sprievodca po fondoch a zbierkach* (Bratislava 1957). For the rest of the municipal archives in Slovakia see Kušík, 'Archive in der Slowakei', 258–9, and *Otázky studia obecných dějin*, II, *Prameny k obecným dějinám vie slovenských archivech a Knihovnách* (Prague 1963) 36 (for Levoča in particular).
29. E. A. Beller, 'The Thirty Years' War', in *The New Cambridge Modern*

History, IV, *The Decline of Spain and the Thirty Years' War* (Cambridge 1970), 315–22.

30. A. Gindely, *Der niedersächsische, dänische und schwedische Krieg...1622 bis 1632. Geschichte des Dreissigjährigen Krieges*, II (Leipzig 1882), 58ff.
31. H. R. Trevor-Roper, 'Spain and Europe, 1598–1621', *The New Cambridge Modern History*, IV, 282.
32. E. H. Kossmann, 'The Low Countries', *Ibid.* 359–84.
33. J. V. Polišenský, *Documenta Bohemica Bellum Tricennale Illustrantia*, I, *Der Krieg und die Gesellschaft in Europa* (Prague 1971), 109–15; 'Der Beginn der zweiten Epoche des Achtzigjährigen Krieges'.
34. O. Odložilík, *Ze zápasů pobělohorské emigrace. Z korespondence pobělohorské emigrace z let 1621–1624.* See also Odložilík's biography of Heinrich von Thurn, *Povstalec a emigrant.*
35. F. H. Schubert, 'Die Niederlande zur Zeit des Dreissigjährigen Krieges im Urteil des diplomatischen Korps im Haag', *Historisches Jahrbuch*, LXXIV (1954), 252–64.
36. *Idem*, 'Die pfälzische Exilregierung im Dreissigjährigen Krieg', 575–680; *Ludwig Camerarius 1573–1651.*
37. J. H. Elliott, 'The Spanish Peninsula, 1598–1648', *The New Cambridge Modern History*, IV, 457–60.
38. C. Pérez-Bustamante, *Compendio de historia de España* (Madrid 1956), 282ff. E. Beladiez, *Osuna el Grande, el Duque de las Empresas* (Madrid 1954). J. M. Castroviejo, F. de P. Fernández de Córdoba, *El Conde de Gondomar. Un azor entre ocasos* (Madrid 1967). See also C. H. Carter, *The Secret Diplomacy of the Habsburgs, 1598–1625* (New York 1964).
39. J. Reglá, 'Hegemonía española', in *Introducción a la historia de España* (Barcelona 1963), 381ff.
40. R. Ródenas Vilar, *La política europea de España durante la guerra Treinta años (1624–1630)*, (Madrid 1967) xiii.
41. *Ibid.* 7.
42. *Ibid.* 10.
43. A. N. Chistozvonov, 'Rol kalvinizma v Niderlandskoy bourgeoisnoy revolutsii XVI veka', *Srednye veka*, XXX (1971), 44–60.
44. J. H. Elliott, *The Revolt of the Catalans. A Study in the Decline of Spain (1598–1640)* (Cambridge 1963), 189.
45. *Ibid.* 190. *Consulta* of 26 July 1618, Archivo General de Simancas (hereafter AGS), *Hacienda*, Leg. 555, no. 212.
46. *Consulta* of 1 February 1619, printed in Gonzáles Palencia, *La Junta de Reformación.* no. 4. See Elliott, *Revolt of the Catalans*, 191. A contemporary transcription is in the MS Collection of the State Central Archive at Prague (hereafter SCA), Těšnov section. P. Fernández Navarrete, *Conservación de Monarquías* (Madrid 1626), is in the library of the Lobkowitzes of Roudnice (hereafter LLR), now in the University Library, Prague.
47. Elliott, *Revolt of the Catalans*, 192, in general follows the conclusions of the pioneering work by A. Domínguez Ortiz, *Política y Hacienda de Felipe IV.* (Madrid 1960), 4ff.
48. J. V. Polišenský, *The Thirty Years' War* (London 1971), 133ff.
49. M. A. M. Franken, 'The general tendencies and structural aspects of the foreign policy and diplomacy of the Dutch Republic in the latter half of the 17th century', *Acta Historiae Neerlandica*, III (1968), 1–42.
50. *Documenta Bohemica Bellum Tricennale Illustrantia*, II, *Der Beginn des*

Dreissigjährigen Krieges. Der Kampf um Böhmen 1618–1621 (Prague 1972).

51. Besides transcriptions from the AGS, the SCA contains microfilms of the correspondence of Diego de Zeelandre, the agent of the Archduke Albert.
52. Most important of the Viennese sources in the Haus- Hof- und Staatsarchiv are: *Spanische dipl. Korrespondenz,* nos. 16–17; *Spanische Hof-Korrespondenz,* no. 4; *Spanische Varia,* no. 3; *Belgische Korrespondenz* (correspondence of the Emperor with the Archduke at Brussels).
53. See J. V. Polišenský, 'La plata americana y los comienzos de la Guerra de los 30 años', *Anuario de Estudios Americanos,* XXVIII (Seville 1971), 209–218.
54. *Lista kayserlicher Kriegs-armada...Anno MDCXX,* SCA, VL, Kriegslisty 2.
55. *Lista...,* 5–10
56. *Ibid.* 15–17.
57. *Ibid.* 23–4.
58. *Ibid.* 24–8.
59. *Ibid.* 35.
60. The information has been gathered from the following collections: *Lista kayserlicher Kriegs-armada...Anno MDCXIX,* State Archive at Prague, branch at Mnichovo Hradiště, Waldstein Family Archive; *Lista A. MDCXX,* SCA, VL; *Eigentliche Fürstellung...Kriegsvölker...1621, ibid.*; *Lista S.K.M. Kriegs-armada...1622, ibid.*; *Verzeichnis gesamtl. Kriegsvölker...1623, ibid.*; *Soupis...1624,* State Archive at Prague, branch at Mnichovo Hradiště, Waldstein Family Archive; *Habsb....Kriegsmacht, ibid.* R 12.
61. The information from the Indexes has been supplemented by printed and unprinted source materials. See Hrubý, ed., *Moravské korespondence a akta,* I *1620–1624,* 455ff.
62. J. V. Polišenský, *Wallenstein* (*I protagonisti della Storia Universale,* Milan 1969).
63. L. Mandová, *Kardinál Dietrichstein a španělská politika ve střední Evropě v letech 1621–1624* (M.A. thesis, Charles University, Prague 1973). V. Šuťák, *Hispanika roudnické lobkovické knihovny* (M.A. thesis, Charles University, Prague 1973).
64. F. Hrubý's article 'Bethlen Gábor a česká emigrace v letech 1622–1623', *ČČH,* XLI (1935), 572–82, contains some of the testimony concerning Bethlen's erratic relations with the Bohemian émigrés.
65. See J. V. Polišenský, *Nizozemská politika a Bílá hora* (Prague 1958).
66. See the edition by A. Duch, *Die Politik Maximilians I. von Bayern und seiner Verbündeten 1618–1651,* Part I, Vol. II (Munich–Vienna 1970).
67. For the situation in the Netherlands in 1621 and in the following years see I. Schöffer, 'De crisis van de jonge Republik 1609–1625', in *Algemene Geschiedenis der Nederlanden,* VI (Utrecht–Antwerp 1953), 50–60. Polišenský, *Nizozemská politika a Bílá hora,* 307ff. J. Presser, ed., *De Tachtigjarige Oorlog,* Part II, *Van het Twalfjarig Bestand tct de Vrede van Munster* (Amsterdam–Brussels 1963), 217ff. J. den Tex, *Oldenbarnevelt,* Part III, *Bestand 1609–1619* (Haarlem 1966), 586–8.
68. Schubert, 'Die pfälzische Exilregierung im Dreissigjährigen Krieg', 675ff.
69. Subsidie aan den Koning. 13 February 1622. General Index no. 340. *Handelingen en Resolutiën van de...Staten Generaal...1576–1698,* sub Bohemen, Algemeen Rijksarchief, The Hague (ARA).
70. Castroviejo-Fernández de Córdoba, *El Conde de Gondomar. Un azor entre ocasos,* 171ff.

71. For the Palatine War, see A. Morel-Fatio, *L'Espagne au XVIe et au XVIIe siècle* (Heilbronn 1878) and Gindely, *Geschichte des Dreissigjährigen Krieges*, IV. See also J. Polišenský, *Třicetiletá válka a český národ* (Prague 1960), 128ff.
72. See Schubert, 'Die pfälzische Evilregierung im Dreissigjährigen Krieg', 632ff. for the quarrel between Christian of Anhalt and Camerarius, and the correspondence of Verdugo with both Anhalts in the Verdugo Family Archive of Doupov, State Archive at Pilsen, branch at Žlutice.
73. For Thurn, see Odložilík, *Povstalec a emigrant*, 30ff. Ehrenfried von Berbisdorf to the States General, 26 January 1623, The Hague. The draft of a reply: ARA, Loketkas–Duitsland, 64, Correspondence with Gabriel Bethlen from 1623 to 1626.
74. Bethlen to the States General, 28 July 1623, Alba Julia, Lat., and the States General to Bethlen, Latin draft, *ibid.* See Gindely, *Geschichte des Dreissigjährigen Krieges*, IV, 493ff.
75. Brederode's correspondence from Strasbourg, Basle, etc., from 1622 to 1631 is in the ARA, Ie Afdeling, Staten Generaal, Lias–Duitsland, 6022–3.
76. Papers connected with the mission of Jan Adam of Víckov from January to March 1624 are in ARA, Loketkas–Duitsland, 64. See Fialová, *Jan Adam z Víckova*, 64ff.
77. The States General to Bethlen, 16 May 1625, The Hague, Latin draft, ARA, Loketkas–Duitsland, 64.
78. *Propositio a Bethlenio Principe Transylvaniae...*, transcription (1626), in ARA, Loketkas–Duitsland, 64. See Polišenský, *Třicetiletá válka a český národ*, 145ff.

4. THE DANISH INTERVENTION AND THE ATTEMPTS AT THE FORMATION OF A GRAND COALITION

1. J. Pekař, *Valdštejn. Dějiny valdštejnského spiknutí* (Prague 1934); *Wallenstein 1630–1634. Tragödie einer Verschwörung*, 2 vols. (Berlin 1937).
2. H. von Srbik, *Wallensteins Ende. Ursachen, Verlauf und Folgen der Katastrophe* (Salzburg 1932).
3. A. Ernstberger, *Wallenstein als Volkswirt im Herzogtum Friedland* (Reichenberg 1929).
4. J. V. Polišenský, 'Zur Problematik des Dreissigjährigen Krieges und der Wallensteinfrage', in *Aus 500 Jahren deutsch-tschechoslowakischer Geschichte* (Berlin 1958), 99–136.
5. J. V. Polišenský, *Wallenstein* (*I protagonisti della Storia Universale*, Milan 1969). Golo Mann, *Wallenstein* (Frankfurt-am-Main 1971).
6. M. Hroch, 'Valdštejnova politika v severním Německu v letech 1629–1630', *SbH*, V (1957), 203–28; B. F. Porshnev, A. S. Kan, 'Novaya tochka sreniya na politiku Wallensteina v gorodach Severnoy Germanii', *Voprosy istorii* (1962), 188–9.
7. M. Hroch, 'Der Dreissigjährige Krieg und die europäischen Handelsbeziehungen', *Wissenschaftliche Zeitschrift der Universität Greifswald*, XII (1963), 533–43.
8. J. V. Polišenský, 'Morava a vztahy mezi evropským východem a západem 1626–1627', in *Macůrkův sborník* (Brno 1961).
9. F. Roubík, 'Valdštejnovo tažení na Slovensko roku 1626', *SAMV*, VIII (Prague 1935).

10. F. Hrubý, ed., *Moravska korespondence a akta z let 1620–1636*, II, *1625–1636* (Brno 1937).
11. B. Indra, 'Odboj města Hranic 1620–1627 a jeho potrestání', *Časopis vlastivědného musej spolku v Olomouci*, LV (1940).
12. F. Stieve, *Der oberösterreichische Bauernaufstand des Jahres 1626* (Vienna 1904–5).
13. G. Mecenseffy, *Geschichte des Protestantismus in Österreich* (Graz–Cologne 1956), 149ff.
14. R. F. Schmiedt, *Der Bauernkrieg in Oberösterreich vom Jahre 1626 als Teilerscheinung des Dreissigjährigen Krieges* (dissertation, Halle 1963).
15. For basic information, see J. Nielsen, *Dänische Wirtschaftsgeschichte* (Jena 1933) and F. Danstrup, *History of Denmark* (Copenhagen 1947). M. Hroch, 'Obchod mezi východní a západní Evropou v období počátku kapitalismu', *ČSČH*, XI (1963); 'Obchod a politika za třicetileté Války', *SbH* XII (1964); 'Úloha západoevropského kupeckého kapitálu ve zprostředkování obchodu s východní Evropou', *Otázky studie obecných dějin*, III (*Acta Universitatis Carolinae*, (Prague 1964).
16. H. D. Loos, *Hamburg und Christian IV. von Dänemark* (Hamburg 1963). P. Vilar, 'Un gran proyecto antiholandés', *Hispania*, LXXXVIII (1962).
17. See J. V. Polišenský, 'Nové práce a nové pohledy na Španělsko "Zlatého věku"', *ČSČH*, XVII (1969), 111–13. J. H. Elliott, *The Revolt of the Catalans. A Study in the Decline of Spain (1598–1640)* (Cambridge 1963), 263ff.
18. C. R. Boxer, *The Dutch Seaborne Empire 1600–1800* (London 1965). M. A. M. Franken, 'The general tendencies and structural aspects of the foreign policy and diplomacy of the Dutch Republic in the latter half of the 17th century', *Acta Historiae Neerlandica*, III (1968), 1–42.
19. J. Presser, *De Tachtigjarige Oorlog*, Part II (Amsterdam–Brussels 1963). *Algemene Geschiedenis der Nederlanden*, VI (Utrecht–Antwerp 1953).
20. H. Sturmberger, *Kaiser Ferdinand II. und das Problem des Absolutismus* (Vienna 1957).
21. E. Winter, *Die tschechische und slowakische Emigration in Deutschland im 17. und 18. Jahrhundert* (Berlin 1955).
22. J. Patočka, 'L'état présent des études coméniennes', *Historica*, I (1959), 197ff. J. V. Polišenský, *Jan Amos Komenský* (Prague 1963). J. Brambora, 'Les problèmes actuels de la coméniologie', *Paedagogica Historica*, VII (1967), 5–49. G. Limiti, *Rassegna e prospettive degli studi comeniani oggi* (Rome 1968).
23. N. Mout, J. V. Polišenský, *Komenský v Amsterodamu* (Prague 1970).
24. A. Ernstberger, *Hans de Witte, Finanzman Wallensteins* (Wiesbaden 1954). Roubík, 'Valdštejnovo tažení na Slovensko roku 1626', 145ff.
25. R. Quazza, *La guerra per la successione di Mantova e del Monferrato (1628–1631)*, 2 vols. (Mantua 1926); *Storia politica d'Italia. Preponderanza spagnuola, 1559–1700* (2nd edn., Milan 1950).
26. See A. Mörath, 'Archivalien des fürstlich Schwarzenbergschen Zentralarchivs in Krumau (1907)', *Archivalien*, I, 12–27.
27. J. Zukal, 'Die Lichtensteinsche Inquisition in den Fürstentümern Troppau und Jägerndorf aus Anlass des Mansfeldischen Einfalles 1626–1627', *Zeitschrift für Geschichte und Kulturgeschichte Österreichisch-Schlesiens*, VII (1912); *Slezské konfiskace 1620–1630* (Prague 1916).
28. F. Roubík, 'Osudy registratury Albrechta z Valdštejna a jeho jičínské

komory', *SAMV*, II (Prague 1929), 115. Josef Kollmann is preparing a description of the contents of the archive, and I have used his information in the following. See also J. Svátek, *Dvorská kancelář Valdštejnova frýdlantského vévodství* (dissertation, Olomouc 1953).

29. V. Budil has prepared a descriptive catalogue.
30. *Státní archiv v Brně. Průvodce*, II, 390ff.
31. A descriptive catalogue has been prepared.
32. See below, 'The Danish War in Moravia and Hungary'.
33. A. Gindely, *Die maritimen Pläne der Habsburger* (Vienna 1890). F. Mareš, 'Die Maritime Politik der Habsburger', *Mitteilungen des Instituts für österreichische Geschichtsforschung* (hereafter *MIÖG*), I, 543–8.
34. E. Bouza, 'Náchodský zámecký archiv a spisovna velkostatku Náchod v období feudalismu a kapitalismu', *Sborník archivních prací* (hereafter *SbAP*) (1961), 115–37.
35. *Průvodce po archivních fondech. Státní archiv v Opavě* (Prague 1955). See above, n. 27.
36. Register of the shoemakers' guild at Frýdek in Moravia, Municipal Archive, Ostrava, C 89, fos. 141v, 142.
37. B. F. Porshnev, *Les rapports politiques de l'Europe occidentale et de l'Europe orientale à l'époque de la guerre de Trente ans. Rapport pour le XIe Congrès International des Sciences Historiques* (Stockholm 1960). Cf. J. V. Polišenský, *The Thirty Years' War* (London 1971), Bibliographical Survey, 266–95.
38. J. Macůrek, *České povstání r. 1618–1620 a Polsko* (Brno 1937); 'České povstanie v rokoch 1618–1620 a severozápadné Slovensko', *Historické štúdie*, II (1956).
39. This view is still defended for example by H. Sturmberger, *Aufstand in Böhmen. Der Beginn des Dreissigjährigen Krieges* (Munich–Vienna 1959).
40. Riksarkivet Stockholm, Germ. A III, Förhandlinger, 5 April 1620. See the work cited above by Macůrek on Poland in the *Časopis Matice moravské* LXI. See also M. Hroch and J. V. Polišenský, 'Švédská politika a české stavovské povstání 1618–1620', *SbH*, VII (1960), 157ff.
42. Of the voluminous works on Denmark in this period the following should be especially noted: E. Arup, *Danmarks Historie*, II (Copenhagen 1932); A. Nielsen, *Dänische Wirtschaftsgeschichte* (Jena 1933); O. B. Andersen in *Schultz Danmarkhistorien*, III (Copenhagen 1942), 3–172. More recent works may be found in H. Bruun, *Dansk historisk bibliografi 1943–1947*. Of the monographs the most important is A. E. Christensen, *Dutch Trade to the Baltic about 1600* (Copenhagen 1941).
43. T. Christiansen, *Die Stellung König Christians IV. von Dänemark zu den Kriegsereignissen im Deutschen Reich und zu den Plänen einer evangelischen Allianz 1618–1625* (dissertation, Kiel 1937).
44. B. Navrátil, *Jesuité olomoučtí za protireformace I*, (Brno 1916), 179ff. F. Cinek, ed., *Matricula Academiae Olomucensis*, in *Ročenka CM fakulty bohoslovecké v Olomouci* (1929), 42ff.
45. See M. Roberts, *Gustavus Adolphus, A History of Sweden 1611–1632*, I (London 1953), 93ff.
46. According to Cinek's edition and Navrátil's information. There are some mistakes in Cinek's transcriptions.
47. The Bohemian Estates to Christian IV, 13 March 1619, Prague, German copy, Riksarkivet Copenhagen, Tyske Kancellis Udenlandske Afdeling

(hereafter RAK, TKUA), Pfalz A II, 14. The same to Gustavus Adolphus, same date and place, German, copy, Riksarkivet Stockholm, Germ. Ständerna. These letters do not appear in the published protocol of the correspondence of the Chancery of the Bohemian Estates (ed. J. Prokeš, SAMV, VII, (Prague 1934)).

48. Christiansen, *Dutch Trade to the Baltic*, 32–3.
49. The Bohemian Directors to Christian IV, 13 July 1619, Prague, RAK, TKUA, Pfalz A II, 14. Christian IV to Frederick of the Palatinate, 5 August 1619; see Christiansen, *Dutch Trade to the Baltic*, 31.
50. The Bohemian Directors and Estates to Christian IV, 19 December 1619, Prague, German, copy, RAK, TKUA, Pfalz A II, 14.
51. Christiansen, *Dutch Trade to the Baltic*, 35.
52. D. Schäfer, *Geschichte von Dänemark*, V (Gotha 1893), 382. See also Christiansen, *Dutch Trade to the Baltic*, 35–6.
53. For the Danish aid, see Nethersole to Carleton, 10 March 1620, English, PRO, S. P., Dom. CXIII, 33; Christiansen, *Dutch Trade to the Baltic*, 37; Anstruther to Carleton, 20 August 1620, Bredstedt, English orig., PRO, S. P. Holland 89/96, 99.
54. Christiansen, *Dutch Trade to the Baltic*, 36. See also G. Das, *Foppe van Aitzema* (Utrecht 1920), 46ff.
55. J. Goll, *Der Convent von Segeberg* (Prague 1875); 'Poměry evropské po bitvě na Bílé hoře', *Časopis Českého Musea*, XIL (1875), 359–72. See also *idem*, *Vybrané spisy drobné II* (Prague 1929), 169ff.
56. Christiansen, *Dutch Trade to the Baltic*, 55.
57. For the efforts of Frederick of the Palatinate and the Bohemian émigrés see O. Odložilík, *Ze zápasů pobělohorské emigrace*, (offprint from the *Časopis Matice moravské*, LVI (1932), LVII (1933)) (Brno 1933). Also valuable is Odložilík's edition *Z korespondence pobělohorské emigrace z let 1621–1624* (Prague 1933), which, however, is not complete.
58. J. V. Polišenský, 'Die Universität Jena und der Aufstand der böhmischen Stände in den Jahren 1618–1620', *Wissenschaftliche Zeitschrift der Universität Jena*, VII (1957–8), 441–7. See also J. Goll, *Die Französische Heirat: Frankreich und England 1624 und 1625* (Prague 1876). *Relationes Abraham Richters, Kammerschreibers, aus Den Haag, wegen Hzg. Johann Ernsts zu Sachsen; Weimar norddeutscher Kriegs Expedition, 14 April 1624–19 May 1625*, Thüringisches Landeshauptarchiv (LHA), State Archive, Weimar, H 38.
59. Receipts of '14 Denemärkischer Rittmeister', 22 and 23 February 1625, Hamburg, German, orig., State Archive, Weimar, H 45.
60. For the 'Danish' War see especially J. O. Opel, *Der niedersächsisch–dänische Krieg*, III (Magdeburg 1894). A. Larsen, *Kejserkrigen. Et Bidrag til de nordiske Rigers Krigshistorie* (Copenhagen 1901). The first to use Wallenstein's Military Chancery was F. Roubík; see 'Valdštejnovo tažení na Slovensko roku 1626', 145ff.
61. Unknown person to Johann Ernst of Saxe-Weimar, 6 November 1625, n.p., German, orig., partly in cipher, State Archive, Weimar, H 18, 174–5. For Bethlen see F. Hrubý, *Ladislav Velen ze Žerotína* (Prague 1930), 167ff. Among more recent work is T. Wittman's *Bethlen Gábor* (Budapest 1952).
62. Instructions for M. Streyff, March 1626, State Archive, Weimar, H 42, 9.
63. Opel, *Der niedersächsisch–dänische Krieg* II, 455.
64. Roubík, 'Valdštejnovo tažení na Slovensko roku 1626', 173. The most

valuable source for the Danish 'Regiment' in Silesia is the *Gründliche und warhaffte Relation der Campagne in Schlesien und Ungarn unter beiden Generalen H. Gfen. v. Mansfeldt und Hzg. von S. Weimar, 1626 et 1627*, Riksarkivet Copenhagen, 5811. I thank Mme. Mag. Gyda Dahm-Rinnan (Oslo) and Mag. W. Thorndahl (Charlottenlund) for the microfilm of this.

65. For the prospects of Johann Ernst the rich documents of the Saxe-Weimar War Chancery are valuable: Bestand H 18 (I. F. Gn. Hzg. Johann Ernsts des Jüngeren Feldzug in Schlesien und Ungarn, 208–76). The *Artillerie Rechnung* of Captain J. E. Trost von Tiefenthal is helpful in reconstructing the itinerary of the Saxe-Weimar contingents (20 February 1626–24 December 1626), German, orig., State Archive, Weimar, H 31, fos. 70ff. The 'Konsultation' mentioned above of 13–23 August 1626 is in the LHA Weimar, H 18, 209–10.

66. *Grafen v. Mansfelds Articul, so wie I. F. Gn. zu unterschreiben und demselben (nach Lukow) zugesandt worden* (around 30 August from Leipnik), German draft, *ibid.* H 18, 272–3.

67. Johann Ernst of Saxe-Weimar to Mansfeld, n.d., n.p., German draft in Duke's hand, *ibid.* H 18, 274–5.

68. Original Latin letters of G. Bethlen to the Duke, of 25 August, 13 September, 23 September and 25 September 1626 are in the Saxe-Weimar Chancery, H 18, 213ff. Lieut.-Col. Peblis to Johann Ernst, 26 September 1626, Proben, German, orig., *ibid.* H 18, 221–4, accompanied by Latin copy.

69. Gabriel Bethlen to Mansfeld and Johann Ernst, 28 September 1626, Balassa-Gyarmat, Latin, copy, *ibid.* H 18, 231–3.,

70. Roubík, 'Valdštejnovo tažení na Slovensko roku 1626', for the meeting near Drégelypalánk. Bethlen to Mansfeld, 1 October 1626, Szécsény, Latin, copy, *ibid.* H 18, 233.

71. *Puncta welche I. Gn. dem Prinzen von Mansfeld durch den Obristen Peblicz proponiret*, 29 October 1626, Tekov, German, copy, *ibid.* H 18, 262–3. *Antwort auf diejenige Puncta, so I. F. Gn. Herzog Johann Ernst zu Sachsen Weimar, mir (Mansfeld) durch den Obristen gesterigen Tage proponiren lasse*, 30 October 1626, Tekov, German, orig.(?), *ibid.* H 18, 264–7. *Des Generals von Mansfeld in zehen Puncten gefasste Antwort...und Replica*, after 30 October 1626, n.p., German, summary, *ibid.* H 18, 268–9. *Ihr Gn. Verantwortungs Puncta gegen den Graf von Mansfeld...*, n.p., n.d., German, draft (holograph), *ibid.* H 18, 270–1.

72. Roubík, 'Valdštejnovo tažení na Slovensko roku 1626', 227.

73. G. Bethlen to Johann Ernst, 21 November 1626, Tekov, Latin, orig., *ibid.* H 18, 242–3. *Instructio pro Egregio et Nobile Francisco Kun*, 21 November 1626, Latin, orig., *ibid.* H 18, 240–1.

74. *Was auf Ihr durch Fürsten in Siebenbürgen Proposition antworten sollen...*, 3 December 1626, n.p., German draft, *ibid.* H 18, 246–9.

75. *Ihrer Durchlaut gestriger Discours...*, n.d., n.p., German draft, *ibid.* H 18, 250.

76. *Unmassgebliche Puncta...Resolution* (from Johann Ernst to G. Bethlen), n.d., n.p., German draft, *ibid.* H 18, 251–2. The Wallachians appear now for the first time in Johann Ernst's correspondence. See J. V. Polišenský, 'Valaši a Valašsko v anglických pramenech 17. století', *Naše Valašsko*, x (1967), 101–7.

77. Hrubý, *Ladislav Velen*, 180–1.

78. *Johann Ernstens Bedenken an den Fürsten von Siebenbürgen...*, Pukanec, n.d., German draft, incomplete, *ibid.* H 18, 253–9.

79. *Capitain Georg Friedrichs von Brandstein Absendung...*, 6 February 1627, *ibid.* H 54.
80. *Rolle der sämtlichen Officiers, so unter Ihr Fürstl. Gn. und Herzog Johann Ernst zu Sachsen Weimar Commando, der königl. Majestät zu Dennemark–Norwegen bestellten General in Schlesien und nach deroselben Absterben bey der Armee gewesen von 20. Juli 1626 bis 20. Juni 1627 Stylo veteri*, German, orig., *ibid.* H 31, 35–6.
81. *Vorschlag und Überschlag, die Garnison zu Troppau betreffend*, 11 June 1627, German draft, *ibid.* H 31, 37–8.
82. J. Zukal, *Paměti opavské* (Opava 1912); 'Die Liechtensteinsche Inquisition'; *Slezské konfiskace 1620–1630* (Prague 1916). The works by Hrubý and Roubík are cited above.
83. For example, the view of this period given in the work by E. Préclin and V. L. Tapié, *Le XVIIe siècle. Monarchies centralisées* (Paris 1949), 66–133.
84. Indra, 'Odboj města Hranic 1620–1627 a jeho potrestání,' V. Fialová, *Jan Adam z Víckova, moravský emigrant a vůdce Valachů 1620–1628* (Brno 1935); *Kronika holešovská 1615–1645* (Holešov 1967). J. V. Polišenský, ed., *Kniha o bolesti a smutku. Výbor 2 moravských kronik XVII. století* (Prague 1948); *idem*, 'O úloze lidových hnutí na východní Moravě v období pozdního feudalismu', *Český lid*, XXXII (1952). F. Dostál, *Valašská povstání za třicetileté války (1621–1644)* (Prague 1956).
85. *The Relation of Sydnam Poyntz*, Fonds Anglais 55, Bibiothèque Nationale, Paris. Published by A. T. S. Goodrich in *Publications of the Camden Society* (London 1908). See also J. V. Polišenský, *Anglie a Bílá hora* (Prague 1949), 190.
86. P. Pach-Zsigmond, *Boje proti Habsburkovcom za nezávislosť v XVII. storočí, Einige Kapitel aus der ungarischen Geschichte* (Bratislava 1952): see particularly 113ff. See also E. Kovács and J. Novotný, *Maďaři a my* (Prague 1959).
87. A. Gindely, *Bethlen Gábor* (Budapest 1890). G. Szekfü, *Bethlen Gábor* (Budapest 1929). D. Angyal, *Bethlen Gábor, Magyar Könyvtár*, 133. D. Kosáry, 'Gabriel Bethlen', *Slavonic Review* (1938), 162ff. (a weak article, though the assessment approaches the more modern ones). M. Depner, *Das Fürstentum Siebenbürgen im Kampf gegen Habsburg* (Stuttgart 1938).
88. The County of Thuróc (Turiec) to Gabriel Bethlen, 10 November 1626, Martin, Latin, orig., LHA Weimar, H 18, 244–5. See also *Artillerie Rechnung, ibid.* H 31, 76–7.
89. J. Petráň, *Matouš Ulický a poddanské povstání na Kouřimsku a Čáslavsku roku 1627 (Acta Universitatis Carolinae – Philologica et Historica*, 1954), 43ff., particularly 51, 60–1.

5. THE SWEDISH–DUTCH PERIOD OF THE CONFLICT 1630–5

1. D. Albrecht, *Richelieu, Gustav Adolf und das Reich* (Munich–Vienna 1959).
2. *Idem, Die auswärtige Politik Maximilians von Bayern, 1618–1635* (Göttingen 1962).
3. G. Marañon, *El Conde Duque de Olivares. La pasión de mandar* (Madrid 1952).
4. A. Domínguez Ortiz, *Política y Hacienda de Felipe IV.* (Madrid 1960); *El Antigquo Régimen: Los Reyes Católicos y los Austrias* (Madrid 1973).

5. F. Tomás Valiente, *Los validos en la monarquía española del siglo XVII* (Madrid 1963).
6. R. Quazza, *La guerra per la successione di Mantova a del Monferrato, 1628–1631* (Mantua 1926).
7. D. Albrecht, *Die deutsche Politik Papst Gregors XV.* (*Schriftenreihe zur Bayerischen Landesgeschichte*, LIII, Munich 1956).
8. A. Leman, *Urbain VIII et la rivalité de la France et de la Maison d'Autriche de 1631 à 1635* (Lille 1920).
9. E. von Frauenholz, *Entwicklungsgeschichte des deutschen Heerwesens*, III, Parts 1–2 (Munich 1935–41). G. Mann, *Wallenstein* (Frankfurt-am-Main 1971). J. Janáček, *Valdštejnova smrt* (Prague 1970).
10. I. Andersson, *Schwedische Geschichte* (Munich 1950).
11. E. F. Heckscher, *Economic History of Sweden* (Cambridge, Mass. 1954).
12. N. Ahnlund, *Gustav Adolf, král švédský* (with an introduction by O. Odložilík) (Prague 1939).
13. M. Roberts, *Gustavus Adolphus: A History of Sweden 1611–1632*, 2 vols. (London 1953–8).
14. *Idem, The Early Vasas: A History of Sweden 1523–1611* (London 1968).
15. *Idem*, ed., *Sweden as a Great Power 1611–1697. Government – Society – Foreign Policy* (London 1968).
16. V. M. Alekseyev, *Tridsatiletnaya voyna* (Leningrad 1961), 171–82.
17. B. F. Porshnev, *Les rapports politiques de l'Europe occidentale et de l'Europe orientale à l'époque de la guerre de Trente ans. Rapport pour le XIe Congrès International des Sciences Historiques* (Stockholm 1960), 136–63.
18. P. Geyl, *The Netherlands in the Seventeenth Century*, I, *1609–1648* (New York 1961).
19. *Idem, History of the Low Countries. Episodes and Problems* (London 1964), 43–78.
20. J. Presser, *De tachtigjarige Oorlog. Van het bestand tot de vrede van Munster* (Elsevier 1963), 381ff.
21. V. L. Tapié, *La France de Louis XIII et Richelieu* (Paris 1952).
22. R. Mandrou, *La France aux XVIIe et XVIIIe siècles* (Paris 1967).
23. G. Mecenseffy, *Habsburger im 17. Jahrhundert. Die Beziehungen der Höfe von Wien und Madrid während des Dreissigjährigen Krieges* (*Archiv für österreichische Geschichte*, (XXI. Vienna 1955)), 26–8.
24. J. M. Jover, *1635. Historia de una polémica y semblanza de una generación* (Madrid 1949).
25. J. A. Maravall, *La philosophie politique espagnole au XVIIe siècle* (Paris 1955).
26. J. Bergl, 'Auf den Spuren Wallensteins', *Bohemia*, XI (1934). *Diarium et itinerarium Johannis Putz à Turraquilla*... (MS 1660, 208 pp.). See also letter of Aitzema to an unknown correspondent, 1634, The Hague, 'Autographs II', 222.
27. Waldstein Family Archive, I 22/29.
28. J. Jeník z Bratřic, *Bohemica*, II/2, 177ff. (Library of the National Museum, Prague).
29. Gallas Family Archive, Military Chancery and Correspondence of M. Gallas, section XV, box 24 with Marradas' correspondence with Count Galena from February 1634; section XVIII, box 4, Leo C. Medici to Gallas, 2 January 1634, Pilsen, 'gli spagnuoli ubediran il Re'; section XXII, box 12, 'Wallensteinsche Konspiration', groups I–IV.

30. The contents of the Schlick Family Archive are well organized and are described in a catalogue of 1966, so that orientation presents no problem. For the Thirty Years' War the most important sections are under the numbers C IV 3c, 1–35 (I, nos. 203–38). See M. Dvořák, 'Hrabata Šlikové a jejich archiv v Kopidlně', *ČČH*, I (1895), 298–307. J. Loserth, 'Über einige Handschriften und Bücher im gräfl. Schlickschen Archiv zu Kopidlno', *MVGDB* (1918), 114–20.
31. A survey of the holdings is provided by K. Tříska's catalogue of the Slavata Family Archive.
32. See J. V. Polišenský, *Wallenstein* (*I Protagonisti della Storia Universale*, Milan 1969).
33. J. H. Hagelgans, *Des Fürsten und Beschürmers Teutscher Freiheit Arminii Thaten*. . .(Nuremberg 1640). See F. Schiller, 'Geschichte des 30 jährigen Krieges', in *Historische Schriften* (Leipzig 1906).
34. L. von Ranke, *Geschichte Wallensteins* (*Sämtliche Werke*, XXIII, Leipzig 1872).
35. H. Hallwich, *Wallensteins Ende*, 2 vols. (1879); *Fünf Bücher Geschichte Wallensteins*, I–III (1910); *Briefe und Akten zur Geschichte Wallensteins 1630–1634*, I–IV, *Fontes Rerum Austriacarum*, 63–6 (1912). A. Gindely, *Waldstein während seines ersten Generalates* 2 vols. (1886).
36. J. Pekař, *Wallenstein 1630–1634. Tragödie einer Verschwörung*, 2 vols. (Berlin 1937). H. von Srbik, *Wallensteins Ende: Ursachen, Verlauf und Folgen der Katastrophe* (Salzburg 1952).
37. The Czech literature to 1934 is in the bibliographical section of the collection *Doba bělohorská a Albrecht z Valdštejna* (Prague 1934). For more recent works see notes to chapters 4, pp. 234–5, and 5, pp. 239–40, and the extensive bibliography in Mann, *Wallenstein*, 1185–204.
38. On the youth of Wallenstein see J. Pekař, 'Valdštejn a česká otázka,' *ČČH*, XL (1934); Mann, *Wallenstein*, 7–38: H. Diwald, *Wallenstein. Eine Biographie* (Munich–Esslingen 1969). *Handbuch der Geschichte der böhmischen Länder*, II, bibliography on 294–5. See also F. Roubík, 'Albrecht z Valdštejna, vévoda Frýdlantský', in *Doba bělohorská a Albrecht z Valdštejna* (Prague 1934), 121–46 and F. Dvorský, 'Albrecht z Valdštejna až na konec r. 1621', *Rozpravy Čes. Akad.*, I. 3.
39. On the Bohemian background see bibliography in Mann, *Wallenstein*, 1190–1.
40. Roubík, 'Albrecht z Valdštejna', 122ff.
41. *Ibid.* 123–4.
42. *Documenta Bohemica Bellum Tricennale Illustrantia*, II (Prague 1972), *sub voce* Wallenstein, 337.
43. *Documenta Bohemica Bellum Tricennale Illustrantia*, III (Prague 1976), *sub voce* Wallenstein, 308.
44. Roubík, 'Albrecht z Valdštejna' 126ff.
45. A. Ernstberger, *Wallenstein als Volkswirt in Herzogtum Friedland* (Liberec 1929); *Hans de Witte, Finanzmann Wallensteins* (Wiesbaden 1954).
46. F. Roubík, 'Valdštejnovo tažení na Slovensko roku 1626', *Sborník archivu ministerstva vnitra*, VIII (1935), 145–232. *Documenta Bohemica Bellum Tricennale Illustrantia*, IV (Prague 1974), *sub voce* Wallenstein, 470–1, and the Preface by Josef Kollmann, 5–35.
47. M. Hroch, 'Wallensteins Beziehungen zu den Wendischen Hansestädten, *Hansische Studien* (Berlin 1961).

48. E. Beladiez, *España y el Sacro Imperio Romano Germanico. Wallenstein 1583–1634* (Madrid 1967), especially 235ff. B. Dudík, *Waldstein von seiner Enthebung bis zur abermaligen Uebernahme des Armee-Ober-Kommandos* Vienna 1885).
49. Mann, *Wallenstein*, 729ff. Pekař-Kristen, *Odhalení o Valdštejnově zradě a smrti* (Prague 1934). New documents, especially the correspondence of Diodati, will be published in *Documenta Bohemica Bellum Tricennale Illustrantia V*, ed. by M. Toegl (in press).
50. J. Janáček, *Valdštejnova smrt* (Prague 1970).
51. See Roubík, 'Albrecht z Valdštejna', 121–46.
52. See the legal opinions of the 'appointed counsellors and commissioners' of April 1634, printed in Hallwich, *Briefe und Akten*, II, no. 1344, *Alberti Fridlandi perduellionis chaos sive ingrati animi abysmus, Anno 1634*. See J. Bergl, 'Wer war Verfasser des Chaos perduellionis?', *MVGDB*, LXXII (1934), 84ff.
53. See the articles in the collection *O Josefu Pekařovi*, ed. R. Holinka (Prague 1937).
54. S. H. Steinberg, *Der Dreissigjährige Krieg und der Kampf um die Vorherrschaft in Europa 1600–1660* (Göttingen 1967).
55. J. V. Polišenský, 'Zur Problematik des Dreissigjährigen Krieges und der Wallensteinfrage', in *Aus 500 Jahren deutsch-tschechoslowakischer Geschichte* (Berlin 1958), 99–135.
56. See Mann, *Wallenstein*, 1127ff. for a discussion of Wallenstein in the correspondence of Slavata, Marradas and Schlick.
57. Correspondence between Maximilian of Bavaria and Wallenstein in the Autograph Collection, State Archive, Mnichovo Hradiště. See Albrecht, *Die auswärtige Politik Maximilians von Bayern*.
58. See J. H. Elliott, *The Revolt of the Catalans. A Study in the Decline of Spain (1598–1640)* (Cambridge 1963), 263, 272, 293.
59. M. Hroch, 'Valdštejnova politika v severním Německu v letech 1629–1630', *SbH*, V (1957), 202–32. See also V. Letošník, 'Polsko, dům Rakouský a Albrecht z Valdštejna za pruské války r. 1626–1629', *Časopis Národního Musea*, CVIII–CXI (1934–7), *passim*.
60. See J. Petráň, *Zemědělská výroba v Čechách v druhé polovině 16. a počátkem 17. století* (*Acta Universitatis Carolinae, Philos. et Hist.*, Prague 1964).
61. K. Stanka, *Die Eisenerzeugung im Friedländer Bezirk im 17. Jahrhundert* (dissertation, Leipzig 1963).
62. Ernstberger's statements in his *Wallenstein als Volkswirt im Herzogtum Friedland* should be understood in this sense.
63. See Mann's *Wallenstein*, 549ff. and the correspondence between Aitzema and Aldringen (Algemeen Rijksarchief, The Hague), between Schwarzenberg and Aldringen (in the State Archive, Český Krumlov), and letters of van Aitzema in the Autograph Collection, Mnichovo Hradiště.
64. See Beladiez, *España y el Sacro Imperio Romano Germanico;* and B. Chudoba, *Spain and the Empire 1519–1643* (Chicago 1952).

6. THE SWEDISH–FRENCH PERIOD, 1635–43

1. J. H. Elliott, *Imperial Spain 1469–1716* (London 1963).
2. *Idem, The Revolt of the Catalans. A Study in the Decline of Spain (1598–1640)* (Cambridge 1963).

3. J. Sanabre, *La acción de Francia en Cataluña* (Barcelona 1956).
4. P. Vilar, *La Catalogne dans l'Espagne moderne;* 4 vols. (Paris 1962), I.
5. F. Mauro, *Le Portugal et l'Atlantique au XVIIe siècle* (Paris 1960).
6. H. Kellenbenz, *Unternehmerkräfte im hamburger Portugal- und Spanienhandel, 1590–1625* (Hamburg 1954).
7. *Idem,* 'Hamburg und die französisch-schwedische Zusammenarbeit im Dreissigjährigen Krieg', *Zeitschrift des Vereins für hamburgische Geschichte* (1964), 49–50.
8. H. Lonchay, *La rivalité de la France et de l'Espagne aux Pays-Bas, 1635–1700* (Brussels 1896).
9. H. Pirenne, *Histoire de Belgique* (Brussels 1948–53), IV. A. Leman, *Richelieu* et Olivares (Lille 1938).
10. A. van der Essen, *Le Cardinal-Infant et la politique européenne de l'Espagne, 1609–1641,* I (Louvain 1944).
11. J. U. Nef, 'War and economic progress, 1540–1640', *Economic History Review,* XII (1942).
12. W. Tham, *Den svenska utrikespolitikens historia 1560–1648* (Stockholm 1960).
13. W. Hubatsch, *Im Bannkreis der Ostsee* (Marburg 1948); *Skandinavien und Deutschland im Wandel der Zeiten* (with M. Gerhardt, 1950); *Unruhe des Nordens* (Göttingen 1956).
14. J. Paul, *Europa im Ostseeraum* (Göttingen 1961).
15. B. Dudík, *Schweden in Böhmen und Mähren 1640–1650* (Vienna 1879).
16. B. Bretholz, 'Neue Aktenstücke zur Geschichte des Schwedenkrieges in Böhmen und Mähren', *Zeitschrift des Vereins für Geschichte Mährens und Schlesiens* (*ZVGMS*) VIII, 12ff.
17. J. Loserth, 'Zur Geschichte der Stadt Olmütz in der Zeit der schwedischen Okkupation', *ZVGMS,* II (1898).
18. P. M. Hebbe, *Svenskarna i Böhmen och Mähren* (Uppsala 1932).
19. S. Göransson, *Den europeiska konfessionspolitikens upplösning 1654–1660* (Uppsala–Wiesbaden 1956).
20. L. Tingsten, *Fältmarskalkarna J. Baner och Lenart Torstenson säsom härforare* (Stockholm 1932).
21. A. Rezek, *Děje Čech a Moravy za Ferdinanda III. až do konce třicetileté války (1637–1648)* (Prague 1890).
22. E. Denis, *Čechy po Bílé hoře,* Part I (Prague 1911).
23. F. Dostál, 'Historie Valachů ve velkém díle o československých dějinách', *Valašsko,* VII (1958), 131.,
24. For descriptions of the holdings see J. Čelakovský, K. Rezek, 'Popis náchodského archivu', *Památky Archeologické* (1878), 495, 505, 507–10. F. Machat, 'Schlossarchiv zu Náchod', *Archivalien,* I, 206–9. F. Roubík, 'Příspěvek k dějinám náchodského archivu Oktavia Piccolominiho', *SAMV,* II (1929), 151–9. E. Bouza, 'Náchodský zámecký archiv a spisovna velkostatku Náchod v období feudalismu a kapitalismu', *SbAP* (1961), 115–37.
25. See M. Dvořák, 'Hrabata Šlikové a jejich archiv v Kopidlně', *ČČH,* I (1895), 298–307. J. Loserth, 'Über einige Handschriften und Bücher im gräfl. Schlickschen Archiv zu Kopidlno', *MVGDB* (1918), 114–20.
26. For the Castle Library, see *Knihovna Národního musea* (Prague 1959), 141. K. R. Fischer, 'Bericht über das Reichsgräflich Desfours–Walderodesche Archiv in Gross–Rohozec', *Archivalien,* I, 446–53.
27. *Státní archiv v Opavě. Průvodce po archivních fondech,* IV (Prague 1961).

28. There is not yet a general survey of the Bohemian question during the Thirty Years' War. O. Odložilík gathered material for the history of the emigrations but did not go beyond the year 1624. B. Šindelář in his work on the Bohemian and Silesian questions in the peace negotiations in Westphalia and W. V. Wallace in his dissertation *The Czech Exiles and the Thirty Years' War* (London 1955) have done no more than raise some of the issues.
29. J. V. Polišenský, *Anglie a Bílá hora* (Prague 1949), 192–4.
30. J. Rushworth, *Historical Collections...Beginning...Anno 1618* (London 1659).
31. *Ibid.* B2.
32. See the brief survey in J. V. Polišenský's article 'Anglická buržoasní revoluce a česká otázka', *Dějepis ve škole* (1955/2), 49–54.
33. Papers in the British Museum, London, Eg 2592, 2593 (Carleton Papers, vol. II–III). Also PRO, S. P. (Holland) 84/88–98 of 1618–20; *Acta Bohemica 1618, 1619*, under Bernburg–Anhalt 9a, 170–3, Staatsarchiv Oranienbaum.
34. V. F. Semenov, 'Anglisky absolutism v pervoy polovine XVII v. i nazrevaniye revolutsii', *Angliskaya bourgeoisnaya revolutsiya....*, I, 69–106, in particular 86. S. I. Archangelsky, 'Vneshnyaya politika angliskovo absolutisma v pervoy polovine XVII veka', *ibid.* 107–27, in particular 114–15 and 117.
35. D. Harris Willson, *King James VI and I* (London 1956).
36. *Ibid.* 339–424 (citation from 421).
37. *Ibid.* 273.
38. *Tom-Tell-Troath*, (n.p. 1622), printed in *Somers Tracts IV*, I (London 1752), 111–25.
39. See J. V. Polišenský, 'Valaši a Valašsko v anglických pramenech 17. století', *Naše Valašsko*, x (1947).
40. C. V. Wedgwood, *The King's Peace 1637–1641* (London 1955), 124–6.
41. *Angliskaya bourgeoisnaya revolutsiya*, I, 470.
42. C. Hill, *Economic Problems of the Church. From Archbishop Whitgift to the Long Parliament* (London 1956), 29ff.
43. Some of the evidence concerning Comenius' relationship to pre-revolutionary England is in G. H. Turnbull's *Hartlib, Dury and Comenius* (London 1947), in particular see p. 301. The selection from Hartlib's papers edited by Turnbull give only the vaguest indication of what might be found among the originals, now in the Library of Sheffield University.
44. Turnbull, *Hartlib, Dury and Comenius*, 343.
45. *Ibid.* 344.
46. J. V. Polišenský, 'Komenský a jeho doba', *SbH*, I (1953), 227.
47. See G. H. Turnbull, *Samuel Hartlib, A Sketch of His Life and His Relations to J. A. Comenius* (London 1920). See also Turnbull's work cited above, and R. F. Jones, *Ancients and Moderns* (2nd edn., Berkeley and Los Angeles. 1965); D. Bush, *English Literature in the Earlier Seventeenth Century* (Oxford 1946), 545ff.
48. Turnbull, *Hartlib, Dury and Comenius*, 343.
49. Wedgwood, *The King's Peace*, 405, 426–7. S. R. Gardiner, *History of England from the Accession of James I to the Outbreak of the Civil War*, x (London 1884), 118–25.
50. Wedgwood, *The King's Peace*, 483.
51. Gardiner, *History of England*, 137.

52. P. Zagorin, *A History of Political Thought in the English Revolution* (London 1954), 67–70.
53. Compare Polišenský, 'Komenský a jeho doba', 229ff.
54. Turnbull, *Hartlib, Dury and Comenius*, 370ff. W. C. Abbott, ed., *The Writings and Speeches of Oliver Cromwell*, III, *1653–1655* (Cambridge 1945). See also Polišenský, 'Anglická buržoasní revoluce a česká otázka'.
55. The misconceptions concerning Comenius' invitation to England were pointed out as early as the 1930s by R. F. Young (*Comenius in England* (London 1932)), whose conclusions were supplemented by D. Stimson writing in *Isis*, XXII (1935). Turnbull's work of 1947 supports Young's conclusions. See R. A. B. Oosterhuis, *Comenius in London* (*Paedag. Studien*, Amsterdam 1937), 1–7.
56. The Pamphlet Collection in the Castle Library at Mnichovo Hradiště, section 'Anglica et Hollandica'; also the State Archive, Zámrsk, Piccolomini Family Archive, Pamphlet Collection, nos. 51,542–56.
57. B. F. Porshnev, 'Angliskaya respublika, frantsuskaya Fronda i Vestfalsky mir', *Sredniye veka*, III (1951), 180–216. See also *Sredniye veka*, IV, 5. *Idem*, 'Angliskaya revolutsiya i sovremenaya yey Frantsia', *Angliskaya bourgeoisnaya revolutsiya*, II, 71–89; *Frantsia, Angliskaya revolutsiya i evropeyskaya politiky v seredine XVII veka* (Moscow 1970).
58. The most important Bohemian sources for the history of the Fronde are in the collection 'Historica' in the Náchod Archive, in the Belrupt Correspondence in the Chudobín Collection in section II of the State Archive at Janovice-Rýmařov, and finally in the Manuscript Collection of the Lobkowitz Library, now part of the University Library at Prague. Those who have written about Oxenstierna's 'betrayal' of the Bohemian interests at the Peace Congress in Westphalia have not taken account of the actual situation. See for example the otherwise valuable study of Václav Clemens Žebrácký (*Universitas Carolinae, Philologia* 1/2, 1955) by J. B. Čapek – particularly p. 164.
59. See C. Hill's review of the efforts to collect this material, in the *English Historical Review*, (1956), 460–1.
60. 'Historica', Correspondence of O. Piccolomini, in particular nos. 30,945–31,017, sections XVI and XXIX (hereafter cited as Náchod, Hist.).
61. G. Shawe to Piccolomini, 12 December 1635, French, orig., Náchod, Hist., 30,945.
62. 'Estratto de lettere di Londra', Italian, copy, 1639, Náchod, Hist., 51,543. 'Abhandlung über die Bischöfe', Mnichovo Hradiště, Castle Library, XXXIII, 629. 'Lat. Berichte aus London 1640', Náchod, Hist., 51,544. 'Humble Petition', French, copy, 1642, Náchod, Hist., 51,545, 51,546.
63. Shawe to Piccolomini, 8 February 1642, Brussels, Spanish, orig., Náchod, Hist. 30,950.
64. Shawe to Piccolomini, 17 May 1642, Malines, Italian, orig., Náchod, Hist., 30,946. 'El message segundo...el coronel Juan Hotham', Spanish, copy, 1642, *ibid.* 51,547.
65. Shawe to Piccolomini, Brussels, 21 April 1642, Spanish, orig., Náchod, Hist., 30,947.
66. Shawe to Piccolomini, London, 13 June 1642, French, orig., Náchod, Hist., 30,948.
67. Shawe to Piccolomini, 27 June 1642, Swiwesword (?), French, orig., Náchod, Hist., 30,949.

68. Edward Herbert to Piccolomini, 15 April 1644, Oxford, French, orig., Náchod, Hist., 30,954. Endymion Porter to Piccolomini, 26 April 1644, Oxford, Spanish, orig., Náchod, Hist., 30,956.
69. Henry Gage to Piccolomini, 4 July 1644, Oxford, Spanish, orig., Náchod, Hist., 30,951.
70. Edward Herbert to Piccolomini, 5 December 1644, Bristol, Italian, orig., Náchod, Hist., 30,955. Patent of Charles I concerning the position of the Fleet, English copy, with French translation, 22 October 1644, *ibid.* 51,548.
71. Henry Gage to Piccolomini, 14 October 1644, Oxford, and same to same, same date and place, Spanish, orig., Náchod, Hist., 30,952, 30,953.
72. F. Foissotte to Piccolomini, 1 February 1645, Waterford, Spanish, orig., Náchod, Hist., 30,958. Also letter of Catholic confederates to Piccolomini, 23 November 1644, Latin, orig., *ibid.* 51,549.
73. F. Foissotte to Piccolomini, 5 March 1645, Kilkenny, Spanish, orig., Náchod, Hist., 30,959.
74. Newcastle to Piccolomini, 15 April 1645, Valenciennes, French, orig., Náchod, Hist., 30,960, 30,961.
75. See the article on Endymion Porter by C. H. Firth in the *Dictionary of National Biography*, XVI, 172.
76. Endymion Porter to Piccolomini, 24 February 1646, Spanish, orig., Náchod, Hist., 30,962.
77. Porter to Piccolomini, 14 April 1646, Paris, Spanish, orig., Náchod, Hist., 30,963.
78. Porter to Piccolomini, 12 May 1646, Paris, Spanish, orig., Náchod, Hist., 30,964.
79. Porter to Piccolomini, 20 May 1646, Paris, Spanish, orig., Náchod, Hist., 30,695. For G. Goring the Elder see C. H. Firth in *DNB*, VIII, 245–51.
80. Porter to Piccolomini, 3 July 1646, St Germain, Spanish, orig., Náchod, Hist., 30,967. Same to same, 21 September 1646 St Germain, Spanish, orig., Náchod, Hist., 30,966.
81. Porter to Piccolomini, 14 November 1646, St Germain, Spanish, orig., Náchod, Hist., 30,967.
82. George Porter to Piccolomini, 2 January 1647, London, French, orig., Náchod, Hist., 30,984. For George Porter, see C. H. Firth in *DNB*, XVI, 172–5.
83. G. Porter to Piccolomini, 5 February 1647, London, French, orig., Náchod, Hist., 30,985.
84. A. Keynes to Piccolomini, 15 March 1647, London, French, orig., Náchod, Hist., 30,989.
85. G. Porter to Piccolomini, 18 March 1647, London, French, orig., Náchod, Hist., 30,986.
86. Keynes to Piccolomini, 26 April 1647, London, French, orig., Náchod, Hist., 30.993. Same to same, 14 May 1647, London, French, orig., *ibid.* 30,990. G. Porter to Piccolomini, 23 April 1647, London, French, orig., *ibid.*, 30,987.
87. Keynes to Piccolomini, 9 August 1647, Brussels, French, orig., Náchod, Hist., 30,996.
88. Letters from G. Goring and A. Keynes from 6 July from Brussels, Lille, Douai, Dixmuiden and Ghent, Spanish and French, orig., Náchod, Hist., 30,970–31,003.

89. Keynes to Piccolomini, 25 April 1648, Brussels, French, orig., Náchod, Hist., 31,004.
90. Keynes to Piccolomini, 2 May 1648, Brussels, French, orig., Náchod, Hist., 31,005. Same to same, 16 May 1648, French, orig., *ibid.* 31,006.
91. Goring to Piccolomini, 11 June 1648, French, orig., Brussels, Náchod, Hist., 31,002.
92. Keynes to Piccolomini, 6 June 1648, Brussels, French, orig., Náchod, Hist., 31,007.
93. Keynes to Piccolomini, 13 June 1648, Brussels, French, orig., Náchod, Hist., 31,008.
94. Keynes to Piccolomini, The Hague, 15 July 1648, French, orig., Náchod, Hist., 31,009.
95. Extract from a document from The Hague, 1649, n.p., German copy, Náchod, Hist., 51,551. Count E. Traun to Piccolomini, *ibid.* 13,319ff.
96. Keynes to Piccolomini, 26 March 1649, London, French, orig., Náchod, Hist., 31,010.
97. Goring to Piccolomini, 21 May 1649 (incorrect dating), French, orig., Náchod, Hist., 30,969.
98. 'Ectract uyt een Brief gesonden uyt Amsterdam', Dutch print, 1650, Náchod, Hist., 51,552. Keynes to Piccolomini, 1650, from Breda and Scotland, French, orig., 31,011–13. Same to same, 1651 Brussels, French, orig., *ibid.* 31,014.
99. 'De Namen der schepe van oorloge van Zijn Majesteit van Denemarken', 1653, Den Haag, Dutch print, Náchod, Hist., 51,542. Dutch and French prints concerning the dissolution of Parliament, *ibid.* 51,533. Charles(II) to the States General, 1653, Paris, French, copy, *ibid.* 51,554. 'Le discours de M. de Neufville...', 1653, French, copy, *ibid.* 51,555. 'Articles de paix... à Westminster', 1654, French print, *ibid.* 51,556. Keynes to Piccolomini, 1655, London and Canterbury, French, orig., *ibid.* 31,015–16. Same to Same, 1656, Vienna, French, orig., *ibid.* 31,017.

7. WAR, REVOLUTION, PEACE NEGOTIATIONS 1643–50

1. J. Reglá, *Introducción a la historia de España*, (Barcelona 1967), 431ff; 'Spain and her Empire', *New Cambridge Modern History*, v (Cambridge 1961).
2. V. Palacio, *Derrota, agotamiento, decadencia en la España del siglo XVII* (Madrid 1956).
3. J. M. Jover, *Política mediterránea y política atlántica en la España de Feijóo* (Oviedo 1956).
4. M. Fraga Iribarne, *Don Diego de Saavedra Fajardo y la diplomacia de su época* (Madrid 1956).
5. C. Hill, *Reformation to Industrial Revolution* (London 1967); *Change and Continuity in Seventeenth Century England* (London 1974). See the polemics between Hill and J. H. Hexter in the late 1975 issues of the *Times Literary Supplement.* See also E. M. Furber, ed., *Changing Views on British History. Essays on Historical Writing since 1939* (Cambridge, Mass. 1966).
6. J. R. Jones, *Britain and Europe in the Seventeenth Century* (London 1966).
7. C. R. Boxer, *The Dutch Seaborne Empire* (London 1965).
8. B. F. Porshnev, 'Anglyskaya respublika, frantsuskaya Fronda i Vestfalsky mir', *Sredniye veka*, III (1951) 180–216. 'Angliskaya revolutsiya i sovremenaya

yey Frantsia', in *Angliskaya bourgeoisnaya revolutsiya*, II, 71–89. *Frantsia, Angliskaya revolutsiya i europskaya politika v seredine XVII veka* (Moscow 1970).

9. J. V. Polišenský, 'Česká otázka, habsburská politika a anglická revoluce 17. století', *SbH*, v (1957), 175–202.
10. P. Geyl, *History of the Low Countries. Episodes and Problems* (London 1964), 43–78, 79–109.
11. C. Smit, *Het Vredesverdrag van Munster, 30 januari 1648* (n.p. 1948).
12. J. J. Poelhekke, *De Vrede van Munster* (n.p. 1948).
13. J. A. van Houtte, *Economische en sociale geschiedenis van de Lage Landen* (Zeist 1964), 136–214.
14. H. A. Enno van Gelder, *Cultuurgeschiedenis van Nederland in vogelvlucht* (Aula–Boeken 1965), 108ff.
15. T. Wittman, *Németalföld aranykora* (Budapest 1965).
16. J. Presser, *Arm in de Gouden Eeuw* (Amsterdam 1965).
17. S. Hart, J. V. Polišenský, 'Praha a Amsterdam 17. a 18. století. Demographische Veränderungen und wirtschaftliche Entwicklung zweier Städte', *ČSČH*, xv (1967), 827–46.
18. B. F. Porshnev, *Narodnye vostaniya vo Frantsii pered Frondoy* (Moscow–Leningrad 1948).
19. R. Mousnier, ed., *Lettres et mémoires adressés au chancelier Séguier (1633–1649)* (Paris 1964).
20. R. Mandrou, 'Les soulèvements populaires et la société française du XVIIe siècle', *Annales*, XIV (1959), 756–65. E. H. Kossmann, *La Fronde* (Leiden 1954).
21. E. Werner, *Die Geburt einer Grossmacht – die Osmanen 1300–1481* (Berlin 1966). See also H. Inalçik, *The Ottoman Empire. The Classical Era 1300–1600* (London 1973).
22. F. Dickmann, *Der Westfälische Frieden* (Münster 1959).
23. M. Braubach, *Der Westfälische Friede* (Münster 1948).
24. *Acta Pacis Westphalicae, Instructionen*, I, *Frankreich, Schweden, Kaiser* (Münster 1962).
25. B. Šindelář, 'Die böhmischen Exulanten in Sachsen und der Westfälische Friedenskongress', *SbFFBU* (1960), 215–50; 'Comenius und der Westfälische Friedenskongress', *Historica*, v (1963), 71–107; *Vestfálský mír a česká otázka* (Prague 1969).
26. S. H. Steinberg, *The 'Thirty Years' War'*...(London 1966), 92–122.
27. R. Ergang, *The Myth of the All-destructive Fury of the Thirty Years' War* (Pocono Pines 1956).
28. K. F. Olechnowitz, *Handel and Seeschiffahrt der späten Hanse* (Weimar 1965).
29. J. A. van Houtte, 'Onze zeventiende eeuw "Ongelukseeuw"', *Mededelingen Koninglijke Vlaamse Academie*, xv (1953).
30. V. Pešák, *Obecní dluhy královských, věnných a horních měst v Čechách, zvláště Starého města pražského po třicetileté válce* (Prague 1933).
31. K. Doskočil, *Popis Čech roku 1654* (*Berní rula*, II, Prague 1953).
32. See J. V. Polišenský, *Otázky studia obecných dějin I* (*Acta Univ. Carolinae, Historica*, Prague 1957), 41.
33. *Ibid.* 33–4. See also Chapter 6, n. 28 above.
34. See J. O. Miltner's article in *Památky Archeologické*, I (1855), 328ff; and F. Šváb, 'Gräflich Clam-Martinicsches Archiv in Smečna', *Archivalien*, I, 518–25.

35. See W. Schulz, 'Das Archiv des Museums des Königreichs Böhmen', *Archivalien*, I, 52–97. F. Count von und zu Trauttmansdorff, 'Die Korrespondenz des Grafen Maximilian von und zu Trauttmansdorff', *ibid.* 133–9. V. Kratochvíl, 'Politischer Aktenbestand des fürstlich Trauttmansdorffschen Familienarchivs', *ibid.* 470–5.
36. M. Kušík ,'Archive in der Slowakei und ihre Bestände', *Studia Historica Slovaca*, III (1965), 230ff.
37. See J. V. Polišenský, 'Rassegna delle fonti per la storia e la cultura italiana in Cecoslovacchia', *Historica* (1967), 271–8.
38. Basic information about Italian writing on this problem may be found in R. Quazza, *Storia politica d'Italia. Preponderanza spagnuola, 1559–1700* (Milan 1950)
39. 'Manifesto del fedelissimo Popolo di Napoli', 17 October 1647, Castle Library, Mnichovo Hradiště, no. 48–7–6, fos. 15ff. See also G. Pepe, *Il mezzogiorno d'Italia sotto gli Spagnuoli. La tradizione storiografica* (Florence 1952).
40. Pepe, *Il mezzogiorno*, 17ff.
41. There are documents concerning the Gallas Duchy of Lucera in the Clam–Gallas Family Archive (State Archive, Děčín), nos. XIX, 25–8. For the Duchy of Amalfi, the Piccolomini Family Archive (State Archive, Zámrsk). nos. 2684ff., 4028–5343.
42. Particularly important for the Masaniello uprising are nos. 51,548–656, Piccolomini Family Archive (State Archive. Zámrsk). The Castle Library at Mnichovo Hradiště contains some propaganda materials: 'Epistole Filomarini', no. 48–6–17; 'Historia Gastaldi Neapolitana', 48–6–18; 'Rivoluzioni di Napoli', no. 48–6–17.
43. Some printed source collections are difficult to obtain: *Cronache e documenti per la storia dell' Italia meridionale dei secoli XVI e XVII* (Naples 1930); and F. Schlitzer, *Diario di Napoli dal 1600 al 1680.* The monograph on the Neapolitan uprising by Angelo Saavedra is also unobtainable. Besides the work by Pepe cited above the best survey is by M. Schipa, *Masaniello* (Bari 1925).
44. L. Salvatorelli, *Sommario della storia d'Italia* (Turin 1942), 450ff.
45. J. Merriman, *Six Contemporaneous Revolutions* (Oxford 1938); see also I. Schöffer, 'Did Holland's Golden Age coincide with a period of crisis?', *Acta Historiae Neerlandica*, I (1966), 82ff. J. H. Elliott, 'Revolts in the Spanish monarchy', in *Preconditions of Revolution in Early Modern Europe*, ed. R. Forster and J. O. Greene (Baltimore–London 1970), 109–130.
46. See J. H. Elliott, *Imperial Spain 1469–1716* (London 1963), 346ff.
47. In the following the contents of Cardinal Filomarino's letters of 8 and 12 July 1647 will be cited as 'Due Lettere', Castle Library, Mnichovo Hradiště, no. 48–7–6. They are supplemented by the works of Pepe and Schipa cited above.
48. 'Due Lettere', fo. 3v.
49. 'Due Lettere', fos. 10–11.
50. *Ibid.* fo. 5. The Viceroy's manifesto of 9 July 1647, no. 51,649, Piccolomini Family Archive, State Archive, Zámrsk.
51. 'Due Lettere', fos. 6–8.
52. Manifesto of the Viceroy, 11 July 1647, Piccolomini Family Archive.
53. 'Due Lettere', fo. 12. The joint manifesto of the Duke d'Arcos and Tommaso Aniello of Amalfi, the head of the Neapolitan people, is in the

Piccolomini Family Archive, 52,652. D'Arcos' manifesto of 15 July is in 51,650.

54. 'Due Lettere', fo. 13.
55. D'Arcos' manifesto against Genoino, Piccolomini Family Archive, 51,651.
56. Proclamation of the Duke di Massa, 16 and 17 October 1647, Castle Library, Mnichovo Hradiště, no. 48–7–6.
57. Most important of these tracts was the anti-Spanish pamphlet 'Il cittadino fedele', n.d., Castle Library, Mnichovo Hradiště, 48–7–6, fos. 67–8. 'Manifesto del fedelissimo Popolo di Napoli', 17 October 1647, Piccolomini Family Archive, 51,648. The Spanish offer is outlined in the pamphlet 'Cinque discorsi a signori Napoletani...', Chieti, 23 October 1647, Castle Library, Mnichovo Hradiště, 48–7–6, fo. 223. The republican programme is defended in the pamphlet 'Nuova instruttione per buon formare la Repubblica in Napoli', *ibid.*, fos. 35, 59, 62. The best source for the October uprising of 1647 is the proclamation of 17 October cited above, n. 56.
58. Guise's correspondence from December 1647 until April 1648 is in the Castle Library, Mnichovo Hradiště, no. 48–6–17, fos. 129–41. Here too are the manifestoes issued in the name of the King of France, fos. 142–66. The pro-French tract 'Lettera scritta da N. N. Napolitano al Popolo di Napoli' is under number 48–7–6, fos. 23–33. Correspondence with the Curia is in number 48–6–17, fos. 1–118, correspondence with Palermo fos. 241–90.
59. Manifestoes of Don Juan José d'Austria are in the Piccolomini Family Archive, nos. 51,653–5, and in the Castle Library, Mnichovo Hradiště, 48–6–17, fos. 169–82. The attempts to intensify the uprising of the Neapolitan people are shown in the 'Discorso, o esortizione fatta alle Provincie del Regno', 4 May 1648, *ibid.* fos. 155–66.
60. 'Discorso politico, intitulato La Zuppa Celeste, sopra le presenti Revoluzioni di Napoli', manifestly anti-French. 'Anticamera di Plutone sopra le Rivoluzioni di Napoli', Castle Library, Mnichovo Hradiště. fol. 321–343 and 233–321. The close is on fo. 320.

8. THE AFTERMATH OF CONFLICT

1. R. Forster, J. P. Greene, eds., *Preconditions of Revolution in Early Modern Europe* (Baltimore–London 1970). R. Mandrou, *Louis XIV en son temps, 1661–1715* (Paris 1973). C. Hill, *Change and Continuity in Seventeenth Century England* (London 1974).
2. See F. Braudel, *Civilisation matérielle et capitalisme XVe–XVIIIe siècle* (Paris 1967); J. V. Polišenský, *The Thirty Years' War* (London 1971). J. U. Nef, *War and Human Progress: an Essay on the Role of Industrial Civilization* (Cambridge, Mass. 1950).
3. Polišenský, *The Thirty Years' War*, 254ff.
4. V. L. Tapié, *Monarchie et peuples du Danube* (Paris 1969), 135ff. ('Ténèbres ou gloire baroque') thinks the glory prevails over the misery.
5. On Comenius, see C. Webster, ed., *Samuel Hartlib and the Advancement of Learning* (Cambridge 1970).
6. Compare the conflicting views of V. L. Tapié, *Baroque et classicisme* (Paris 1957) and J. V. Polišenský, 'Società e cultura nella Boemia del barocco', in *L'Arte del Barocco in Boemia* (Milan 1966), 1–12. Cf. J. Neumann in *Karel Škréta 1610–1674* (Prague 1974), 7ff.
7. See V. L. Tapié, 'Méthodes et problèmes de l'histoire de l'Europe centrale',

in *Mélanges Pierre Renouvin. Études d'histoire des rélations internationales* (Paris 1966), 33–49.

9. CHANGES IN THE COMPOSITION OF THE BOHEMIAN NOBILITY

1. *Teoreticheskye i istoriograficheskye problemy genezia kapitalizma* (Moscow 1969), particularly the contributions by Chistozvonov: 'Some aspects of the problem of the origin of absolutism', 64ff.; 'Classes, class struggle, and the origins of capitalism', 89ff.; 'Preconditions for the rise of absolutism in Austria', 87. R. Mousnier, ed., *Problèmes de la stratification sociale* (Paris 1968), with contributions by K. Bosl, W. Conze and I. Schöffer.
2. V. L. Tapié, 'The Habsburg Lands, 1518–1657', *The New Cambridge Modern History*, IV (Cambridge 1970), 503–30.
3. V. L. Tapié, *Monarchie et peuples du Danube* (Paris 1969).
4. O. Placht, *Lidnatost a společenská skladba českého státu v 16.–18. století* (Prague 1957).
5. H. Kamen, *The Iron Century. Social Change in Europe 1550–1660* (London 1961), 424ff.
6. L. Stone, *The Crisis of the Aristocracy 1558–1641* (Oxford 1965). P. Goubert, *Problèmes généraux de la noblesse française. Rapport pour le XIIIe Congrès International des Sciences Historiques* (Moscow 1970), 1–8.
7. J. Meyer, *Noblesse d'Europe centrale au XVIIe siècle*, *ibid.* 8–22.
8. H. Rössler, *Deutscher Adel*, II, 1555–1740 (Darmstadt 1965). V. L. Tapié *Baroque et classicisme* (Paris 1957).
9. Meyer, *Noblesse d'Europe centrale*, 16.
10. *Ibid.* 18, 20.
11. J. Honc, 'Populační vývoj šesti generací 125 českých panských rodů v letech 1502–1794', *Historická demografie*, II (1969).
12. This is true particularly of Placht's work; see above n. 4.
13. E. Perroy, 'Social mobility among the French noblesse in the later Middle Ages', *Past and Present*, XXI (1962), 25–38.
14. Register of incolats from the *Tabulae regni*, compiled for Karel of Žerotín the Elder. Czech MS in the Library of the Hus Museum at Prague.
15. A. Míka, 'Majetkové rozvrstvení české šlechty v předbělohorském období', *SbH*, XV (1967) 45–75.
16. More detailed documentation in F. Snider *The Restructuring of the Bohemian Nobility 1610–1656* (dissertation, University of California, Berkeley 1972).
17. New information on this point has been found in the papers of Cardinal Dietrichstein in the State Archive, Pilsen, branch at Žlutice, and in the State Archive, Prague, branch at Mnichovo Hradiště.
18. *Paměti strany rebelie 1618*, drafts of cases prepared by Jeníšek, Archive of the Municipal Museum, Jindřichův Hradec, MS. B/a 10. T. Bílek, *Dějiny konfiskací v Čechách po r. 1618* (Prague 1882–3). B. Jelínek, *Die Böhmen im Kampfe um ihre Selbständigkeit 1618–1648* (Prague 1916).
19. L. Mikeštíková-Kubátová, *Jak se přijímali cizinci do Čech po roce 1627* (dissertation, Charles University, Prague 1952).
20. For more detailed information see Snider, *The Restructuring of the Bohemian Nobility*.

21. J. Goll, *Válka o země koruny české (1740–1742)* (Prague 1915). The question is not explored in this work, though there is much useful material.
22. For the 'old' and the 'new' nobility see J. V. Polišenský, *The Thirty Years' War* (London 1971), 254ff.
23. J. Kočí, *Odboj nevolníků na Frýdlantsku 1679–1687. Příspěvek k povstání nevolníků v Čechách v roce 1680* (Liberec 1965). J. Kašpar, *Nevolnické povstání v Čechách roku 1680* (*Acta Universitatis Carolinae*, Prague 1965).

Appendix
Tabular survey of archives, libraries and individual collections

(references are to page numbers)

Central Bohemia

Southern Bohemia

Western Bohemia

Northern Bohemia

Gallas Military Chancery (Děčín): 103, 127, 160
Aldringen Papers (Děčín): 51, 98, 103, 127
Thun-Hohenstein FA (Děčín): 69, 98, 103, 127, 161
Desfours-Walderode FA (Děčín): 161

Eastern Bohemia

State Archive, Zámrsk: 24
Kolowrat FA: 52, 160
Coloredo-Mansfeld FA: 52, 128, 160
Piccolomini Military Chancery: 52, 72, 104, 127, 158, 183
Schlick FA: 72, 103–4, 128, 159, 184
Morzin FA: 127
Leslie FA: 160

Southern Moravia

State Archive, Brno: 24, 44, 129
Žerotín FA: 45
Collalto Military Chancery: 45, 98, 102
Dietrichstein FA: 46, 68, 105, 129, 163
Rottal FA: 162
Magnis FA: 162–3, 186
Brno and Moravian Libraries: 24
Brno and Moravian Municipal Archives: 24

Northern Moravia

State Archive, Opava: 24, 105
Dietrichstein Papers (Olomouc): 47, 129
Various FA (Janovice): 163, 186

Slovakia

State Central Archive, Bratislava: 25
Pálffy FA: 53, 186
Illésházy FA: 72
Municipal and District Archives: 25, 73
Libraries: 26
State Archive, Bratislava: 25
State Archive, Banská, Bystrica: 26, 53
State Archive, Košice: 26

Index